TITANIC
OR
OLYMPIC

WHICH SHIP SANK?

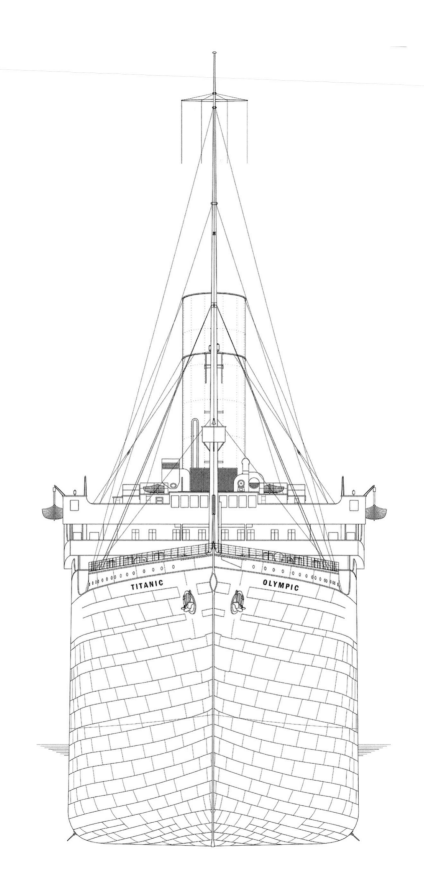

TITANIC
OR
OLYMPIC

WHICH SHIP SANK?

THE TRUTH BEHIND THE CONSPIRACY

STEVE HALL   BRUCE BEVERIDGE
ART BRAUNSCHWEIGER

FOREWORD BY MARK CHIRNSIDE

The
History
Press

Frontispiece: Drawing by Robert Hahn.

First published 2012

The History Press
The Mill, Brimscombe Port
Stroud, Gloucestershire, GL5 2QG
www.thehistorypress.co.uk

British Library Cataloguing in Publication Data.
A catalogue record for this book is available from the British Library.

ISBN 978 0 7524 6158 8

Typesetting and origination by The History Press
Printed in Great Britain
Manufacturing managed by Jellyfish Print Solutions Ltd

CONTENTS

ACKNOWLEDGEMENTS

Unless otherwise credited, all images are from the authors' collections.

Scott Andrews, for sharing his considerable knowledge of period shipbuilding practices and providing the information on *Olympic* and *Titanic*'s propulsion machinery.

Mark Chirnside, for taking the time to review the text on *Olympic* and *Britannic*.

Roy Mengot, for providing access to the analyses done by the Marine Forensics Panel of the Society of Naval Architects and Marine Engineers.

Ray Lepien and Robert Compton, who contributed so much to the original manuscript.

George Behe, for sharing his substantial knowledge of *Titanic*'s passengers and crew.

Daniel Klistorner, who supplied some rarely seen images of *Titanic*.

Jonathan Smith, for providing rare photographs and postcards from his collection.

Cyril Codus, for his *Titanic* and *Olympic* drawings.

Tom Cunliffe, for checking the navigational information cited for the waters in and around the Solent.

Charles C. Milner, for allowing us to use several of his period postcards.

Samuel Halpern, for providing additional information on *Titanic*'s lifeboats and the White Star Line.

John White, with special thanks for allowing us to use photographs taken of his extensive White Star Memories collection of *Olympic* artefacts. Photographs by Liza Campion (copyright White Star Memories).

R. Terrell Wright, for allowing the use of his rare photographs.

Josha Inglis and Stewart Kelly, for their interior woodwork photos.

Bernhard Funk, for his dive footage.

Mark Darrah, for his support and the use of his *Engineering* and *The Engineer* photos from the Harland & Wolff archives.

Alastair Arnott of the Southampton City Archives, who also assisted with photographs.

Charles Haas and Jack Eaton, for the use of photographic material from their book *Titanic: A Journey Through Time*.

The Titanic Historical Society, Indian Orchard, Massachusetts.

Frank and Dennis Finch and Kyogle Maritime Museum.

R. J. Thomson, Manager, Marine Crews at the Australian Maritime Authority (1997).

Bob Read, Steve Rigby, the British Titanic Society, Ralph White, Peter Quinn, Remco Hillen, the folks at the Bridgeview Public Library and any other contributors we may have missed.

Karen Signell Andrews, for editing the original 2004 version of this text.

The staff of The History Press, and in particular, Amy Rigg and Emily Locke, who have worked closely with us on our many *Titanic* projects, and who have somehow always managed to remain calm during our many requests for deadline extensions.

And Robin Gardner, for giving us something to write about.

FOREWORD

'From the assassination of JFK in November 1963, through Watergate and Lockerbie, conspiracies beset popular culture.' So writes Jane Parish in *The Age of Anxiety: Conspiracy Theory and the Human Sciences*. 'Television programmes about mysteries and "inexplicable" events command peak-time viewing schedules, reinterpreting "old" conspiracy theories with new evidence. Sky television devotes a single channel to programmes about mysterious happenings. In the tabloid papers, conspiracies have caught the public imagination... Reflecting this trend, the best-selling books of the 90s reflect a widespread fascination with conspiracy, intrigue and secret organisations...'

Perhaps it is unsurprising that one of the most famous maritime disasters in history, *Titanic*'s sinking, became the subject of an extraordinary conspiracy theory: that *Titanic* did not sink at all. According to the theory, the ship that sank on 15 April 1912 was actually her near-identical sister ship *Olympic*, which sustained damage during a collision with HMS *Hawke* on 20 September 1911. Theorists believe that the damage was so serious that *Olympic* was an economic write-off, and so she was switched with her sister. The plan was to deliberately scuttle *Olympic*, but she struck an iceberg accidentally and began to sink far more quickly than was originally anticipated.

The theory is far-fetched, and yet – is it possible? Conspiracies suggest deception and intrigue, and none is quite as intriguing as the idea that the White Star Line pulled off such a massive cover-up. However, dismissing such a claim out of hand is not enough. It requires rigorous analysis by researchers who have the relevant expertise and objectivity to assess it. It demands examination of the *all* the claims put forward point by point, by looking at the evidence and seeing whether it supports them. Moreover, it demands that the evidence be presented in such a way that the non-technical layperson can assess it for himself

If such a theory is absurd, then why is it necessary to examine it in such detail? Might not a conspiracy theorist simply dismiss such a critical analysis in any case? Perhaps so, but a detailed analysis also provides a service to the intelligent layman by pointing to the specific problems with the theory. There is much to be said for ignoring it – few would debate seriously with the argument that the earth is flat – but any theory should be assessed objectively by examining whether there is any evidential basis for it. While this volume looks for flaws in the conspiracy theory, it also provides a lot of historical information. It documents the hundreds of differences between *Olympic* and *Titanic*, all of which must be considered in answering the question 'could it have really happened?'

When someone puts forward an idea or theory, then it is incumbent on them to prove it. There will always be people who believe what they want to believe, rather than what can be demonstrated to have happened, but that is their choice. Herein lie the facts – decide for yourself.

Mark Chirnside
October 2011

PREFACE

'*Titanic* is unsinkable.' This phrase strikes a chord in the mind of any *Titanic* enthusiast and is reiterated in nearly every *Titanic* book printed. These same words are frequently cited as proof of shipbuilder and ship owner's arrogant overconfidence in what they had created, and yet no one ever uttered them. They are quoted inaccurately from a period trade publication *The Shipbuilder,* which described *Titanic* and *Olympic* as '*practically* unsinkable'.

Inaccurate stories are not new. Immediately after the sinking, there were even reports of Capt. Smith being seen on the streets of New York City. Some researchers, however, have used elements from the information available on *Titanic* to form 'conspiracy theories'. Many are far-fetched, completely ridiculous, or both. The Jesuit conspiracy theory is one: there are many variations of this story, all of which are based on the belief that the Jesuits have been controlling world events behind the scenes for hundreds of years.

In the early 1900s in the United States, there was no national banking system – what is known today as the Federal Reserve System. As the Jesuit conspiracy theory claims, in 1910 a clandestine meeting supposedly occurred on J.P. Morgan's Jekyll Island off the coast of Georgia, attended by Nelson Aldrich and Frank Vanderlip of the Rockefeller financial empire; Henry Davidson, Charles Norton and Benjamin Strong representing J.P. Morgan (a member of the Jesuit order); and Paul Warburg of the Rothschild banking dynasty of Europe, reportedly the banking agent for the Jesuits. Their common interest was the centralisation of America's financial resources and elimination of outside competition in the banking world. This would ultimately ensure that more wealth flowed to the Roman Catholic Church and would also ensure that the United States had the financial means to fund a world war, favoured by the Jesuits in pursuit of their aims.

However (according to conspiracy theorists), the concept of a Federal Reserve was opposed by three of the most wealthy and influential men in the country: Benjamin Guggenheim, Isidor Straus and John Jacob Astor. Their opposition had to be eliminated in order for the Jesuits to succeed. Plans were made in which J.P. Morgan would arrange for the three to take passage aboard *Titanic*, which was then being built, for a pre-arranged fatal maiden voyage.

The theory claims that *Titanic*'s captain, Edward John Smith, was a 'Jesuit temporal coadjutor': not a priest, but a Jesuit who served the order through his profession. Through him, an accidental sinking could be arranged. A Jesuit master – a passenger from the order named Frank Browne – would board the liner for the short trip between Southampton and Cherbourg. Browne would order Smith to run his ship at full speed through an ice field on a moonless night, ignoring any ice warnings, including those from the lookouts, with the purpose of hitting an iceberg severely enough to cause the ship to founder and cause Guggenheim, Astor and Strauss to drown. In other words, the ship and her crew and passengers were to be sacrificed to eliminate three men. As their evidence, these theorists point out that after the sinking, all opposition to the Federal Reserve disappeared. In December of 1913 it was established in the United States, and eight months later (according to the conspiracy theorists) the Jesuits had sufficient funding to launch a European war. This particular theory, however, has never addressed why the conspirators in 1910 would feel that sinking a ship was a practical way to eliminate enemies of the Jesuits, to say nothing of how they would arrange for all three victims to board a specific ship on a specific voyage two years later. This is but one conspiracy theory involving *Titanic*; this book deals with another quite different.

Until 1985, the wreck of *Titanic* was a much sought-after prize that many considered equal to the quest for the Holy Grail. Over fifty books had been published covering the disaster from every conceivable angle. In the years following the discovery of the wreck, an estimated 120 new books were written, generally retelling the same old story, albeit with a wealth of new technical data and photographs acquired during the numerous return expeditions to the wreck site. Added to this has been an exponential increase in research on *Titanic*'s construction as well as forensic analysis of surviving photographs and the technical information they yield. While answering many long-standing questions, new questions have been raised that were never considered prior to her discovery and which have not been fully answered. Uncertainty spawns conjecture, and thus are born conspiracy theories. Some defy credibility, yet we cannot help but think 'what if …?'

Complicating the picture is the fact that many of the original builders' plans have disappeared over time, and many last-minute changes were made during construction that were never redrawn on the plans. Photographs are incomplete. Recollections of the surviving passengers and crew following the sinking are maddening in their contradictions. As an example, the testimony of nearly a dozen different officers and crewmen never established exactly what engine orders were rung down from *Titanic*'s bridge following the collision. Most of the testimony gained in formal hearings took place well after the event. With the passage of days and weeks memories fade and become corrupted by hearing what others remembered. Over the course of time, theory and fact have a way of becoming intertwined. Evidence can also be interpreted selectively to suit one's convenience: holding some up as proof of a claim, while conveniently ignoring that which contradicts it. Then there are the technical aspects. Frequently one theory or another fails simply because those promoting it lack technical knowledge of period shipbuilding, maritime practices or other aspects and what is claimed simply could not have happened that way.

This book, originally titled *Olympic and Titanic – The Truth Behind the Conspiracy*, was first published in 2002. It is not a book that promotes a conspiracy theory. It presents a wealth of photographic evidence and examines, with objectivity and analysis, the claims supporting one particular theory. It is the intent of this book to examine that theory in light of some of the mysteries surrounding *Titanic* and her nearly identical sister, *Olympic*. In doing so, it also catalogues and compares the differences between the two ships, which were far more numerous than a casual glance would suggest.

The ship that today lies more than 12,000ft below the waters of the icy North Atlantic is nothing more than a rapidly collapsing and disintegrating hulk. Is it really *Titanic*?

Titanic leaving the dock at Southampton at the start of her first and last voyage. (*R. Terrell-Wright Collection*)

INTRODUCTION

On 20 September 1911, nearly seven months before *Titanic* entered service, an event took place on what started out as a routine beginning of an eastbound crossing for *Olympic*. A sudden collision between *Olympic* and a Royal Navy cruiser, the RMS *Hawke*, left *Olympic* with major damage and the prospect of expensive and time-consuming repairs. She was withdrawn from service, and the damage was found to be even more serious than originally feared. Thus was born the 'switch theory'. Simply put, it holds that the wreck lying over 12,000ft below the surface is not *Titanic* but her sister ship *Olympic* and that the severe, crippling damage that *Olympic* suffered in the collision with RMS *Hawke* was concealed because she was too costly to repair. The cost of the repairs was not covered by insurance, nor would she recover the revenue lost while out of service. Therefore, the theory claims, *Olympic* was switched with her younger sister *Titanic* and deliberately sunk as *Titanic*, for whose loss insurance claims would be paid.

Support for this theory is partially based on the following points:

* Photographs taken of *Titanic* on 2 April in Belfast and on 10 April in Southampton show hull plates that appeared to be as faded and discoloured as those of a ship that had been at sea for over twelve months – not those of a ship that had been recently painted.
* There were remnants of white paint found on the hull of the wreck – a colour painted only on *Olympic*, never on her younger sister, *Titanic*.
* The fact that *Titanic*, the world's newest and largest ship, was never opened for public inspection while she was at Southampton as was customary. (The theory

holds that such public inspection may have revealed that the ship was, in actuality, *Olympic*.)

★ During the American investigation into the loss of the ship, Senator William Smith persistently tried to establish whether the ship's lifeboats were new since almost none of the lifeboats had lanterns as required by the Board of Trade and some started leaking once lowered into the water. (The lifeboats of *Olympic*, being older, were in theory susceptible to leakage, unlike new boats as would have been installed on *Titanic*.)

★ Supposedly there was a conversation years later in which a person claiming to be a surviving *Titanic* crewman stated that when he joined the ship at Belfast, he heard rumours that the two ships had been switched and that the true reason for the sinking of the ship had been covered up.

Would it have been possible to successfully switch the two ships?

There was one opportunity – if it succeeded, it would be the greatest sleight of hand of all time.

SUNSET, The Pacific Monthly   APRIL 1913   Advertising Section

THE WHITE STAR LINE

NEW YORK
PLYMOUTH
CHERBOURG
SOUTHAMPTON

BOAT DECK   BOAT DECK

PROMENADE   PROMENADE

THE NEW "OLYMPIC"
VIRTUALLY "TWO SHIPS IN ONE"

PROMENADE DECK B   HEIGHT OF EXTENDED WATERTIGHT BULKHEADS   PROMENADE DECK B

BULKHEADS 40 Ft. ABOVE WATER LINE — WATER LINE — OUTER SKIN — INNER SKIN

WATER TIGHT
G DECK
BULK-HEAD
D DECK
WALLS
E DECK
BULK-HEAD
F DECK
WALLS
G DECK

Fitted with

DOUBLE SIDES as well as DOUBLE BOTTOM | WATERTIGHT BULKHEADS extending from the BOTTOM TO THE TOP OF THE HULL

THUS AUGMENTING THE

FLOTATION CAPACITY

and enhancing
TO THE UTMOST

THE SAFETY OF THE VESSEL

The New "Olympic" is the greatest production of the premier British shipbuilders — the highest achievement of their long and fruitful experience in constructing many of the largest steamers of recent years—and in her, will be embodied everything that human foresight has devised for the safety of the passengers and crew.

Sailing from NEW YORK **April 12, May 3**

MAY 24. JUNE 14. JULY 5

and regularly thereafter.

White Star Line, 9 Broadway, New York
Offices and Agencies Everywhere

INNER SKIN

DOUBLE BOTTOM

In writing to advertisers please mention SUNSET, The Pacific Monthly
11

I

ISMAY'S TITANS

The *Olympic*-class liners – *Olympic* and *Titanic,* and later *Britannic* – represented a 50 per cent increase in size over the Cunard vessels *Lusitania* and *Mauretania*, which were the largest and fastest liners in the world at that time. Although the *Olympic*-class liners would not be as fast as the two Cunard greyhounds, White Star Line policy was to emphasise the luxury of its ships' passenger accommodations rather than speed.

To facilitate the construction of these three colossal vessels, Belfast shipbuilder Harland & Wolff would be required to make major modifications to its facilities. Two new slips were constructed in an area previously occupied by three. The William Arrol Company Ltd was contracted to construct two huge new gantries over these slips to carry the travelling cranes that would service them. When completed, the gantries covered an area 840ft long by 270ft wide.

Although the *Olympic*-class ships were originally conceived by J. Bruce Ismay, managing director of the White Star Line, and Lord William Pirrie, managing director of Harland & Wolff, their actual planning and design was carried out by the shipyard's principal naval architect Alexander Carlisle. Thomas Andrews was head of the yard's design department and oversaw the creation of the plans of the class prototype (*Olympic*) but Carlisle took charge of the details until he resigned in 1911. Throughout all stages of design and planning, all drawings and specifications were submitted to Ismay for his approval. Any modifications or suggestions he believed necessary were, without a doubt, carried out.

Of the three ships, *Olympic* and *Titanic* were built first, side by side in the two new slips, whereas *Britannic* would not begin building until three years later. When completed, *Olympic* and *Titanic* registered at just over 46,000 gross tons each and

A photograph of the massive Arrol gantry taken on 27 March 1909, the day *Olympic*'s keel was laid. (*White Star Photo Library/Daniel Klistorner Collection*)

measured 882ft 9in long and 92ft 6in wide at their maximum breadth. As a comparison to later ships, the German *Imperator* of 1913 was 909ft long and the *Queen Mary* of 1936 was just over 1,000ft. In an age of industry and accomplishment, these new ships would be true leviathans and would secure for the White Star Line a pre-eminent position in the North Atlantic steamship trade for years to come. Having a trio of the same class would also permit the White Star Line to guarantee a weekly service in each direction.

The *Olympic*-class ships were driven by a triple-screw arrangement powered by three engines of two different types. The port and starboard wing propellers were driven by two giant reciprocating engines, a form of motive power that was well established and highly reliable. These engines worked in much the same fashion as an automobile engine – with giant pistons and crankshafts – save that steam pressure was used to move the pistons within the cylinders. These engines were of the four-cylinder, triple-expansion type with a high-pressure, an intermediate-pressure, and two low-pressure cylinder bores of 54in, 84in, and 97in diameter respectively; each one had a 75in stroke. They were designated 'triple expansion' because the high-pressure steam from the boilers was fed first into a high-pressure cylinder, then, after it had expanded and moved the piston in that cylinder, it was exhausted into an intermediate-pressure cylinder to expand further and move that piston, and thence into two low-pressure cylinders to expand further and move those pistons. It was an economical means of propulsion in that the steam was made to do its work three times, although this type of engine did not yield speeds as high as a newer type of engine: the marine steam turbine.

The turbine engine – the motive power used aboard the *Lusitania* and *Mauretania* – functioned by directing steam past a series of vanes, closely grouped and fitted around a shaft directly attached to the propeller. In the same way that a windmill functions, the high-pressure steam expanding and passing through the turbine forced the vanes to spin the shaft. Higher speeds were possible than could be attained with reciprocating engines, albeit at the cost of more coal. As the White Star Line's goal was luxury and not speed, this design was not favoured as the principal means of propulsion for the *Olympic*-class ships. However, the turbine could be used in another way. By incorporating a low-pressure turbine engine in addition to the other two, use could be made of the latent energy that still remained in the steam even after it had been exhausted at sub-atmospheric pressure from the low-pressure cylinders of the reciprocating engines and before it was condensed to water and returned to the boilers. This low-pressure turbine drove the central propeller shaft, although it could only operate at higher speeds. After trials on various ships, the combination of two reciprocating engines and a single low-pressure turbine engine was found to be the most economical in terms of coal consumption and yielded a service speed that was eminently satisfactory. Each of the reciprocating engines developed 15,000IHP (indicated horsepower) at 75RPM (revolutions per minute). The low-pressure turbine developed around 16,000SHP (shaft horsepower) at 165RPM. Combined, the three engines within each of the *Olympic*-class ships could generate up to 51,000HP (and just over 59,000 if forced), giving the ships a service speed of 21 to 21½ knots with up to 24 knots possible when required.

The steam required to power the three massive engines on each ship was provided by twenty-nine huge boilers arranged side by side in six boiler rooms. Each had multiple furnaces within which the coal burned to heat the feedwater into steam. The five boilers in the aftermost boiler room were single-ended, with furnaces at one end only. The remaining twenty-four were double-ended, and were twice as long, with furnaces at each end. With three furnaces in the five single-ended boilers and six in the double-ended ones (three furnaces at each end), this required up to 159 furnaces to be kept burning with coal simultaneously. All had to be fired in a never-ending rotating sequence, and every piece of coal had to be shovelled by hand. This required a 'black gang' of 175 firemen, plus more than seventy-five trimmers whose job was to move the coal from the bunkers to the boilers. With the ship running at its normal service speed of 21 to 22 knots the furnaces could consume 620 to 640 tons of coal per day. The ship's coal bunkers, situated between the boiler rooms, had a combined

This image taken on 2 July 1909 shows *Olympic*'s partially plated Tank Top and wing tanks. In the slip to the left, *Titanic* is being constructed.

capacity of 6,611 tons and an additional 1,092 tons of coal could be carried in the reserve bunker hold just ahead of the forward-most boiler room.

Steam from the boilers not only powered the engines that drove each ship, it also generated electricity. Four powerful 400kW dynamos, or generators, were driven by steam and provided electricity for the ship's lighting, supplemental heating, much of the galley equipment, telephones, Marconi wireless equipment and myriad other needs. There were literally hundreds of miles of electrical cable throughout these massive ships; the lighting alone was provided by way of approximately 10,000 incandescent lamps. The four main dynamos were positioned in two side-by-side pairs within the Electric Engine Room aft of the Reciprocating and Turbine Engine Rooms, just forward of where the propeller shafts exited the hull. Two smaller 30kW emergency dynamos were located five decks higher up in the ship, and could function to provide emergency lighting in the event of catastrophic flooding around the propeller shafts putting the main dynamos out of service. A completely independent emergency lighting circuit could provide limited illumination in the event that the main lighting circuit was out of commission.

A ship of any size requires strength, stability and structure. The principal longitudinal strength centres on the keel, which in each *Olympic*-class vessel was a massive built-up construction of steel plating 1½in thick amidships and just under 1¼in thick at the bow and stern. Resembling a beam lying on its narrow edge, this vertical keel was 53in wide and 63in high, increasing in height to 75in in the Reciprocating Engine Room to provide additional strength to carry the massive reciprocating engines.

Hydraulic riveter at work on the vertical keel of *Olympic*. (Engineering/*Authors' Collection*)

Four smaller longitudinal members running parallel to the keel on either side provided additional strength in a fore-and-aft direction, and vertical steel plates running in a cross-ways direction between them completed the bottom. From the outer curve of the bottom extending outward and upward were the ship's frames, resembling a series of parallel ribs. These were constructed of 10in steel channels and were spaced 36in apart amidships, with the spacing gradually reduced to 27in at the stern and 24in at the bow where greater strength was needed to withstand the pounding of heavy seas as well as any light ice that might be encountered in New York Harbor in winter. Completing the framework of the hull were web frames called stringers or 'side keelsons', which connected the frames in a longitudinal direction and which gave added belts of great strength along the hull.

The outer skin of each ship was its shell plating – large steel plates riveted to the frames. On average, the shell plates were 6ft wide and 30ft long and weighed between 2½ and 3 tons each, with the largest being 36ft long and weighing 4¼ tons. The thickness of the plates averaged 1in amidships and thinned toward the ends but was thicker in other areas depending on the need for extra strength. The shell plates were fastened with rivets that were applied both by hand hammering and hydraulic press. It is a common misunderstanding that all of the rivets were hydraulically applied. In fact, hydraulic riveting had its limitations – for example, the massive jaws of the

Hydraulic riveter at work on *Olympic's* sheer strake. (Engineering/*Authors' Collection*)

hydraulic riveting machine could not be worked around more than moderate bends in the plates or get into confined areas. More than half a million rivets were used on each double bottom, and the weight of these rivets alone was estimated to be 270 tons. When completed, each ship had about 3 million rivets with an estimated weight of over 1,200 tons.

Much has been made in recent years of steel that became overly brittle in freezing temperatures, with suggestions that *Titanic* was somehow flawed in her construction from the start. In reality, the shell plating and the rivets that held them together and fastened them to the ribs were, in the collision with the iceberg, subjected to shearing forces that they were never designed to withstand. Inspectors from the British Board of Trade – an entity entirely separate from the shipyard and beholden to no private firm – rigorously inspected the ship's riveting in an ongoing basis for tightness and integrity, and any that failed inspection resulted in a deduction from the riveters' wages. While these steel plates were tremendously strong, the term 'shell plating' is quite appropriate as they were only intended to form the ship's outer shell and were never designed to be impervious to any major collision such as with another ship at speed – or an iceberg.

The lowest part of the hull was formed not by a single layer of steel plating, but by the heavily reinforced bottom structure with the keel as its backbone. With the outer bottom plated with steel to form the 'skin' of the ship and the inner bottom also plated, a cellular 'double bottom' resulted. The inner bottom was termed the Tank Top, so named because the double bottom, divided as it was by the keel and its longitudinal and transverse members, was comprised of forty-four separate watertight compartments. These compartments were used as tanks to carry water for ballast, boiler feed, and for domestic use. In addition to holding water, the double bottom added to the safety of the ship. As the Tank Top formed a second skin, it could save the ship from sinking if the ship struck a sunken obstruction or ran aground. Even with the outer bottom torn open, the watertight inner bottom would limit the flooding to the tank space and prevent entry of water into the holds or machinery spaces.

The principal safety feature of the *Olympic*-class ships, and certainly the one that gave rise to the 'unsinkable' myth, was the division of the space within the hull into sixteen watertight compartments by strong transverse watertight bulkheads. The forward, or collision, bulkhead was carried as high as C Deck, whereas those from the forward end of the reciprocating engines and aft were carried to D Deck. The remainder of the bulkheads – the ones between the boiler rooms amidships – only went as high as E Deck, but the lowest of these (there being a slight rise, or sheer, fore and aft from amidships) was still almost 11ft above the maximum-load waterline. This arrangement would allow *Olympic* and *Titanic* to easily survive a breach of two adjacent compartments amidships, the damage that would be expected through a collision with another large ship. Furthermore, each ship was capable of remaining afloat with all of the first four compartments flooded, providing ample protection if the ship rammed a floating body in her path. Thus *Olympic* and *Titanic*'s builders and owners were confident that their ships would remain afloat even in a worst-case collision scenario, and in fact the ships' watertight subdivisions met and exceeded many of the regulations for large ocean-going passenger vessels of today. In short: an *Olympic*-class ship would not be easy to sink.

Access through each of the transverse watertight bulkheads was gained by means of vertical-sliding watertight doors, which were held in the open (upper) position by a friction clutch. The doors could be released by means of a powerful electromagnet that was controlled by a switch on the bridge. These doors could also be closed by a releasing lever at the door itself, or from the deck above. The doors were also coupled to a float-activated switch that would close them automatically in the event that the compartment flooded and the water reached a pre-determined level. Although the speed of each door's descent was controlled by a hydraulic cylinder, the system was engineered to permit the doors – which weighed nearly three quarters of a ton – to drop the last 18 to 24in unrestricted. This ensured that they would crush or cut any obstruction (such as chunks of coal) which remained in the doorway, which was especially important since several of the watertight doors gave passage through the coal bunkers.

Any ocean-going ship must be designed to rid itself of water that makes its way into the lower part of its hull, and even the watertight *Olympic*-class ships were no

Period image of *Olympic* showing deck letter designations.

exception. A complex arrangement of piping connected to drain wells along the centreline of the ship in each watertight compartment provided for the removal of water in any area; a slight upward rise of the Tank Top from the centreline outward on each side ensured that any water would naturally flow into the wells. If necessary, the ship's entire pumping power could be brought to bear on a single compartment, and in an emergency, large volumes of water could be removed from the engine room by utilising the powerful condenser-circulating pumps that cooled the steam from the engines into water that was piped back to the boilers. Combined, either ship's pumping system could move 1,700 tons (over 400,000 gallons) per hour.

Olympic and *Titanic* were each fitted with a cast-steel rudder with a weight of 101¼ tons, an overall height of 78ft 8in and a width of 15ft 3in. It is commonly believed that *Titanic's* rudder was undersized and was one of the critical design flaws that contributed to the ship's inability to turn away from the iceberg in enough time to avert disaster. Like many 'facts' that often appear in print and online, this is a fallacy. Unlike warships, which had as a design requirement the ability to manoeuvre quickly, ocean liners had no such requirements. When manoeuvring in a narrow channel they normally utilised their engines in conjunction with the rudder, such as going half ahead on one engine while backing slow on the other. In a 1997 report by the Marine Forensics Panel of the Society of Naval Architects and Marine Engineers, naval architects Chris Hackett and John Bedford stated that: 'It must also be remembered that, although the rudder area was lower than we would adopt nowadays, *Olympic's* turning circles compare favourably with today's standards.'[1] Their conclusion was based on hard data rather than the speculation and conjecture on which statements to the contrary have been based.

Communication with ships and shore was made possible by the Marconi wireless apparatus fitted to a suite of rooms within a few steps of the Navigating Bridge. No longer was a ship isolated at sea when out of sight of other ships; no more did 'speaking' another ship require them to heave to within hailing distance. Day or night, fine weather or fog, ships could communicate with each other and have messages relayed to one side of the Atlantic or the other when in mid-ocean. Passengers could enjoy the novelty and convenience of sending messages through the ether, and in fact bridge-to-bridge messages from the master of one vessel to another enjoyed no priority over that of a passenger sending the equivalent of an electronic postcard.

The 5kW wireless transmitter was connected to four parallel aerial wires suspended between the ship's towering masts. From these aerial wires, cables led directly to the equipment in the wireless room. The wireless installation consisted of two complete sets of apparatus: one for transmitting and the other for receiving transmissions, plus an emergency transmitting set with limited range that could operate independently of the ship's power supply for 6 hours. The main transmitter had a guaranteed minimum range of 400 miles; however, at night or during certain atmospheric conditions, its range extended to more than 2,000 miles. The wireless apparatus was manned

24 hours a day by two operators holding nominal ranks of Junior Officers with the White Star Line, although their 'real' employer was the Marconi International Marine Communication Company Ltd.

For visual signalling, each ship was fitted with two electrically operated Morse lamps mounted on the roofs of the wing cabs outboard of the Navigating Bridge on either side. By pressing a sending key on a portable box plugged into a socket inside either wing cab, an officer could 'Morse' another ship via the flashing lamp above. In clear visibility the Morse lamps could be seen at 10–15 miles' distance. In addition, for distress signalling the ships were equipped with a large number of pyrotechnic rockets, described later in this book.

On their Boat Decks, *Olympic* and *Titanic* were each fitted with sixteen pairs of Welin davits, eight on each side of the ship. Rigged under the davits were sixteen wooden lifeboats: fourteen 30ft boats with a combined capacity of 910 persons, and two smaller emergency cutters (25ft 2in) with a combined capacity of eighty persons. The cutters were rigged under the foremost davits near the Bridge and were kept permanently swung out while at sea in order that they could be lowered quickly if needed. It was quite common for large vessels, steaming in excess of 20 knots, to collide with fishing boats on the Grand Banks off Newfoundland, and the cutters also had to be kept in readiness in case someone fell overboard.

Each of the ships was also equipped with an additional four Engelhardt collapsible boats (27ft 5in long) with a combined capacity of 188 people. The collapsibles were so named because they had wooden bottoms and adjustable canvas sides that could be pulled up and snapped taut by means of hinged steel braces. Two of the collapsibles were secured to the deck beneath the emergency cutters and the remaining two were secured to the roof of the Officers' Quarters deckhouse on either side of the No. 1 funnel. The latter could be raised up off the roof and lowered to the deck below by means of block-and-tackles that could be rigged to eyes spliced into the funnel shrouds (guy wires) above them.

Each ship had a total lifeboat capacity for 1,178 persons, well in excess of the official requirements – but more than 2,000 short of the number each ship was certified to carry. Provision of sufficient lifeboats became one of the most contentious issues that arose in the wake of the *Titanic* disaster. Much of the blame was levelled at the outdated regulations set by the British Board of Trade, which had not been amended since 1894. At the time of the last revision of the Board of Trade lifeboat regulations, the 12,950-ton Cunard vessel *Campania* was the largest ship afloat. In the years following this revision, no allowance was made for the dramatic increase in the size and passenger capacity of subsequent ships. At the time the plans were drawn for the construction of the *Olympic*-class ships in 1908, the regulations showed no distinction between the 12,950-ton *Campania* and the 46,000+ ton *Olympic* and *Titanic*. Under the regulations in force at that time, all British vessels of more than 10,000 tons with sufficient watertight subdivisions only had to carry sixteen lifeboats with a total

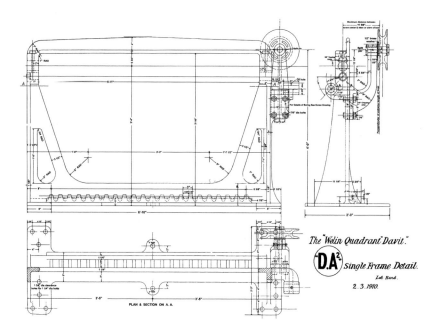

QUADRANT DAVIT FOR DOUBLE-BANKED BOATS.

CONSTRUCTED BY THE WELIN QUADRANT DAVIT, LONDON.

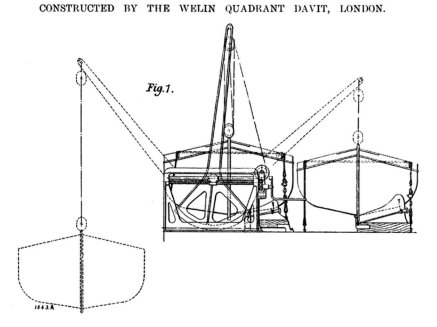

Top: A period advertisement for the Welin quadrant davit.
Bottom: The Welin double-quadrant davit, showing its capability to accommodate an inboard row of lifeboats.

capacity of 7,750 cubic feet; however, the lifeboat capacity on each of the *Olympic*-class ships totalled 11,325 cubic feet.[2] By fitting four Engelhardt collapsibles, the White Star Line actually exceeded the Board of Trade requirements by 46 per cent.

While the Board of Trade requirements were outdated, the White Star Line was by no means alone in its belief that more lifeboats would be unnecessary. In 1912, the need for 'lifeboats for all' was never seriously considered by many. Since the second half of the nineteenth century the flow of shipping across the Atlantic from New York to England had been known as the 'Atlantic Ferry' and for good reason: it was the most heavily travelled sea route in the world. With the advent of the Marconi wireless, ships were rarely out of communication with each other and any ship in distress could count on others coming to her aid long before she was in danger of foundering. Thus, in 1912, the utility of lifeboats was seen in their ability to convey passengers to a nearby ship rather than to provide a refuge for all aboard. It was considered inconceivable that a ship could ever founder with such rapidity that all persons would need to be taken off at once, rather than shuttling passengers to other vessels and then returning for additional loads. Even after the *Titanic* disaster, the author of *Practical Shipbuilding*, a widely respected authority on large steel-ship construction, opined that when a ship had been designed to remain afloat after the worst conceivable accident, 'the need for lifeboats practically ceases to exist, and consequently a large number may be dispensed with.'[3]

The Welin double-acting davits had been designed to attach and lower three lifeboats in succession and could easily have been adapted to increase this number to four. After launching the boats beneath them, the davit arms could be cranked inboard to be rigged to additional boats nested there. It is stated that during the significant planning stages of the *Olympic* and the *Titanic*, between 4 and 5 hours were devoted to discussing the ships' interior fittings and decor, with only 10 minutes given to discussing lifeboat capacity. Harland & Wolff's chief naval architect, Alexander Carlisle, had grave misgivings about the British Board of Trade's seemingly outdated lifeboat regulations. Carlisle's original sketch incorporated a provision for sixty-four lifeboats, which would have been sufficient for all on board; however, as discussions proceeded between Harland & Wolff and the White Star Line, Carlisle was obliged to modify his original plans. The number of lifeboats for *Olympic* and *Titanic* was first reduced to forty-eight, then to thirty-two, and then, some time between 9 and 16 March 1910, to only sixteen – the minimum number required by the Board of Trade.

Titanic's palatial First-Class passenger accommodations are well known and photographs of her public rooms and staterooms appear in countless books. They were luxurious indeed, and rivalled the finest hotels and restaurants ashore. Walnut, sycamore, oak and satinwood panelling were used liberally in the best First-Class rooms; imitation coal fires providing electric heat burned within wrought-iron grates set within ornate fireplaces; and stateroom washbasins were mounted in veined marble. Electric lighting and electric heat – all within the passenger's control – added to the

First-Class Stateroom B-59 on *Titanic.* (*H&W/Daniel Klistorner Collection*)

comfort, and bell pushes could conveniently summon a steward to provide a cup of tea or anything else that was desired.

The culinary facilities of the *Olympic*-class ships were no less impressive. The First-Class Dining Saloon could seat 554 passengers in one sitting, yet the service did not suffer from catering to such numbers: there was, on average, one steward for every three passengers. The galleys were immense and served everything from roast duckling to Waldorf pudding. A separate *à la carte* restaurant catered to passengers who did not want to dine according to a fixed schedule or partake of set courses, and passengers in either dining venue had their choice of wine, mineral water, cigars, fresh fruit, ice cream … virtually any drink, dish or delicacy found ashore could be had in First Class on *Olympic* or *Titanic.*

No less luxurious were the accommodations for Second and Third Class. Far from being in steerage, Third-Class passengers slept and dined as well as Second-Class accommodations on other ships, and better than on some. Clean linens, separate cabins, and meals served at table by stewards were the standard in Third Class. Making their new ships attractive to prospective emigrants was not out of compassion, but was good for business: despite the prices paid by First-Class passengers, which equalled the proverbial king's ransom for the finest suites, emigrant traffic was the bread and butter of the transatlantic steamship trade. While the *Olympic*-class ships could carry 735 in First Class and 674 in Second Class, they were designed to carry 1,026 Third-Class passengers. Without the income realised by the passage of emigrants in large numbers, neither the White Star Line nor any other major steamship company would have been able to afford these palatial liners.

The carriage of passengers was not the only income realised by *Olympic* and *Titanic*, however. Each ship could carry nearly 2½ tons of cargo in three spacious holds, and while no bulk cargoes were carried, bags, barrels, cases and crates in various quantities could be readily accommodated. Even motor cars could be carried, appropriately crated. No less important was the carriage of Royal and US Mail under contract to their respective governments, with 'RMS' before the ships' names to designate them as Royal Mail Steamers. There was even a special strong room for specie (coin money) and bullion. 268 tons of mail, parcels and specie could be carried, with four to eight British and American Sea Post clerks employed aboard to sort the thousands of bags of mail carried on each trip.

All in all, the *Olympic*-class ships were the pinnacle of shipbuilding achievement and would be highly profitable for their owners, and the White Star Line's prestige and prominence was riding on them. To have one damaged beyond repair – an event that would not be covered by insurance – would be catastrophic. As fate would have it, however, less than four months after *Olympic*'s maiden voyage, an unexpected event would take her out of service for a period of two months. Would it be grave enough to imperil the ship's future?

2

OLYMPIC AND TITANIC

Work on the construction of *Olympic* – Harland & Wolff yard number 400 – commenced on 16 December 1908. By New Year's Day a few weeks later, her hydraulically riveted keel had been completed. By this time the workforce at the shipyard had grown to well over 10,000. Three months later, when the keel of her sister ship *Titanic* was laid in the adjacent slip, the workforce had increased to by an additional 4,000 men. However, it should be noted that not all of these workers were actively engaged in the construction of these two ships. Harland & Wolff had contractual arrangements with other shipping companies, and work on those contracts proceeded in other parts of the yard. Approximately 6,000 men were directly involved with the building of the *Olympic*-class ships, about one-sixth of whom were on nightshift.

While work on *Olympic* and *Titanic* was in progress, construction was underway on two new White Star Line tenders to service the new leviathans at Cherbourg. Because the *Olympic*-class ships were too large to dock there, tenders would be required to ferry passengers, mail and baggage between ship and shore. These new tenders, *Nomadic* and *Traffic*, were purpose-built for this role and would be kept at Cherbourg.

After *Olympic*'s keel was laid, work proceeded at a brisk pace. Photographs reveal that by late November 1909 all but the last of the ship's frames had been raised into position. By late April 1910 her hull was completed. As with the ship's keel, hydraulic riveting had been adopted whenever possible. The seams of *Olympic*'s bottom hull plating were double riveted (two parallel rows of rivets where two shell plates met), whereas the topside hull plating had been triple and quadruple riveted for extra strength.

Over the course of six months, work continued within the hull. This included the laying of deck plating, installation of the transverse watertight bulkheads, plumbing,

In this image taken on 18 February 1909, hydraulic riveters are attaching the vertical floor plates to *Olympic*'s vertical keel plate. (*Authors' Collection*/The Engineer)

By mid-July, steel plating largely covered *Olympic*'s Tank Top and the stern frames (seen in the background) had been raised into place. (*Authors' Collection*/The Engineer)

Titanic and *Olympic* in mid–August 1910. The plating of *Titanic*'s hull is well advanced. (*Authors' Collection*/The Engineer)

Olympic's hull is freshly painted, as seen here two weeks before her launch. (*Authors' Collection*/*Harland & Wolff*)

electrical work, and the fitting of auxiliary equipment. The ship's heavy machinery such as boilers and engines would be lowered into the hull after the ship had been launched. For this reason the ships were not launched with their funnels installed, as the heavy machinery would be lowered into the hull through large openings in the funnel casings.

On 20 October 1911 *Olympic* was ready for launch. Photographs reveal something curious about her appearance: the hull had been painted a very light grey, except for the red ochre-coloured anti-fouling paint applied below the ship's intended water-line. This was at the direction of Lord Pirrie, who wanted to give the ship a dramatic visual appearance while she slid down the slipway into the River Lagan. The light paint would give the hull an overwhelming appearance of size, providing excellent photographic opportunities for the press to capture what was to be the world's largest ship.[1] Pirrie's decision to paint the ship's hull as such was intended to grab maximum press coverage, which would later pay handsome dividends as the photographs were seen worldwide. Following the launch, *Olympic*'s hull would be painted with the traditional graphite-grey undercoat above her waterline, eventually to be followed by her final coats of black for the majority of the hull and white on the uppermost

Olympic at time of her launch, 20 October 1910. (*Authors' Collection/Harland & Wolff*)

Titanic prior to launch on 31 May 1911. (*Charles Milner/Harland & Wolff*)

strake. The practice of painting the ship's hull in a very light-coloured paint was a common shipyard practice for the first of a class or for a special ship in order to draw attention to the launch. *Olympic*'s sisters *Titanic* and *Britannic* would both be painted in their standard colours when they were launched.

It was stated that on 20 October 1910 well over 100,000 people witnessed the launching of *Olympic*, with the press, dignitaries, and senior management of Harland & Wolff and the White Star Line present. *Olympic*'s launch weight – excluding the launch cradle at the bow that would keep her upright – was 24,600 tons, and the downward pressure on the bearing surface would be 2.6 tons per square ft. To lubricate the slipway and reduce the friction on the ways, some 15 tons of tallow and 3 tons of train oil mixed with 3 tons of soft soap were used. Just before 12.15p.m. the last of the supporting shores had been removed, leaving *Olympic* resting solely on the fore and aft poppets and the sliding ways. Only 62 seconds after the launch triggers had been released the ship gracefully slid stern first into the river. The 24,600-ton hull reached a maximum speed of 12½ knots before being brought to a standstill by six anchors and 80 tons of drag cable and chain.

At 12.15p.m. on 20 October 1910, *Olympic* was successfully launched.
(*Charles Milner/Harland & Wolff*)

On 31 May 1911, seven months after *Olympic*'s launch, *Titanic* slides stern first into the River
Lagan. (*R. Terrell-Wright collection*)

Following her launch, *Olympic* was taken in tow by tugs to the new deep-water Fitting-Out Wharf, located at some distance from the main shipyard. To bring all the heavy machinery from the shops to the ship's new location, Harland & Wolff operated a steam tram with small rail trucks. Everything that would be put aboard the ship from this point forward – boilers, funnels, engine bedplates, turbines, condensers, and other equipment and fittings – would be brought by rail. An extensive network of rail lines ran throughout the yard and terminated at the Fitting-Out Wharf.

To transfer of all the heavy equipment and machinery from the rail trucks into the ship, Harland & Wolff purchased a 200-ton floating crane with a maximum lifting weight of 150 tons, a lifting height of 150ft, and a loading radius of 100ft. The crane also had a smaller cable-operated hook capable of lifting 50 tons. By the end of December 1911, all of the heavy machinery such as the boilers, reciprocating engines, turbine engine, and so on, had been lowered and secured to their bedplates, after which the ship's four funnels were fitted.

On 1 April 1911, *Olympic* was transferred to the new graving dock (dry dock) adjacent to the Fitting-Out Wharf for the installation of her massive propellers. This new dry dock had been specifically constructed for the *Olympic*-class liners and was quite impressive in its dimensions. With concrete walls 15ft thick, its floor was 850ft in length and could be extended to over 886½ft if a caisson were placed against the outer quoins. The depth at the centre, below the level of high water of ordinary spring tides, was 37ft 3in. Once a ship had been carefully shifted into the dock and the gates had been closed, the water was pumped out and the ship rested on her keel on a series of blocks spaced close together. Strong timbers braced against the ship's side ensured that the hull could not shift to either side.

Olympic and *Titanic's* wing propellers (port and starboard) were each three bladed, had a diameter of 23ft 6in and weighed a massive 38 tons each. They were of 'built-up' construction, having manganese bronze blades bolted onto a cast-steel hub. The centre propeller had a diameter of 16ft 6in and weighed 22 tons. It had four blades and was cast as a single piece in manganese bronze.[2] Because the turbine was not equipped to move in reverse, the centre propeller operated only in the 'ahead' direction. On 2 May 1911, *Olympic* underwent her basin trials, during which the engines were turned for the first time.

In the months that *Olympic* spent in dry dock, most members of the workforce that had been actively engaged in the ship's construction were now completing the interiors. This consisted of painting, laying carpet and tile, installing plumbing and electrical fixtures, and otherwise transforming her interiors from bare steel spaces into rooms that would rival the finest hotels ashore. By this stage the ship was receiving her final coat of black paint on the lower hull and the white of the upper hull strake and superstructure.

Before departing on her sea trials on the morning of 29 May 1911, the world's newest and largest liner was opened for public inspection. A small admission fee was

Olympic at the Fitting-Out Wharf. (*Charles Milner*/The Engineer)

A similar view of *Titanic* at the Fitting-Out Wharf, August 1911. (*Ray Lepien*)

Olympic back in dry dock for port–side propeller replacement, 2 March 1912. (*Charles Milner/Harland & Wolff*)

Titanic in dry dock for the first time, 3 February 1912. (*Daniel Klistorner*)

charged, and thousands of people took the opportunity to see the new liner. All of the money collected was donated to various Belfast hospitals. On 29 May, having been loaded with over 3,000 tons of Welsh coal a few days prior, she was guided by tugs up the Victoria Channel toward Belfast Lough for her sea and acceptance trials. In command was the White Star Line's most senior and experienced captain, E.J. Smith, with Board of Trade surveyor Francis Carruthers aboard to cast his critical eye on the ship's performance. Carruthers was no stranger to the ship, and is believed to have inspected *Olympic* on no fewer than 2,000 occasions during her construction and fitting out.

The sea trials took place over a period of two days, and showed that the ship was slightly faster and more manoeuvrable than her designers had originally expected. At the completion of her trials, Carruthers issued a seaworthiness certificate valid for one year. Following the completion of the trials *Olympic* returned to Belfast in time to witness, from a distance, the launching of her younger sister *Titanic*. Her stentorian whistles added a congratulatory note to the occasion.

Olympic sailed on her maiden voyage at 4.30p.m. on 31 May 1911, stopping first for a courtesy call at her official port of registry, Liverpool. It was at this time that *Olympic* was officially handed over from the builders to her new owners, the White Star Line, who now had the world's largest and most luxurious liner afloat. On her arrival at Liverpool on 1 June, *Olympic* anchored in the River Mersey and was once again opened for public inspection. Just before midnight that same evening, *Olympic* weighed anchor and steamed for Southampton. Once there, arriving in the early hours of 3 June, she was berthed at the her new dock. The ship was provisioned, last-minute

Olympic departing Belfast on her sea trials, 29 May 1911. (*Jonathan Smith*)

Titanic departing Belfast on her sea trials, 2 April 1912. (*Authors' Collection / Harland & Wolff*)

mechanical adjustments were made, and some furniture and fittings were installed that had been waiting at Harland & Wolff's facility at the port. By 14 June *Olympic* was ready to depart on her maiden voyage and was scheduled to depart at midday.

When *Olympic* sailed for New York she had 1,316 passengers and 850 crew on board; her first port of call was Cherbourg, France. After collecting passengers at Cherbourg, she proceeded to Queenstown (now Cobh), Ireland, her final port of call before her first transatlantic crossing. *Olympic* arrived in New York on 21 June 1911, five days, 16 hours, and 42 minutes after departing Queenstown, having travelled an average speed of 21.17 knots. After coming up the Hudson River (known by mariners as the North River), *Olympic* was manoeuvred into the White Star Line's newly lengthened Pier 59, but her docking was not without incident. One of the tugs at her stern, the *O.L. Hallenbeck*, was caught up in the suction created by the liner's propellers and pulled under her stern, damaging her mast.

On *Olympic*'s return voyage from New York to Southampton on 28 June 1911, she averaged nearly 22.3 knots, arriving at Southampton on 5 July 1911, an excellent time considering that not all of the boilers had been fired. *Olympic* was never intended to be a contender for the Blue Riband (the title held by the fastest liner

Different view of *Olympic* departing on her trials. (*Ray Lepien*)

to cross the Atlantic) and her owners knew that she would never be a greyhound like the *Lusitania* and *Mauretania*. But she did prove that once all three *Olympic*-class liners were in service, they could easily maintain weekly service out of New York and Southampton. The Cunarders were not quick enough to operate a two-ship weekly return service from New York, so the additional 4 or 5 knots of speed that the Cunard ships had over White Star was to prove to no great advantage. Although many passengers enjoyed travelling on the fastest ships, the White Star Line had an unassailable position in size, luxury, and safety over their Cunard competitors.

Before *Olympic* entered service, the White Star Line was already operating a weekly transatlantic service between Southampton and New York, with the 21-knot *Oceanic* (17,274 GRT (gross register tonnage)), the 17-knot *Adriatic* (24,541 GRT) and the two 20-knot liners *Teutonic* (9,984 GRT each) and *Majestic* (9,984 GRT). It was planned that when *Olympic* entered service she would replace the *Adriatic* and that *Titanic* would replace the *Majestic*. The *Oceanic* would operate with *Olympic* and *Titanic* until *Britannic* was in service. When *Britannic* took over the transatlantic route, the *Oceanic* would then be transferred to other service but would be placed back in transatlantic service when an overhaul of any of *Olympic*-class liners required their temporary removal from service.

Titanic's construction had begun on 31 March 1909, only three months after *Olympic's* keel had been completed. Her construction schedule mirrored that of her sister, although with a seven-month difference, and both ships rose side by side within the Arrol gantry for more than a year and a half. Experience gained with *Olympic's* construction made work on *Titanic* somewhat easier, and it is recorded that by 6 April 1910, *Titanic* had been fully framed and by 19 October her hull was fully

A different view of *Titanic* departing Belfast on her trials. (*Daniel Klistorner*)

plated. Because of less interest in her building – *Olympic* having commanded most of the attention as the first in the class – *Titanic*'s construction details are somewhat sketchy. To this day, much of the media coverage and construction documentation on *Titanic* have yet to come to light.

As noted, the White Star Line benefitted from a fortunate coincidence in timing when *Titanic* was ready for launch on 31 May 1911 – the same day that *Olympic* returned from her sea trials prior to her final departure from Belfast. Dressed in holiday attire, J. Bruce Ismay, J.P. Morgan and other distinguished guests travelled to Belfast in the chartered ferry *Duke of Argyll* to witness the event. *Titanic* towered overhead in the gantry as more than 100,000 people turned out to see the spectacular event. Despite the impressive turnout, her launch attracted a visibly smaller crowd than had been in attendance to witness *Olympic*'s launch seven months earlier. It was said that many of those present were marvelling over *Olympic* at where she was anchored and paid less attention to *Titanic*. It was still a noteworthy event though, as the sheer size of the ships had no equal anywhere in the world.

Titanic was launched at 12.15p.m., and just over a minute later was afloat in the river. Yard workers in rowing boats proceeded to detach the steel-wire hawsers from the river anchors and drag chains, which had been used to arrest the massive hull to an eventual standstill. She was taken in tow by five tugs, which escorted her to the Fitting-Out Wharf. Back on land, the attendant dignitaries remained at Queen's Island while their guests dined at the Grand Central Hotel in Belfast. Later, all boarded the tender *Nomadic* for the transfer to *Olympic*, which sailed at 4.30p.m. for Liverpool. It had been a memorable day, and a cause for celebration in more than one way: it was also Lord and Lady Pirrie's birthday.

When first conceived, *Titanic* was to be nearly an identical replica of *Olympic*. Photographs taken when *Titanic* was launched in 1911 show how similar the two hulls were. The only obvious difference was the colour of the hull. If one closely examines the photographs one will notice that, externally, the only differences were in the porthole arrangements in the plating around and below the Poop Deck (the area painted in white at the stern) and the porthole arrangement along the sides of the hull. Looking at the area painted in white in the general area amidships, one can see a difference in size of some of these portholes.

In the weeks following *Titanic*'s launch, and following observations made during *Olympic*'s maiden voyage, Bruce Ismay decided that certain modifications should be made to *Titanic* to add more First-Class staterooms as well as making some of the existing accommodations even more luxurious. *Olympic* originally had two full-length promenade decks, one on B Deck as well as the one on A Deck that *Titanic* would have. As it turned out, *Olympic*'s B Deck promenade was little used and Ismay felt that this was a waste of valuable space. By removing this promenade on *Titanic*, her First-Class accommodations on B Deck could be extended out to the side of the hull, thereby creating a series of luxurious suites. From the space remaining, a private Promenade Deck could be added to each of the two B-Deck Parlour Suites. Aft on the starboard side, the remainder of the B-Deck promenade was turned into the chic Café Parisien, and on the port side the First-Class *à la carte* Restaurant was extended out to the ship's side. This also had the advantage of eliminating what was originally a Second-Class promenade directly outside the Restaurant.

These alterations required the removal of almost all the original external windows and framing on B Deck. The result was a distinctly less uniform pattern than that on *Olympic*. There was also another significant alteration made to *Titanic*: the enclosing of the forward part of the A Deck promenade with steel-framed screens with windows to protect passengers from sea spray. On *Olympic*'s maiden voyage, the strong winds blowing aft along her hull – typical of a westbound crossing – carried large amounts of spray with them, and caused the deck area along the forward half to be wet and unpleasant much of the time. Thus it was decided to enclose the deck for part of its length. Ultimately, this alteration would be the most readily identifiable difference between the two ships.

After these alterations were complete, the White Star Line began to refer to *Titanic* as the largest ship in the world in its advertising. When one considers that the hulls of *Titanic* and *Olympic* had been constructed from the same set of plans, how could *Titanic* be larger than *Olympic*? The answer is simple, and needs only a basic understanding of the differences between the various tonnage ratings that can be given to a ship. The 24,600-ton weight of the empty hulls should not be confused with the approximately 45,000+ gross register tonnage of each ship, which was a measurement not of deadweight but rather the volume of the interior revenue-producing portions of the completed ships. Because of the added accommodations into the space formerly occupied by the B-Deck promenade on *Titanic*, she was 'larger' even though the added weight from her alterations was negligible. Even so, the difference in gross registered tonnage was minimal, just a little over 1,004 tons.

Work on *Titanic* continued apace until 6 October 1911, when *Olympic* returned for unforeseen and extensive repairs. This required a large percentage of the workforce to be shifted from *Titanic* to her sister, and while work continued on *Titanic*, her progress was delayed. As a consequence, the White Star Line was forced to reschedule her maiden voyage from 20 March 1912 to 10 April.

A photograph taken in January 1912 shows *Titanic* with all four of her funnels in place. This indicates that all her boilers and heavy machinery had been lowered into place. She was now ready for dry docking for the installation of her three massive propellers and the painting of her lower hull. *Titanic* entered the huge graving dock on 3 February 1912, and the event was captured in a short 2-minute newsreel. That film is, to this day, the only known moving pictures taken of the ship. Two weeks later, on 17 February, the necessary work in dry dock was completed and she was removed and shifted back to the Fitting-Out Wharf.

Only one week later, *Olympic* was once again forced to return to Belfast after losing one of her port propeller blades some 750 miles off Newfoundland under curious circumstances. The cause was never definitively established. *Olympic* was moved into the graving dock on 2 March and replacement of the blade was completed in record time. On the morning of 4 March, *Olympic* was ready to return to service.

In order for her to proceed down the Victoria Channel, she would need to be swung around so that her bow faced in the opposite direction. On the day that she was backed out of the graving dock, the weather deteriorated. With high winds acting against the hull and superstructure, the tugs assisting the vessel had difficulty in controlling her. It soon became obvious that it would be too dangerous to attempt to swing the huge vessel in the restricted waters of the turning basin. With *Titanic* occupying the nearby Fitting-Out Wharf, the only safe option under the circumstances was to place *Olympic* back in dry dock. By the next morning the weather had not improved and *Olympic* was forced to remain in place. With pressure mounting to return her to service, Harland & Wolff undertook something that had never been done before: taking *Olympic* out of dry dock and moving *Titanic* in on the same tide, thereby freeing up space at the Fitting-Out Wharf for *Olympic*, which could remain there until the weather moderated.

Olympic was finally able to cast off her mooring lines and leave Belfast on 7 March. The following day *Titanic* was promptly taken out of the graving dock, turned in the basin and moved back to the Fitting-Out Wharf. Less than four weeks remained until her sea trials and official handover to the White Star Line, and time was pressing.

Titanic's sea trials had been planned for Monday 1 April. The required tugs, owned by the Alexander Towing Company, had been dispatched from Liverpool to Belfast on 31 March. Some of these same tugs had escorted *Olympic* to her sea trials ten months earlier. The weather was bitter and cold with a strong northwesterly wind, turning the normally calm Victoria Channel rough and choppy. By 10.00a.m., the scheduled time of *Titanic's* departure, it was decided that the conditions in the channel presented too great a risk for safe ship handling and the trials were postponed until the following day. By the next morning conditions had improved considerably, and a clear sky and calm waters no doubt caused more than one officer and tug captain to breathe more easily. The tugs *Herculaneum, Hornby, Hercules, Herald* and *Huskisson* escorted *Titanic* up the channel with Captain Edward Smith in command, Smith having handed over command of *Olympic* to Captain Herbert James Haddock a short time earlier.

Once in the open waters of Belfast Lough *Titanic* was put through a series of manoeuvres to test her turning and stopping capabilities and other aspects of her performance. Although her sea trials were not as rigorous as those that *Olympic* had undergone the year before, they were by no means perfunctory. As both ships had identical hulls and propulsion machinery, there was no need to determine what *Titanic's* handling characteristics were, only to verify that she performed as expected and required.

While the ship was being put through her paces, *Titanic's* two wireless operators, John (Jack) Phillips and Harold Bride, were tuning and testing the ship's Marconi system. The equipment was in constant use as messages about the details of the sea trials were being transmitted to Ismay. Other Marconi-equipped vessels were also being contacted to test the equipment's range. At one point Phillips and Bride experienced freak atmospheric conditions and established communications with Port Said in Egypt, some 3,000 miles distant.

Titanic returned to Belfast at 6.30p.m. that evening and was obliged to lower both starboard and port anchors under the critical eye of the Board of Trade surveyor. Carruthers, being satisfied with the ship's performance throughout the trials, signed the certificate of seaworthiness, valid for one year. With this document in hand, the directors of the White Star Line would have seen the obligations of the contract finalised, thereby acknowledging the official transfer of the vessel from builder to owner.

With the formalities dispensed with, and the transfer of the officials ashore, *Titanic* weighed anchor at or around 8.00p.m. Departing Belfast Lough, she briefly tracked eastward into the Irish Sea and made for Southampton. During the 570-mile trip the officers took the opportunity to perform additional engine and manoeuvring trials. One notable highlight of the trip was a short run at maximum speed, during which the new ship reached an impressive 23.5 knots.

Making an average of 18 knots, it was expected that *Titanic* would conveniently arrive at Southampton on the tide. Although the ship was inconvenienced by fog 6 hours into the voyage, it cleared just after 6.00a.m. Just after noon that same day, *Olympic* departed Southampton for Cherbourg, Queenstown and New York.

At approximately 10.00p.m. that evening *Titanic* arrived off Spithead, passed the Nab lightship and slowed to embark the Southampton pilot. With the pilot now on the bridge, she proceeded cautiously at half-ahead past Cowes and negotiated the twisting, turning channel into Southampton Water. A short time later, five Red Star tugs – *Ajax*, *Hector*, *Hercules*, *Neptune* and *Vulcan* – assisted the new ship into the calm waters of the River Test. The time was just after 11.30p.m. With her bow facing downstream, it was then necessary to bring the ship through a 130-degree turn to port to bring her parallel with the dock. Using a push-pull action, the tugs manoeuvred the huge hull slowly astern. It was just after midnight when the ship was finally secured alongside Berth 44.

Titanic was never opened up for public inspection like *Olympic*. The reason given was the delays in her fitting out caused by *Olympic* having to return to Belfast for repairs on two separate occasions. Work was still being completed on her interiors (painting, laying of carpet and the like) during her trials, as well as on her trip to Southampton. This is further evidenced by the fact that *Titanic* was unable to make a courtesy call at Liverpool as *Olympic* had. In fact, *Titanic* was never officially opened up to the general public at any time. Was this circumstantial – or intentional?

During *Olympic's* construction more than 150 photographs were taken of her at Harland & Wolff, while only 100-odd images chronicled *Titanic's* construction and fitting out. It is quite apparent that *Titanic* attracted less photographic and media attention during her beginnings than her sister did. The lack of progressive construction photographs has been disappointing and frustrating over the years for liner enthusiasts, historians and researchers. For much of that period, we are forced to rely on photos of *Olympic* with *Titanic* in the background, 2 minutes of moving pictures taken during the ship's dry docking in February 1912 and images that were taken primarily by press photographers. Very few official images of *Titanic* were taken by Harland & Wolff's photographers.

Both *Olympic* and *Titanic* were constructed from the same set of plans. When launched, their hulls, machinery and deck arrangements were almost identical. Even when completed they were indistinguishable unless one knew exactly what to look for. Apart from the different window spacing on *Titanic's* B Deck and her enclosed forward promenades on A Deck – modifications made only after her launch – the casual observer would have been hard-pressed to tell them apart. Would it have been possible, then, to eliminate these differences altogether and change one ship into the other?

3

SEEDS OF THE CONSPIRACY

At 11.25a.m. on 20 September 1911, *Olympic* departed Southampton to begin her fifth voyage across the Atlantic. Aboard were 885 crew and 1,279 passengers; an additional 824 would board at Cherbourg and Queenstown. Aboard were a number of prominent passengers, including the president of the New York Central Railroad Company and Member of Parliament Waldorf Astor. As with *Olympic's* four previous voyages she was under the command of Captain Edward J. Smith. As these were pilotage waters, a Trinity House pilot would direct the ship's navigation as far as the Nab lightship. On this trip it was Captain George Bowyer, a senior pilot who had known Smith for years and who was thoroughly familiar with the handling of the *Olympic*-class ships.

To reach the open sea from Southampton Water, *Olympic* would have to negotiate a narrow channel that led south-west into the Solent. Bowyer would then guide the huge liner through a tight turn to port around a shoal known as the Bramble Bank before entering the main channel that led to Spithead. From there, she would pass to the south of the Ryde Middle Bank and make for the Nab lightship at the entrance to the English Channel, where Bowyer would disembark. These were not deep waters, and ships had to keep to the designated channels in order not to run aground on the many sandbanks and other shallow areas.

Leaving Southampton Water, *Olympic* turned to starboard past the Calshot Spit light vessel. She steadied on a course of S 65 W (245 degrees)[1] down the deep-dredged Thorn Channel. Meanwhile the HMS *Hawke*, a Royal Navy cruiser[2] under command of Captain William F. Blunt, was going up the Solent in the process of making her annual power trials. The vessels sighted each other at a distance of 3 to 4 miles. By that time *Olympic* was passing the North Thorn buoy and the *Hawke* was in the vicinity of the Gurnard Ledge buoy approaching Egypt Point.

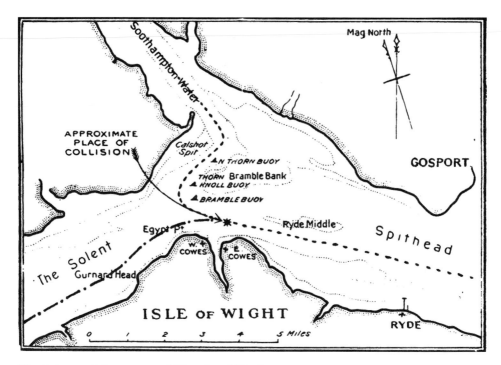

The Solent and the courses of *Olympic* and *Hawke*.
(Pacific Marine Review, *Vol.9, No.2, February 1912*)

About 4 minutes later, three-quarters of the way between the Thorn Knoll and West Bramble buoys, *Olympic* gave two blasts on her whistle to signal to the *Hawke* that she was beginning her turn to port into the eastern passage through the channel into Spithead. By now the distance between the ships had decreased to between 1 and 1½ miles and *Olympic* had the cruiser on her starboard bow. To safely negotiate the sharp turn around the West Bramble buoy, *Olympic*'s rudder would need assistance from her engines. With the starboard engine continuing to turn ahead, the port engine was ordered full-astern, then slow-ahead. The helm was then put to port and the port engine was stopped and briefly backed. With the turn completed, the ship was put on a heading of S 59 E (121 degrees). Both engines were put full-ahead, slowly increasing her speed from 12 to 16 knots. The time was 12.43p.m.

As *Olympic* was completing her sweeping turn to port into the channel, the *Hawke* was rounding Egypt Point to get into the same channel. With *Olympic* having just completed her turn in front of him, Captain Blunt altered his course slightly from S 77½ E to S 74 E (102.5 to 106 degrees) to move further south in the channel. The ships were now converging at an angle of 15 degrees.

By now *Olympic*, her speed still increasing, was making an estimated 14 knots. Slowly the *Hawke,* making 15¼ knots, started to overtake *Olympic* on her starboard side. As *Olympic* finally matched and then exceeded the *Hawke*'s speed, she began drawing away from the cruiser. By how far the *Hawke* overtook *Olympic* up to this

Hawke prior to the accident. (*Jonathan Smith Collection*)

point is open to debate; varying statements never established a definitive answer. Captain Smith estimated that the *Hawke's* bow had reached a point as far forward as his ship's compass tower between the Nos. 2 and 3 funnels before she started to drop back. Bowyer estimated that the *Hawke's* bow was even with *Olympic's* Navigating Bridge, testifying that he saw her stem through the window of the Bridge wing cab. Chief Officer Henry Wilde believed the *Hawke* reached a point opposite *Olympic's* forward funnel, while a local Cowes boatman who had taken a photographer out in the Solent stated that the bow of the cruiser reached the No. 1 funnel. Whichever estimate one accepts, it is clear that the *Hawke's* bow did not pass forward of *Olympic's* Bridge – or did it?

Suddenly the *Hawke* began to swing to port, toward *Olympic's* towering hull in the area of the liner's No. 3 funnel. On *Olympic's* Bridge, Smith and Bowyer noticed that the *Hawke* was moving close to *Olympic's* side. Thinking that the *Hawke* might have been attempting to cross his wake astern, Smith stated, 'I don't believe she will get under our stern, Bowyer'. Bowyer replied, 'If she is going to strike, sir, let me know in time so I can put the helm hard over to port.'[3] Smith replied, 'Yes, she is going to strike us in the stern.'

On the Bridge of the *Hawke*, Captain Blunt had ordered 5 degrees of starboard helm to open the distance between the two ships. Instead, the cruiser swung 4 or 5 points in the opposite direction. Instead of turning away from *Olympic*, she now angled toward her. Believing the helmsman had turned the wheel the wrong way, Blunt yelled: 'What are you doing? Port, port, hard aport![4] Stop port engine, full astern starboard.' From the Wheelhouse below the helmsman called up: 'The helm's jammed!' With the rudder now at 15 degrees to port, the *Hawke* was being pulled into *Olympic's* starboard quarter. The 45,000-ton liner towered over the 7,350-ton cruiser; collision was imminent. Captain Blunt quickly jumped down the ladder to the Wheelhouse and rang full-astern on the port engine. On *Olympic*, Bowyer ordered the ship's helm put over hard to starboard, hoping to swing the liner's stern clear of the rapidly closing *Hawke*.

Olympic's bow had swung 7 degrees to starboard when the cruiser's cement-reinforced bow struck her hull, 86ft forward of the stern post. The collision almost capsized the aging cruiser. Fortunately for the *Hawke*, *Olympic's* forward momentum resulted in the cruiser being sheared away to one side with the ram from her bow falling off in the process, and she quickly returned to an even keel. At the moment of collision, Smith had ordered the closing of the lower watertight doors and 'All Stop' was rung down to the Engine Room to minimise any damage to the propellers. *Olympic* continued for a short distance before coming to a stop, well clear of the *Hawke*. Most likely, Smith ordered one or both of the anchors lowered as well.

Smith, the Chief Engineer and the Carpenter quickly assessed the damage below decks, although a full evaluation of the damage was not possible. The inspection showed that the ship was no longer seaworthy, and the voyage would have to be cancelled. Unable to return to Southampton because of the state of the tide, *Olympic* anchored in Osborne Bay off Cowes to the north of the Prince Consort buoy, about ¾ mile from shore. Her non-essential crew and some of her passengers were taken off, including 600 Third-Class passengers who were put up by the White Star Line at

Hawke after the collision with her prow seriously damaged. (*Jonathan Smith Collection*)

This group of images shows *Olympic* being towed into Southampton after the *Hawke* collision. Her stern is noticeably down in the water. (*Jonathan Smith Collection*)

"S.S. Olympic" at Southampton. Docks after. Collision 20.9.1911

DAMAGE TO WHITE STAR R.M.S. OLYMPIC after collision with H.M.S HAWK SEPT 20 1911

The images on these two pages show the serious damage resulting from the *Hawke* collision. Only the gash above the waterline is visible here; far more serious damage occurred below the waterline from the *Hawke*'s underwater bow ram. (*R. Terrell-Wright collection*)

The damage to *Olympic* as seen from the inside. (*Jonathan Smith Collection*)

its emigrant home in Southampton. *Olympic*'s passengers had nothing but praise for her crew and were unanimous in blaming the warship for the collision.

Although *Olympic*'s two aftermost compartments had been breached and flooded, the ship was in no danger of sinking and the following day she was towed back to Southampton for a full damage evaluation at Harland & Wolff's maintenance facility there. An assessment by divers revealed that all three starboard propeller blades were severely chipped and would require replacement, and 18ft of the starboard propeller boss arm plating was deformed and fractured. The starboard propeller shaft had been bent out of alignment and rendered unusable. Eleven hull plates had been damaged above the waterline; eight of these were beyond repair and would have to be replaced. A 7ft-high hull breach with a pear-shaped opening 12–14ft in size rose from the waterline to D Deck, and a gash approximately 40ft wide was found below the waterline. Many of the ship's frames in the damaged area had been bent and twisted, and thousands of her hydraulically fitted rivets were no longer watertight.

Olympic would have to return to Belfast as she required resources far beyond what was available at Harland & Wolff's maintenance facility at Southampton. She required dry docking, and the huge graving dock at Queen's Island was the only one that could accommodate a ship of her size. In order that she could steam safely to Belfast, the workforce at Southampton attached temporary steel plates to the breached hull

plating below the waterline and secured the opening above the waterline with timbers. The temporary repairs required about two weeks to complete. At first glance,
this seems to be an excessive amount of time for what amounted to no more than a
rough patch over the hull. Did she undergo more work than that, or did the divers
find something that required more investigation?

On Wednesday 4 October 1911, the crippled *Olympic* departed Southampton for
the 570-mile run to Belfast. Because the starboard shaft had been rendered unusable,
she steamed the distance to Belfast on only her port engine. With her speed reduced
to 8–10 knots, *Olympic* arrived at Belfast just before midday on Friday 6 October.
Although the temporary hull patches done at Southampton were intended to prevent the stern compartments from flooding they were only marginally successful, for
when she arrived in Belfast the damaged compartments were filled with water. It
appeared that there might be other breaches in the hull not yet located and only a full
inspection in dry dock would reveal them.

In researching the number of hull plates that had been either damaged or replaced
after the *Hawke* collision, the authors obtained a drawing from Harland & Wolff's
Technical Services Department. This drawing indicates the areas near the stern where
plating was either removed to expedite internal repairs or was replaced because of
collision damage. Knowing that the damage was concentrated about 86ft from the
ship's stern post, and in light of the fact that the *Hawke*'s bow had allegedly reached
a point only as far forward as *Olympic*'s Navigating Bridge, the damage indicated on
the drawing in this area revealed no surprises. It showed that shell plating had been
replaced along five of the aftermost compartments on the starboard side. The two
compartments furthest aft were where the hull had been directly breached by the
bow of the *Hawke*. The next three compartments forward of these also had their
plating removed. It is not clear how far forward in this area the damage extended;
as individual steel plates could be up to 30ft long, some of them may have extended
well beyond the damaged area. Some damage could have also been done to the
frames within, requiring removal of the overlying plates.

Harland & Wolff sent a second drawing as well, however. This one was of *Olympic*'s
bow area. It showed that she had apparently sustained hull damage in the area below
the waterline as far forward as the ship's second watertight compartment from the
bow (well forward of the Bridge), and indicated that shell plating between watertight compartments 2, 3, and 4 may have been either damaged or breached. If this
occurred in the *Hawke* collision, why is it not mentioned in any of the contemporary
reports available? On the basis of this new information, we must ask if *Olympic* was
more extensively damaged than was known at the time outside Harland & Wolff and
the White Star Line.

This new information would also seem to indicate that the *Hawke* first collided with
Olympic 100ft forward of the Bridge, causing 115ft of damage extending forward from
the Bridge. If this were the case, then the casual observer would not have seen any

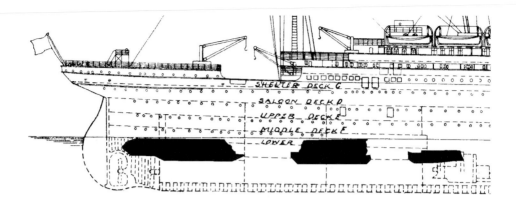

On 10 January 1997, the administration manager of Harland & Wolff's Technical Services was asked to specify the area of damaged shell plates on *Olympic*, which were repaired or removed after the *Hawke* collision. The diagram shown above is what was provided to the authors.

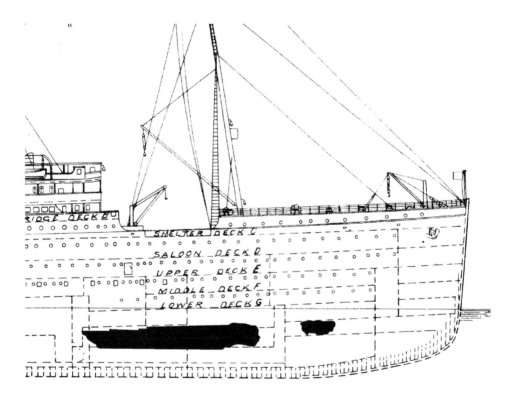

This diagram from Harland & Wolff shows areas of the shell plating further forward that were replaced at the same time, although no explanation was provided as to why.

Olympic in the graving dock at Harland & Wolff. The damage to the propeller blades is clearly evident here. (*Authors' Collection/Harland & Wolff*)

visual damage to *Olympic* besides the breached hull plating on her stern. These damaged plates would have been visible only when the ship had been placed in dry dock. It would appear that the White Star Line managers were going to receive a few costly surprises when the dry dock was drained. Or were they aware of this fact all along?

Although the shell plating in the bow area may not have been damaged enough to cause the ship to take on water in the affected areas, it is clear that 115ft of the ship's hull plating had been sufficiently damaged to require replacement or repair. If the plating had been damaged, there would be a possibility that the 10in steel channel frames inside had been damaged and required replacement as well. Had her structural integrity been compromised in this area?

If this was the case, then replacing the shell plating would not be sufficient unless all the damaged frames were replaced as well. These frames extended over multiple decks; therefore, replacement would require the removal of all the attached hull plating. Removal and replacement of such a large area of shell plating, plus replacement of the frames would have been extremely expensive, labour intensive and time consuming.

The White Star Line management no doubt wanted their flagship repaired and returned to service as quickly as possible. The longer *Olympic* stayed at Belfast, diverting workers who were normally engaged in *Titanic's* fitting out, meant further delays in *Titanic's* completion. Therefore, *Olympic's* hull frames may have been simply bent back into place and reinforced and the shell plating in that area replaced. Even if such a repair failed at some point, the ship could remain afloat with the first four compartments opened to the sea. However, if this was the case, *Olympic* might now have an Achilles heel on her starboard side forward, below the waterline between watertight compartments 2 and 4.

By the end of October, her repairs were expected to cost £100,000 ($500,000). The loss of revenue from the three round trips cancelled thus far was expected to cost the White Star Line another £50,000 ($250,000), none of which was covered by insurance. The company carried a risk of £100,000; anything above that was covered by its insurance underwriters. However, under the terms of the policies covering the ship, a claim would only be paid if it exceeded £150,000 ($750,000).

But the White Star Line was facing an even greater worry. The British Naval Court of Inquiry had just ruled that *Olympic* was at fault for the collision, not the *Hawke*. This meant that the White Star Line might have to bear the financial burden of repairing – or replacing – the *Hawke*. At the time it was seriously considered that the *Hawke* might be a total loss, and her cost when built in 1893 had been £401,000. The limit on liability in such cases was £8 per ton, but owing to *Olympic's* tonnage her potential liability amounted to almost £350,000 ($1,750,000). The implications were staggering.

After six and a half weeks the repairs to *Olympic* were completed, and she returned to service on 29 November. There is no question that the White Star Line lost a substantial amount of money due to cancellations by people who would have otherwise chosen to travel on *Olympic*. But the fact remains that the White Star Line had other ships available – although not as new, large or luxurious – and many passengers simply sailed on them. The court also ruled that while the collision was the result of negligent navigation on the part of *Olympic*, neither her captain nor the White Star Line were at fault because the ship was under compulsory pilotage at the time. It ruled that the pilot was ultimately responsible for the collision, which meant that the White Star Line would not be liable for the cost of the damage to the *Hawke*. Management could breathe easier.

However the incident was still a double blow. Aside from the costs of repairs and lost revenue, the forced diversion of workers from *Titanic* to *Olympic* had set back *Titanic's* maiden voyage from 20 March to 10 April. If *Olympic* had not collided with the *Hawke*, *Titanic* would have departed Southampton three weeks earlier, and history may have changed. However, even if her maiden voyage had occurred as originally scheduled, she was scheduled to operate on a two-week turnaround out of Southampton and would have made another westbound crossing on 10 April. In this case – with Captain Smith supposedly intending to retire after the maiden voyage – someone else would have been aboard in his place, but the ice in the North Atlantic would have been exactly in the same place. If that voyage had been her second crossing, would the same events have occurred that gave *Titanic* her place in history?

There is a curious omission in evidence admitted to the resulting court cases that attempted to ascertain who was at fault in the *Hawke* collision. The court ruled that *Olympic* had turned too wide into the channel and that the movement of her huge hull through the water had resulted in a suction effect between the two ships. The *Hawke*, said the court, was drawn into the liner's side. Although the *Hawke's* jammed helm contributed to the collision, the court ruled that *Olympic* had a duty to keep out of the *Hawke's* way since at the moment of collision *Olympic* had the greater speed and was not, therefore, being overtaken by the *Hawke*.[5] Therefore, the court passed down a verdict in favour of the Admiralty based on negligent navigation on the part of *Olympic*, ruling that she had been steered too far to the south and crowded the *Hawke* out of the channel.

The White Star Line appealed the verdict, claiming that the *Hawke* had in fact been overtaking *Olympic* at the time of collision rather than *Olympic* pulling ahead. To prove its contention, the White Star Line set out to recover the *Hawke's* sheared-off bow ram to pinpoint the exact position of the collision. The court dismissed this on the basis that the *Hawke's* ram had fallen from the ship some time after the collision. This raises a question: if *Olympic* had sustained damage by the *Hawke* forward of the bridge, then why did the White Star Line choose not to cite this damage as evidence that might have proved that the *Hawke* had indeed been overtaking *Olympic* when struck the liner's side? The officers of the White Star Line would have the proof they needed. The appeal was heard in January 1913, eight months after *Titanic* had sunk. Is it possible that White Star Line officials could not produce hard evidence because they no longer had *Olympic* to put forth?

In the appeal, the court again ruled in favour of the Admiralty. The White Star Line appealed once more, this time to the House of Lords. In a judgment handed down on 9 November 1914, the case was again lost. Right to the end, White Star management maintained that they were in the right. Now, having lost all avenues for appeal, the White Star Line had to accept a loss of at least £125,000.

Why the White Star Line had played down the damage to *Olympic's* bow is in need of explanation, but it leaves one wondering what other damage, if any, she suffered in the collision. Could *Olympic* have been deemed an economic liability – not in the short term, but perhaps in the longer term? If the ship's keel had been damaged, it might mean that the ship was an economic write-off.

Was there any evidence that the *Olympic's* keel had been damaged in the collision? Sources at Harland & Wolff stated that *Olympic* sailed from Southampton on only her port engine, the starboard engine having been rendered inoperable. They further stated that the centre turbine was not engaged – not because it had been rendered unusable, but by choice. The centre turbine and, therefore, the centre shaft, was driven by the exhaust steam from the port and starboard main engines. With only the port reciprocating engine in operation on her 570-mile run back to Southampton, would there have been sufficient exhaust steam to operate the centre shaft, albeit at reduced speed? Could the centre turbine, which is located on the centreline of the ship, resting directly over the keel, have been kept idle in order to avoid any undue vibration to a suspected damaged keel?

It is on this point that conspiracy theorists make their case. For argument's sake, we will explore the following theory: if *Olympic's* keel had been damaged, this damage would have occurred near the Reciprocating Engine Room based on the fact that the starboard reciprocating engine would have been damaged when the *Hawke's* bow came into contact with *Olympic's* rapidly turning propeller blades on that side. The resulting shock of each blade successively striking an unyielding object would have been transmitted along the starboard shaft and momentarily impeded the engine's free-flowing cycle, placing extremely high torsional loads on the engine's crank-shafts. This would have occurred regardless of how quickly the engine was stopped. Something would have had to give, and it did. Part of the starboard propeller's shaft was damaged and needed to be replaced. Could the shocks and vibrations have been transferred through the engine to the engine bedplates? Could the resultant stresses have been transferred from the engine bedplates to the ship's keel or double bottom structure and damaged either or both? There may have been no external evidence of the keel or double bottom being damaged, but had the integrity of either of these vital structures been compromised, *Olympic's* hull would no longer be as strong amidships as it had been prior to the collision. Under normal operating conditions this might present no problems, but if the hull were subjected to excessive stresses such as hogging or sagging in heavy seas,[6] either the keel or double bottom – or both – might be at risk of failing. To this day there has been much speculation as to why *Titanic's* keel broke at three places.[7] Could the answer be simply that it was not *Titanic* but *Olympic* that broke in two on the tragic night of 15 April 1912, as a result of part of the lower hull that had been previously weakened?

We address this possibility later in this book. In the meantime, it can be said with certainty that if *Olympic* had been more severely damaged than revealed, she would not pass the Board of Trade inspection for the renewal of her certificate of seaworthiness, due in May 1912. The ramifications of this would have been catastrophic. Renewal of her certification would then depend on whether all the damaged areas could be repaired adequately to pass the rigorous examination by Board of Trade surveyors. The full cost of such repairs and associated loss of revenue from the ship being out of service for so long might have even been beyond the interest of the International Mercantile Marine Company, the ultimate owner of *Olympic* and the White Star Line. Yet the company could hardly advise its shareholders that one of the company's prime assets was now an economic write-off.

Olympic was again returned prematurely to Belfast following the loss of one of her port-side propeller blades at 4.26p.m. on 24 February 1912. After departing New York on a routine eastbound crossing, she was about 750 miles off the coast of Newfoundland[8] when a sudden shuddering vibration required shutdown of her port

Olympic's port-side propeller boss missing one blade. (*Authors' Collection/Harland & Wolff*)

reciprocating engine. It was later reported that she had lost one of her port-side propeller blades, believed to have occurred by passing over and striking an underwater
obstruction. This is a most curious supposition when one considers that the average
depth of the Atlantic Ocean at that point is more than 12,000ft. If *Olympic* had passed
over an obstruction, why was there no evidence of damage done to the hull of the
ship? The ship's hull would have had to pass along the obstruction for its entire length
before coming into contact with the propeller. The only other possible explanation
is if *Olympic* passed something just close enough to strike the propeller. Regardless,
though, she would have to return to Harland & Wolff for inspection and replacement
of the blade.

    Olympic continued her eastbound crossing to Southampton at a reduced speed,
arriving on 29 February. After the passengers had disembarked, all unnecessary crew

were discharged and the cargo and mail were unloaded. *Olympic* departed for Belfast the following day for the graving dock and a replacement blade.

At this point it may be interesting to note the fact that Harland & Wolff is believed to have carried only one full set of replacement propeller blades for the *Olympic*-class ships. If Harland & Wolff did not carry any spare blades for *Olympic*, the only alternative may have been to fit her with one of *Titanic*'s spare (reserve) blades. Mention of this may seem like a mere technical postscript, but is important to mention for another reason: on 13 August 2005, a dive to the wreck of the *Titanic* revealed the number '401' stamped on one of the propeller port-side blades that was not buried in the bottom. As 401 was the yard number assigned to *Titanic* by Harland & Wolff, this is of no consequence, and in fact should confirm that the ship on the bottom of the Atlantic is, indeed, *Titanic*. But if *Olympic* was indeed fitted with replacement blades intended for *Titanic,* it provides a ready explanation as to why the ship on the bottom could be *Olympic* even though the port-side propeller indicates otherwise.

Finally, there is some controversy over the time *Olympic* should have spent at Belfast. The fitting of a replacement blade should have taken only two days; however she was at Belfast for six. The additional inspection had delayed her departure from Belfast until 7 March. *Olympic*'s westbound trip scheduled for the day before had been cancelled, as was her return trip from New York.

Thus the seeds for a conspiracy had been sown. In the collision with the *Hawke*, significant and costly damage had resulted, perhaps great enough to spell financial disaster. We have unexplained evidence of damage other than what was cited in court – evidence which may have exonerated *Olympic* – yet it was never submitted for consideration in the appeal that was heard after *Titanic* sank. After the *Hawke* collision, *Olympic* struck an underwater obstruction where none should be. Finally, on both occasions when *Olympic* returned to Belfast for repairs, she spent far more time there than she seemingly needed.

There is no doubt that at the time the White Star Line despaired over what had happened. 'It is the most cruel case on record,' said General Manager Harold Sanderson. Whether or not the company would, or could, resort to a solution borne out of desperation will be explored in the pages that follow.

4

MYSTERY OR HISTORY?

The two stories in this chapter are intriguing in what they claim. They involve people who were very real, yet who did not exist. Rational thinking demands a logical explanation, yet unlike suppositions based on technical data, their stories are not so easy to prove or disprove. If the reader accepts each as true, however, they add more weight to the belief that a switch actually happened.

We will address the story of James Fenton first. Fenton, a retired seaman, alleged that he was a surviving crewman from *Titanic*, and claimed that when he joined her at Belfast other crewmen told him that the ship he boarded was actually *Olympic*. Was his bizarre story, as told to a young Dennis Finch back in 1971, simply something invented on the spur of the moment? Apparently not – Fenton had been telling the same story for more than sixty years to anyone interested in hearing it.

On 31 July 1996, an interesting letter to the editor appeared in the *Northern Star*, an Australian newspaper. The letter was written by Frank Finch, a retired seaman, who at the time operated a modest but well-run maritime museum in a small town on the far north coast of New South Wales. The letter was written in response to an article on the alleged *Titanic–Olympic* switch theory previously published in the *Northern Star* weeks before. Finch's letter, handwritten in pencil, related what he had learned on the subject in conversation with his eldest son, Dennis Finch.

Dennis, an experienced seaman actively employed in the Australian maritime industry at the time, had the occasion to visit his parents for a few days in early July 1996 while on leave. On this particular occasion, Dennis recalled a conversation he had had with an old boatswain named James Fenton while serving on a cargo ship called the *Kooliga* back in 1971. Up to the point of that conversation elder Finch had never read or even heard of any story centring on a switch between the two ships.

James Fenton in Brisbane, Australia, in 1962. (*Steve Hall Collection*)

Finch's son related how Fenton claimed that he had not only served aboard the ship the world knew as *Titanic*, but that the ship that sank was never *Titanic* at all – she was *Olympic*. The family discussed the possibility. Frank's initial opinion concerning the possibility of the mammoth liners being switched was less than favourable; in fact, he later confided that he thought the whole idea or even the suggestion that these two ships were switched was farcical.

The following is a partial quote from Frank Finch's letter. In it, he paraphrases what his son Dennis recalled from the conversation he had with James Fenton while both were serving together on the *Kooliga*:

[James] Fenton first went to sea in 1898 as an 8-year-old cabin boy aboard a sailing ship called the *Red Rock*. They went missing for 180 days in the Indian Ocean; the vessel was 'becalmed.' In 1912 Paddy [claimed he] was a 22-year-old ordinary seaman aboard *Titanic*. He always maintained that the iceberg alone did not sink *Titanic*, that it had a fire burning in the coal bunkers for a week and that the Captain and the company knew about it. Paddy also said that when the crew joined *Titanic* there was [*sic*] rumours that the company had switched ships at layup and that an insurance scam was going on.

They sailed in a great hurry from Belfast and said that when they hit the iceberg it did not do serious damage but when the cold water hit the coal fire, it exploded and caused the fatal damage. The Chief Mate put Paddy in charge of a lifeboat, keeping older hands on deck for lowering boats. When the surviving crew got to port they were all taken aside and met by two men, one in a high position in the company, the other man was in a very high position in the Government. The Government man read the crew the 'Official Secrets Act' explaining that if they told of the real reason for the sinking, or the rumours of an insurance scam, they would serve a minimum of 20 years in jail and would never get a job when they got out. Paddy said that the guilt of keeping quiet all those years had taken a great toll on his health and the sanity of the surviving crew.

To verify the accuracy of Fenton's story some information must first be established. Was there a ship called the *Kooliga*? Yes. The 2,495-ton *Kooliga* was built in 1958 and was operated by a company called Associated Steamship Pty (Propriety) Ltd. Her port of registry was Melbourne, and she was crewed by thirty-eight to forty men. She operated between Melbourne, Adelaide, and numerous other western Australian ports.

Was there a man by the name of James Fenton? Yes; he was born James Anthony Fenton in the small Northern Ireland town of Dundalk, County Louth, in 1892. His claim that he was twenty-two years old while serving on *Titanic* is a little off; if he was born in 1892, then he would have been only twenty, not twenty-two, as he claimed. However, either age was acceptable to be employed in this position at the time.

Did Fenton and Finch ever sail together on the *Kooliga*? Again, the answer is yes: records from the Australian Marine Crews Manager reveal that a James A. Fenton served as a Boatswain on board the *Kooliga* between 9 July and 6 September 1971. Finch served as an Ordinary Seaman on board the same vessel between 6 July and 5 October of that year.

With the elements of Fenton's existence validated, we now look into the facts pertaining to the identity of this man and his claimed service aboard *Titanic* in greater depth. Was Fenton's name listed on any of *Titanic's* crew lists at either Belfast or Southampton? No. However, before rejecting Fenton's story out of hand, consider the example of an alleged crewman who appeared to vanish into thin air. Mrs H. W. Bishop, who left *Titanic* in lifeboat 7, made the following statement about those in her lifeboat: 'The conduct of the crew, as far as I could see, was absolutely beyond criticism. One of the crew was Jack Edmonds and there was another man, a lookout [Hogg], of whom we all thought a great deal.'

One could assume that Edmonds must have been one of the more active or helpful crewmen aboard the lifeboat; otherwise, why would Mrs Bishop ever have cause to recall the name? Given the fact that her statement acknowledges Edmonds' presence based mainly on his conduct that night, would it not be feasible to consider the opposite view? If Fenton had not at any time drawn undue attention to himself, but stoically manned the oars in silence like many others of his kind that night, it may

MV *Kooliga*. (*Steve Hall Collection*)

well have contrived against anyone remembering him. If one accepts this, it is not surprising that Fenton faded into obscurity as just another guernsey-clad[1] seaman aboard the lifeboats that night.

Was there a Jack Edmonds aboard *Titanic*? There is no definitive answer. Edmonds' name, like Fenton's, fails to appear among any crew or passenger lists taken on board the *Carpathia*. Compounding the mystery is that neither name appears on the hand-written crew rosters or even in the crew discharge documents. But since Mrs Bishop presumably was not hallucinating or lying, we must allow for the possibility that she may have heard or recalled the man's name incorrectly. George Behe, an advisor of the *Titanic* Historical Society, said that: 'The fact that the name is missing from the crew documents is very significant, since it means that 'Edmonds' was never paid for his *Titanic* voyage. I think it's unlikely that a crewman would voluntarily abandon money that he had earned in such a trying circumstance, and that's what leads me to believe that Mrs Bishop misheard the man's name while she was in the lifeboat.'

The passenger and crew lists from *Titanic* are sometimes unreliable. Greaser Thomas Ranger and Bath Room Steward Samuel Rule, both of whom testified before the British inquiry, appear only on the ship's handwritten crew list, and Rule's name fails to appear on the list of survivors taken aboard the *Carpathia*. With this in mind, one is forced to wonder how many other unlisted crew members were actually aboard *Titanic* when she went down.

The figures given for the number of passengers and crew aboard *Titanic* vary depending on the source. In some cases the numbers varied as the investigations moved further ahead. Some members of the crew deserted ship at Queenstown and possibly at Cherbourg. Other points of confusion surround the number saved in the lifeboats, as those numbers conflict also. Walter Lord wrote in his book *A Night to Remember* that there were 2,207 people aboard *Titanic*. He further stated that: 'The British Board of Trade figure seems more convincing, less fireman J. Coffy, who deserted at Queenstown.' The British Board of Trade lists the total number of people aboard *Titanic* as 2,201.

Fenton stated that *Titanic* sailed in a great hurry from Belfast. Certainly if any unusual work had been done on *Olympic* preparatory to a switch, it would be noticed if she remained in Belfast for any length of time. After all, there were thousands of men at Harland & Wolff who would know both ships intimately from working aboard them and who would readily talk among themselves in the streets and pubs of Belfast if anything odd were noticed.

The next part of Fenton's statement requires greater attention. Fenton claimed that when the crew joined *Titanic* there were rumours that the company had switched *Titanic* with *Olympic* during her layup and that there was an insurance scam going on. Fenton did not mention where these rumours among the crew began circulating. Obviously, it was either at Belfast or Southampton. As to who he heard them from, it is also reasonable to assume that it was not from any of the ship's officers or any crew members holding specialised positions in the Deck Department. Because most seamen mix only with others of their own ranks, the rumour of a switch most likely came from another Able Seaman, or possibly one of the ship's Quartermasters or Lookouts. Even today in the merchant marine there is a hierarchical system on any ship: officers normally mix only among themselves, stewards mix with other stewards, and so on. There is no doubt that in 1912 the situation would have been the same. The seamen's mess or berthing areas would have been the place where any such talk would have started.

According to Fenton, while *Titanic* was sinking Chief Officer Henry Wilde put him in charge of a lifeboat, electing to keep the older and more experienced hands on deck for lowering the boats. Wilde was active in the loading and lowering of only three lifeboats: Boat No. 2, lowered at 1.45a.m., Boat No. 14, lowered at 1.30a.m., and Collapsible C, lowered at 1.40a.m. This does not rule out the possibility of Fenton being present, but he was definitely not in charge of any of these lifeboats. The position of Chief Officer aboard *Titanic* was originally assigned to William Murdoch, who made the voyage as First Officer. Wilde had replaced him at the eleventh hour at Southampton. Therefore, some of the crew may have still been unaware of this fact even at the time of the sinking. If Fenton had been placed in charge of a lifeboat believing that Murdoch was still the Chief Officer, any of the lifeboats loaded and lowered under the Murdoch's direction could be a potential candidate for the one Fenton was in. (Murdoch was active in loading and lowering of six lifeboats.)

Fenton's claim that he was placed in charge of a lifeboat on the pretence that the officer wanted experienced seamen to remain on board would indicate that he likely left in one of the earlier boats. There are several possibilities.

Next we turn to the damage caused by the collision with the iceberg. The common perception in 1912 after the sinking was that the iceberg had torn the hull wide open, leading to catastrophic flooding. Fenton, on the other hand, said: 'The iceberg did not do serious damage to the ship.' Exactly how much damage was there? Was it enough to sink the ship?

Fenton also mentioned the fire in the coal bunker. Like the proverbial bad penny, this story keeps turning up. Immediately after the sinking, stories began circulating about this fire and how it had weakened one of the watertight bulkheads. Some conspiracy theorists also believe that a resultant coal dust explosion was responsible for blowing a large hole in the side of the ship underwater, and that this damage – not the damage from the iceberg – was responsible for the flooding that ultimately sealed the ship's fate. The area of the hull allegedly damaged in this explosion was almost directly above the reserve coal bunker.

Fenton stated that the crew had been advised that if they told anyone of the real reason for the sinking or about the rumours of an insurance scam they would serve a minimum of twenty years in prison and would never get a job when they got out. Did this happen?

The *Carpathia* arrived in New York at 9.35p.m. on 18 April with *Titanic*'s survivors. Thirty-eight of the surviving crew members, including the four surviving officers, were subpoenaed to appear before the US Senate inquiry led by Michigan Senator William Alden Smith. The remaining 172 crew members were permitted to return to England aboard the Red Star Line's *Lapland*. The *Lapland* arrived at Plymouth on 29 April. After the American inquiry, the thirty-four crewmen who had been detained by order of the Senate committee returned to Liverpool aboard the *Celtic*. *Titanic*'s officers returned aboard the *Adriatic* four days later.

Fenton said that when the surviving crew members disembarked at Plymouth, they were all taken aside and met by two men, one in a high position in the White Star Line and the other from the government. History does tell us that Harold Sanderson and E.C. Grenfell, both White Star Line directors, met the crew aboard the *Lapland*. Representing the government was a Mr W. Woolven, Receiver of Wrecks. These men would, without a doubt, have cautioned the returning crewmen that any spreading of rumours or speculations regarding *Titanic*'s sinking would not be tolerated. Silence would have been the safest and wisest option available to all involved.

A few months following the Frank Finch's letter in the newspaper, one of the authors had the opportunity to speak with his son Dennis. Finch was asked if he could recall any additional information from his conversation with Fenton. Finch said that only one more thing came to mind: '[Fenton] said that when he joined the ship she had false portholes painted on her side.'

DAILY SKETCH.

No. 979.—MONDAY, APRIL 29, 1912.   THE PREMIER PICTURE PAPER.   [Registered as a Newspaper.]   ONE HALFPENNY.

FIRST SURVIVORS OF TITANIC TO REACH ENGLAND.

The Lapland, the Red Star liner, arriving in Cawsand Bay, off Plymouth, yesterday morning with the Titanic survivors on board. The crew of the lost liner were not brought ashore immediately, but waited on the tender (Sir Richard Grenville) until the mails and passengers were got away from Plymouth. In the lower photograph the Titanic men are seen leaning against the taffrail of the tender.—*Daily Sketch* Photographs.

Front page of the *Daily Sketch*, 29 April 1912. (*Steve Hall Collection*)

Is this additional information relevant? With very few exceptions, the porthole sizes and locations on the two ships were identical, but there were several on *Titanic* where none existed on her sister. One area where this was more readily noticeable was on the port bow along the white-painted strake of plating directly below the railing (C Deck). Here, *Titanic* had sixteen portholes to *Olympic's* fourteen. *Olympic* supposedly had only fourteen until 1914. Harland & Wolff advised that the additional two portholes were added in 1914 during her conversion to a troopship. However, as far back as March 1912, *Olympic* had sixteen portholes, as is evidenced in photographs. If the additional two had been painted onto *Olympic* that month in order to make the two ships appear identical, then this would support Fenton's claim.

All in all, Fenton told an amazing tale. What is even more amazing is that he had been telling the same story to anyone who chose to listen, for some sixty years. Was it true?

Our second mystery surrounds the tale of Constance Evans and her husband, David. It is alleged that David was attached to the Harland & Wolff Guarantee Group that joined the ship at Belfast. The Guarantee Group was a select group of workmen and experts who had sailed on *Titanic* in the shipyard's employ to consult on and assist with problems on any of the mechanical equipment on board. The mystery arises when we find that there is no record of a David Evans – or his wife – ever having been aboard.

The following recollections come from Peter Quinn, a retired businessman who had the story passed down to him from his late father. Constance Evans was Peter's aunt. Many years earlier, in January 1912, she married a young engineer from Harland & Wolff named David Evans. Constance came from a family that would have been considered upper-middle class at the time and so it is not surprising that she married a professional man.

According to Peter Quinn, in April 1912, David and Constance Evans planned to take a belated honeymoon in New York. Their intent was to book second-class passage aboard one of the White Star Line ships from Queenstown to New York, stay a week, then return. As it turned out, David Evans was offered the option to travel on board *Titanic* from Belfast to New York as part of the Guarantee Group. If agreeable, he would receive payment for his services while on board. He naturally accepted. Harland & Wolff officially sanctioned the arrangement, and because Constance would be accompanying David, the couple received an unexpected bonus: their passage was upgraded to First Class.

Constance Evans claimed that on the evening of 14 April, she and her husband dined with the captain in the First-Class *à la carte* Restaurant. Constance stated that also present at the table that evening for a period of time was Thomas Andrews, whom both she and David knew very well. For the short period that Andrews was in the restaurant, he and Evans reportedly discussed the ship's Engineering Department. It was during this conversation that Andrews acknowledged that there was a vibration problem. Evans confirmed this observation that apparently the starboard engine or starboard propeller shaft was increasingly producing an occasional but severe vibration. Evans' recommendation was short and simple: 'Until we can accurately identify the probable cause, we may have to recommend reduced revolutions.'

After the meal, David and Constance Evans made their apologies and left the restaurant early. David allegedly went below to the engineering spaces and Constance never saw him again.

The foregoing is the story told by Peter Quinn, as recalled from the conversation with his father; his father would have heard it from Constance herself. In the years following the *Titanic* disaster, Constance spent the remainder of her reclusive life living in the small Welsh town of Rhyl. Sometime in 1935 or 1936 the *Times* of London approached her for her story; however it was never published. Documentation held by Constance's family in Cardiff supports the fact that she received a token pension from Harland & Wolff for the loss of her husband. Peter Quinn stated that his Aunt Connie lived well into her nineties and that even to the last her mind was as sharp as a tack. She passed away in either 1983 or 1984 and was buried in Rhyl.

The vibration reported by Constance Evans was also noted by First-Class passenger Mahala D. Douglas and her husband, who by coincidence also dined in the restaurant that evening. Mrs Douglas stated that the vibration was very noticeable as one passed the stairway in the centre of the ship. This is not a surprising comment. After all, this stairway (the after Grand Staircase) was directly above the reciprocating engines. We can only wonder if Mrs Douglas had overheard the discussion between Andrews and Evans.

Is it purely coincidental that *Titanic* suffered starboard engine or propeller shaft problems during her crossing seven months after *Olympic's* collision with the *Hawke*? In that collision, as described in Chapter 3, the plating around *Olympic's* starboard propeller shaft boss had been damaged along with the propeller blades and the shaft itself. Although all of these were repaired or replaced, some conspiracy theorists believe that the starboard engine would have been suspect under load afterwards. The question has also been raised as to whether *Olympic's* damaged propeller blades were replaced with spares intended for *Titanic*: these may not have been of the same size and would have caused vibration when run at higher speeds. If the ship that sailed as *Titanic* was really *Olympic*, then we have a ready explanation for the vibration recalled by Constance Evans and Mahala Douglas, both in support of the theory that the ships were switched.

It is necessary to examine David Evans a little more. None of the passenger lists for Southampton, Cherbourg, or Queenstown list a David or Constance Evans. Does Constance Evans appear on either the official White Star Line list of survivors or the list compiled on board the *Carpathia* by her officers? No. At first glance, it would appear they were not aboard at all, and at this point the story, like Fenton's, appears doubtful. However, there is a possible lead.

On the fifteenth day of the US Senate inquiry after the sinking, surviving passenger Daisy Minahan submitted a letter stating that she had seen a couple known to her as Mr and Mrs Blair taking tea with the Widener party in the *à la carte* Restaurant. The letter submitted to the Senate inquiry states that on the evening of 14 April, Daisy was in the Restaurant with her brother, William Minahan, and his wife, Lillian. It reads, in part:

> Dear Sir: I have given you my observations and experiences after the disaster, but I want to tell you of what occurred on Sunday night, April 14.

> My brother, his wife, and myself went to the café [*sic*] for dinner at about 7.15p.m. When we entered, there was a dinner party already dining [*sic*], consisting of perhaps a dozen men and three women. Capt. Smith was a guest, as also were Mr. and Mrs. Widener, Mr. and Mrs. Blair, and Major Butt. Captain Smith was continuously with his party from the time we entered until between 9.25 and 9.45, when he bid [*sic*] the women good night and left. I know this time positively, for at 9.25 my brother suggested my going to bed. We waited for one more piece of the orchestra, and it was between 9.25 and 9.45 (the time we departed), that Captain Smith left.

The Blairs, like Constance Evans and her husband, fail to appear on any passenger list. Could they be the same people?

At this point it is necessary to ask: would David Evans have been given a First-Class berth? The answer may well be yes. Like Thomas Andrews, two other members of the Guarantee Group – William Parr, Assistant Manager of the Electrical Department, and Roderick Chisholm, Chief Ship's Draughtsman, both travelled First Class. The other six members of the Guarantee Group all travelled Second Class. Could Evans have been a tenth member of this group, added at the last moment and not on any passenger or crew list because he was neither passenger nor crew?

The mysterious stories told by the two people in this chapter – James Fenton and Constance Evans – will, perhaps, forever remain mysteries. A definitive case for or against either may never be proven. At this point in our discussion they remain two unknowns that add to the controversy as to what happened.

5

THE LIFEBOAT EVIDENCE

A great deal of mystery surrounds *Titanic*'s lifeboats, from the time they were fitted to their recovery following the sinking. It is not the authors' intention to pursue what happened on each individual lifeboat. However, there are some discrepancies that could be used to help determine whether *Olympic* and *Titanic* were switched.

We begin our discussion with the recovered lifeboats and the question of why all of the salvageable lifeboats were not taken aboard the *Carpathia*. We next look into survivors' accounts of missing equipment and give attention to the possibility that the lifeboats aboard *Titanic* were not new, as would be expected. We then turn to an odd discrepancy in the number of boats and then consider their mysterious disappearance from New York.

Lifeboat Nos. 1, 2, 3, 5–13 and 16 were all unloaded alongside the *Carpathia* and then taken aboard and returned to New York. The two collapsible lifeboats that made it to *Carpathia* – C and D – were abandoned after unloading, as were Boat Nos. 4, 14 and 15. It is perfectly understandable that the collapsibles were abandoned, as they were not much more than rafts, but why were the latter three lifeboats not recovered? Why Captain Rostron of the *Carpathia* allowed them to simply

Captain Arthur Rostron of the *Carpathia*.

drift away remains a mystery, made more perplexing when one considers that they were all only five months old and in as good condition as any of the others taken on board. Some of these abandoned lifeboats were partially filled with water, but one would assume that this would not have precluded their recovery.

We now examine *Titanic's* lifeboats in more detail to determine if we can identify any clues to support the theory that *Olympic* and *Titanic* were switched. One item of emergency equipment that was supposed to be provided to each of *Titanic's* boats was an oil lamp. In addition to providing light for those on board, the oil lamps could have also been used to make their presence known to other lifeboats or rescue ships in the area. We know that on the night of the sinking, almost all of *Titanic's* boats were separated in the dark and the absence of lamps was keenly felt.

It is reasonable to assume that all *Titanic's* lifeboats and safety equipment had been inspected by Board of Trade surveyors following their installation on *Titanic*. Would it also have been reasonable to expect the oil lamps and other lifeboat equipment to have been in place and available for use when the boats were launched? The lamps were reportedly stored in the ship's Lamp Room when not in use, yet most had no oil in them. Listed below are some excerpts of testimony regarding the oil lamps or lack thereof. Unless otherwise noted, all individuals were passengers:

> Boat No. 3, Elizabeth Shutes: 'We were told to hunt under seats, any place, anywhere, for a lantern, a light of any kind. Every place was empty. There was no water-stimulant of any kind. Not a biscuit."
>
> Boat No. 4, Emily Ryerson: 'We had no lights or compass.'
>
> Boat No. 5, Henry Etches, Steward: 'There was no lamp in number 5.'
>
> Boat No. 7, James McGough: 'There was no light in the boat.'
>
> Boat No. 9, Walter Wynne, Quartermaster: 'There was no lamp or compass in the boat.'
>
> Boat No. 12, John Poigndestre, AB (Able Seaman): 'No light. No compass.'
>
> Boat No. 13, Washington Dodge: 'Our lifeboat was found to contain no lantern, as the regulations require.'

There is no doubt that Dr Dodge had been sufficiently disturbed by the lack of a lantern to establish that it should have been there. To have made the comment, it would appear that he had confirmed that, by law, a lamp should have been in the lifeboat:

> Boat No. 14, Daisy Minahan: 'Fifth Officer Lowe had asked us all to try and find a lantern, but none was to be found.'
>
> Boat No. 15, Samuel Rule, Bath Room Steward: 'No lamp.'
>
> Collapsible D, Arthur Bright, Quartermaster: 'They had a lantern in the boat but no oil to light it.'

Lifeboat No. 14 towing Collapsible D to the *Carpathia*.

Collapsible D approaches the *Carpathia*.

For lifeboats 1, 10, 11, and 16, no oil lamps were listed among the when the surviving lifeboat equipment was inventoried at New York. Although these oil lamps may well have been stolen while they were in storage at the White Star Line pier, there is no reference by any passengers or crew to any of these lamps having been either found on board or even used during the hours of darkness:

> Boat No. 2, Mahala Douglas: 'The rowing was very difficult, for no one knew how. We tried to steer under Mr. Boxhall's orders, and he put an old lantern, with very little oil in it, on a pole, which he held up for some time.'

An 'old lantern' on a supposedly new ship?

> Boat No. 6, Helen Candee: '[Quartermaster Robert Hichens commanded] some of the other ladies to take the light and signal to other lifeboats.'
> Boat No. 8, Ella White: 'The lamp in the boat was worth absolutely nothing.'

During the US Senate inquiry, Senator William Smith put the following questions to J. Bruce Ismay, perhaps to call into question the condition of the lifeboats fitted to *Titanic*:

> Sen. Smith: Can you tell us anything about the inspection, and the certificate that was made and issued before sailing?
> Mr Ismay: The ship receives a Board of Trade passenger certificate; otherwise she would not be allowed to carry passengers.
> Sen. Smith: Do you know whether this was done?
> Mr Ismay: You could not sail your ship without it; you could not get clearance.
> Sen. Smith: Do you know whether this ship was equipped with its full complement of lifeboats?
> Mr Ismay: If she had not been, she could not have sailed. She would not have received her passenger certificate; therefore she must have been fully equipped.
> Sen. Smith: Do you know whether these lifeboats were the lifeboats that were planned for Titanic?
> Mr Ismay: I do not quite understand what you mean, sir. I do not think lifeboats are ever built for the ship. Lifeboats are built to have a certain cubic capacity.
> Sen. Smith: I understand that; but I mean whether these lifeboats were completed for the ship coincident with the completion of the ship, or whether the lifeboats, or any of them, were borrowed from the other ships of the White Star Line?
> Mr Ismay: They certainly would not have been borrowed from any other ship.

First-Class passenger Mrs Frederick Spedden, in Boat No. 3, stated in her account of the sinking that number plates with '3' and '5' were both on her boat, and that 'Our seaman told me that it was an old one taken from some other ship, and he didn't seem sure at the time which was the correct number.' Could this have simply been an oversight while the lifeboat identification numbers and nameplates were switched from *Olympic*'s boats to *Titanic*'s?

> Sen. Smith: Do you recollect whether the lifeboat in which you left the ship was marked with the name Titanic on the boats or the oars?
> Mr Ismay: I have no idea. I presume the oars would be marked. I do not know whether the boat was marked or not. She was a Collapsible Boat.

On a collapsible, the name was painted onto the timbers as opposed to there being a metal plate as on the wood lifeboats. The fact that Smith pursued this line of questioning was odd. Was he trying to establish whether there was a reasonable suspicion regarding the true identity or origin of the lifeboats on board *Titanic*?

Then we come to the matter of some of the boats leaking. Describing the moment when her boat reached the water, First-Class passenger Daisy Minahan stated that: 'Almost at once the boat began to leak and in a few moments the women in the forward part of the boat were standing in water. There was nothing to bail with and I believe the men used their hats.'

Titanic's lifeboats were constructed in the clinker style. This means that they were made of planks of wood that tightly overlapped each other. This was a traditional method of boat building, practised for hundreds of years, but clinker-built boats were

Close-up detail of the nameplates on one of *Titanic*'s lifeboats.

susceptible to the plank seams leaking when they were older, especially when out of the water for an extended period of time. All *Titanic*'s lifeboats had been tested for leaks prior to being placed aboard the ship in February 1912. A lifeboat with plank seams that were no longer watertight would seem to be more consistent with one fourteen months old – for example, the ones on *Olympic*. If the ships had been switched, the original lifeboats on *Olympic* would have remained secured below their davits, and only the identification and number pennants would have been switched over.

The lack of lanterns, compasses, provisions, seaworthiness, and other essential boat equipment on *Titanic*'s lifeboats would be far more consistent to a ship such as *Olympic*, which had been at sea for more than twelve months. It is certainly not uncommon for a ship's lifeboat to suffer from theft; however, this normally takes place over an extended period of time, yet all of *Titanic*'s lifeboats had been outfitted just over two months prior to the disaster, and were supposed to be new – or were they?

Another clue to the possible origin of *Titanic*'s lifeboats lies with the adjustable canvas sides of Collapsible A, which had been stored on the roof of the Officers' Quarters deckhouse. On the night of the sinking, the collapsible lifeboat sides proved to be impossible to raise and lock into position. As a consequence of this, the lifeboat filled with water when it was washed overboard as the ship went under. Passengers who were in this boat were transferred to another one later. Collapsible A was set adrift with two, possibly three bodies remaining in it. Why the adjustable sides could not be raised seems odd for a new boat; after all, they would have been tested prior to their being fitted onto the ship. Could the boat have been from *Olympic?*

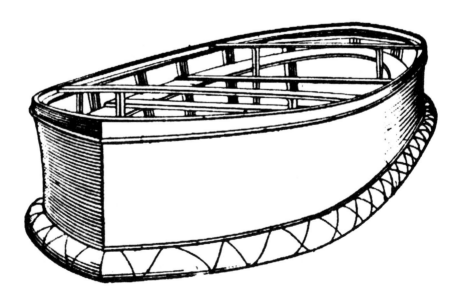

Engelhardt collapsible with canvas bulwark raised.

One of *Titanic*'s cutters being brought aboard *Carpathia*.

To bring in the thinking of some conspiracy theorists to the question of the age of the lifeboats and equipment, many of the lifeboat falls[1] became partially jammed in the davit blocks during their operation. Would this be consistent with equipment that was not properly or regularly maintained and serviced? We know that there were no real lifeboat drills, nor was every boat regularly raised and lowered as is done today. If the crew of *Olympic* believed the ship to be unsinkable, this may explain the lack of inspections and preventive maintenance that appears to have been a factor in the condition of *Titanic's* lifeboats.

Titanic carried twenty wooden lifeboats and four Engelhardt collapsible boats. As noted at the start of this chapter, all the 30ft boats were recovered by the *Carpathia,* with the exception of Boat Nos. 4, 14 and 15. The two emergency cutters were also recovered, but the four collapsibles were not. This means that seven lifeboats were left behind. All of *Titanic's* lifeboats were therefore accounted for. However, Captain Rostron of the *Carpathia* believed that one of *Titanic's* collapsibles was not launched and remained secured to the roof of the Officers' Quarters when the ship went down. Rostron knew that *Titanic* carried only twenty lifeboats, and he had taken aboard passengers from eighteen of them, Collapsibles A and B having been abandoned during the night after the people in them transferred to other boats. The total number of lifeboats recovered by the *Carpathia* and returned to New York was thirteen. This accounts for the twenty, but if one adds the collapsible that Rostron believed went down with the ship, then that makes twenty-one. If one of the collapsibles did go down with *Titanic,* then where did it come from? First-Class passenger Marian Thayer, who was aboard Boat No. 4, stated: 'We passed an overturned lifeboat shortly after reaching the water.' But this was well before any of the collapsibles had been launched. What could be a possible explanation for Mrs Thayer's sighting?

Could one dismiss the supposedly inverted lifeboat sighted by Mrs Thayer as a mistaken witness account? No, because there is more to the story. Also in the same lifeboat with Mrs Thayer was crewman Jack Foley, who stated that: 'Scarcely any of the lifeboats were properly manned. Two, filled with women and children, capsized before our eyes.'

Except for the reported five First-Class women who elected to stay aboard the sinking *Titanic* with their husbands or for other reasons, all female First-Class passengers were saved. However, fifteen women were lost from Second Class. Could these fifteen women have been lowered in a lifeboat that for some reason was capsized at the time it was launched? We know that at some boat stations the crew had difficulty lowering the boats evenly because of the lack of illumination coupled with the fact that the officer directing the boats' lowering had difficulty gauging the trim from above. Given Foley's testimony, the possibility of a lifeboat with fifteen female Second-Class passengers capsizing is entirely possible.

Could this capsized lifeboat have been hauled back up to the Boat Deck and then reloaded? If so, it would explain why the loading of the boats on the port side was

Collapsible A being recovered by *Oceanic*.

completed 25 minutes later than on the starboard side. We can reject this idea out of hand. A 30ft boat is very heavy, and while a large enough group of men in the water might, with a coordinated effort, be able to right an overturned boat, its oars would still have to be recovered in the darkness and the boat itself would have to be bailed, rowed back to the ship, made fast to the falls, and hoisted aboard. Even if there had been sufficient crewmen aboard this boat when it capsized, to expect them to carry out all of this after feeling the effects of hypothermia from the ice-cold water is stretching credibility too far. Furthermore, there is no testimony to even suggest that any of the survivors righted a capsized boat, bailed it and boarded it. If there was an overturned boat in the water as seen by Marian Thayer and Jack Foley, it remained overturned. Yet all twenty of the wooden lifeboats that *Titanic* carried arrived at *Carpathia*'s side.

We know that Collapsible B overturned when it went into the water, because it has been testified to, and accepted, that Second Officer Charles Lightoller and a group of survivors balanced themselves on top of this collapsible for most of the night before being transferred to other boats. Mrs Thayer's lifeboat was Boat No. 4, lowered at 1.55a.m. from the port side of the ship. Could the lifeboat she saw have been the inverted Collapsible B? This is impossible, because Collapsible B was still secured to the roof of the deckhouse at the time Boat No. 4 was launched.

Titanic's boats being lowered from the *Carpathia* upon her arrival in New York.

When one carefully analyses all of this information there would appear to be at least one, possibly two lifeboats more than there should have been. This discrepancy, considered alongside all the names listed as survivors that never appeared on *Titanic's* passenger or crew lists, raises the question 'where did they come from?'

Another point of interest is the testimony of First-Class passenger William Sloper, who described how he had seen, from Boat No. 7, a number of passengers afloat on an inflated life raft (not a standard or collapsible lifeboat). The fact that the *Titanic* did not carry any such rafts raises the question: where did this life raft come from? However, Able Seaman Joseph Scarrott, in Boat No. 14, described how his boat picked up approximately twenty people from a raft constructed of air boxes. During the US Senate inquiry the subject of rafts was raised by Senator Smith when taking evidence from Bruce Ismay. The following testimony is of interest:

Sen. Smith: Can you describe those rafts?

Mr Ismay: There were none on board the ship.

Sen. Smith: Did you see any rafts actually in service?

Mr Ismay: No, sir.

Sen. Smith: Is it customary for the White Star Line to carry rafts?

Mr Ismay: I believe in the old days we carried rafts.

Sen. Smith: Recently that has not been done?

Mr Ismay: Not in the recent ships; no, sir.

The decks of the *Carpathia* crowded with *Titanic* survivors and recovered lifeboats.

At this point we introduce another element of the conspiracy to switch the two ships: the rescue ship. *Titanic's* sinking was not supposed to involve a horrific loss of life – instead, everyone was to have been saved by a ship that 'happened' to be nearby. According to conspiracy theorists, a ship was standing by for that purpose, her lights darkened so as to remain undetected, and it was this ship that *Titanic* struck – not an iceberg. The possibility of such a collision sinking *Titanic* (or *Olympic*) will be discussed at a later point. For now though, it would readily explain the presence of an unaccounted lifeboat overturned in the water.

The *Carpathia* arrived in New York on the evening of 18 April, carrying the thirteen lifeboats that she had recovered. Seven of these boats were lowered into the water, and four were lowered to the deck of the tug *Champion*. From there, they were towed or carried to the White Star Line's Pier 59. The final two lifeboats were unloaded the following morning and then rowed across to join the other eleven lifeboats already tied up to the pier. Collapsible A would later be added to the group

Titanic's remaining lifeboats as seen in the White Star Line berth in New York. By the time this picture was taken, many of the lifeboat nameplates and other items had already been stolen.

after being recovered by the *Oceanic*. Sometime during the night, souvenir hunters removed and stole many of the lifeboats' nameplates, number plates and some of the boats' equipment.

Within a few days the thirteen boats disappeared. Whatever happened to them remains a mystery. It is believed that they remained alongside the pier for another 48 hours and then were all hoisted to a second-floor storage loft between the White Star Line's Piers 58 and 59. Conspiracy theorists make the case that their disappearance was deliberate, to prevent any further examination of them that might reveal that they were from *Olympic* and not *Titanic*. What cannot be proven remains speculation, all of which leads us further down the path to the possibility of a switch having occurred.

6

A WINDOW OF OPPORTUNITY

When *Olympic* arrived back in Belfast on 9 October 1911, after the *Hawke* collision, she was down by the stern and badly damaged. Some 1,000 men were immediately put to work on her, diverted from *Titanic* which by now was well along in her fitting-out process. Seven weeks later repairs were completed, and on 29 November *Olympic* returned to Southampton. If, for argument's sake, it was established by Harland & Wolff's engineers and senior management that *Olympic* was beyond permanent repair, an elaborate scheme might well have been hatched at that time to switch the ships. She could have been repaired sufficiently to return her to service for a time, although with hidden damage to the keel and/or double bottom that could not be rectified. So conspiracy theorists would have us believe.

However, it would not have been possible to switch the two ships that time. *Titanic* was far from a completed ship, and only had one funnel when *Olympic* joined her in Belfast. Clearly, the only opportunity for a switch would have been when work on *Titanic* was nearly at an end. This occurred on only a few occasions.

One possible window of opportunity would have been on *Olympic*'s second unscheduled return to Belfast the following year, on 1 March 1912. This trip was occasioned by the need for replacement of the propeller blade lost on 24 February off Newfoundland. As noted in Chapter 3, the circumstances of that incident were somewhat odd. Could it have been a carefully contrived excuse to get the liner back to Harland & Wolff for a switch?

There is a photograph[1] of *Olympic* (or more specifically, an *Olympic*-class ship with the name '*Olympic*' on her bows) taken on Sunday 3 March at the graving dock at Belfast, and history records that *Olympic* was ready to be returned to service on 4 March. If a switch had been made by 3 March, shipyard workers would have had

The picture above is of *Titanic* at Southampton with the contrast enhanced. Her hull paint was touched up on the port side for appearance sake, but her starboard side remained in the same condition from when she left Belfast. Notice the similarity between the discoloured plates in the bow area here and the area of shell plating replaced as shown on the second diagram provided by Harland & Wolff in chapter three.

only two days to alter all the B Deck windows and the forward ends of the Promenade Decks on both ships. In addition, *Titanic* would have had to have been completely painted within that time, and much of her furniture had not been delivered yet, including her pianos. Plain and simple, her fitting out was just not far enough along for a switch to have been feasible that week. On top of that, this same photograph shows a number of well-dressed men and even ladies walking around the perimeter of the graving dock as though on holiday. Had Harland & Wolff just perpetrated a switch, such public scrutiny of the ship would never have been permitted. But there was another, later, occasion on which a switch might have occurred – one involving an incident with *Olympic* that almost went unnoticed.

Many years after his retirement, George Larwood, a dock worker at Southampton, recounted to his granddaughter, Cara Baverstock,[2] how he had been in a unique position to witness the arrival and departure of many of the great liners from 1910 to

1915. On the occasion of 30 March 1912, five days before *Titanic* berthed there for the first time, he witnessed the arrival of her elder sister, *Olympic*. Larwood remembered that when she moored alongside Pier 44 that day, she was uncharacteristically positioned 'bow in' instead of being backed in to the slip as was customary. After the passengers had disembarked and the mail, baggage and cargo had been unloaded, the ship then vacated her berth. At the time, Larwood reasoned that this berth change had likely been necessitated by the congestion in port from ships laid up by the recent coal strike. In support of Larwood's observation, a picture postcard of *Olympic* offered for auction in 1999 presented a handsome starboard quarter view of the ship at the White Star Line dock. The back of the card reads: '*Olympic* departs Southampton, leaving the dock clear for the arrival of world's newest and largest ship.' If *Olympic* had initially been positioned bow-in as Larwood remembered, then the postcard indicates that by the time she sailed three days later she was back in her usual berth and positioned as usual. Where did she go in the intervening time period?

Prior to *Olympic*'s arrival at Southampton on 30 March, the American Line's *St Louis* had occupied pier 44. The *St Louis* was obliged to vacate this berth in expectation of *Olympic*'s arrival later that day, and was shifted to the northwest corner of the docks and moored to the port side of the steamer *Philadelphia*. That morning, *Olympic* had weighed anchor and departed the French port of Cherbourg just after 7.00a.m. The standard duration for the crossing of the English Channel was about 5½ hours, varying occasionally depending on the weather, the tides and shipping movements in the approaches to Southampton. On this particular occasion, all the necessary conditions prevailed for an on-time arrival at Southampton – just after noon. Instead, the ship was inexplicably delayed for 30 minutes during her crossing. This delay is noted in an obscure record held within the Southampton City Museum.[3] Unfortunately, the text within the document does not elaborate on the actual cause, the reference simply being a short by-line within a larger piece of writing. Based on this, the incident could be dismissed as having no significance or relevance, if not for a curious reference in a '*Titanic* Information Booklet' put out by the Ulster Folk and Transport Museum. In this booklet is a notation that: '*Olympic* had been laid up for repairs following a minor collision in the English Channel, so her Chief Officer H. T. Wilde had been transferred from *Olympic* to *Titanic*.'

How badly damaged was *Olympic* after this reported collision? Despite being 'minor', something must have happened to require inspection or repair. It was obviously bad enough to have referred to her as having been 'laid up', which implies removal from service and going to a shipyard for inspection and/or repair. Yet the damage must either have been repaired during this period or deemed insufficient to warrant delaying or cancelling her upcoming voyage. *Olympic* did, without a doubt, depart Southampton as scheduled just after noon on 3 April 1912.

Could this inspection and/or repair have been carried out at Southampton? Harland & Wolff did maintain a yard there for the express purpose of being able to do just that, in order that ships requiring attention would not have to go all the way back to Belfast. But there were no facilities at Southampton for dry docking a ship of *Olympic's* size. That leaves the Queen's Island facility in Belfast as the only other option. Is it possible that *Olympic* made an unknown trip back to Belfast for repairs without this being recorded?

If there were no other references to *Olympic* being 'laid up' prior to her 3 April departure from Southampton, the above would have to be dismissed as a frustrating and unsubstantiated piece of information. But another reference to the same incident does exist. In the early 1930s, *Titanic's* former second officer, Charles Lightoller, penned his autobiography[4] in which he detailed his years at sea. His account of his time aboard *Titanic* is fairly detailed, and at one point reads as follows:

> Unfortunately, whilst in Southampton we had a reshuffle amongst the Senior Officers. Owing to *Olympic* being laid up, the ruling lights of the White Star Line thought it would be a good plan to send the Chief Officer (H.T. Wilde) of *Olympic*, just for the one voyage as Chief Officer of *Titanic* to help with his experience of her sister ship.

This gives us a vital second reference, but there are more pieces to the puzzle. One is a photograph that appears in countless books and websites captioned as '*Titanic's* Officers' (Fig. 1). In attempting to match names with the faces in the picture, one point of disagreement among researchers is whether the man sitting to the left of Captain Smith is Chief Officer Wilde. The image of Wilde that usually appears in

Figure 1. This image has been widely reproduced over the years and captioned as *Titanic's* officers. (*George Behe Collection*)

Figure 2. Henry Tingle Wilde.

books on *Titanic* (Fig. 2) is that of a much younger man. It is quite possible that this photo was taken much earlier in Wilde's career. But if the man sitting next to Smith is not Wilde, who else could he be? Occasionally he is captioned as being Chief Engineer Bell, but this is incorrect as the Chief Engineer had four stripes on each sleeve, the same as the Captain. He is wearing the three sleeve stripes of a Chief Officer, which was Wilde's position on both *Olympic* and *Titanic*.

Perhaps the reason for the confusion among researchers and historians over this image is that it was not taken aboard *Titanic* – it was taken aboard *Olympic*.

If the many captions listing these men as the officers of *Titanic* are correct, the men would be as follows: sitting, left to right, Sixth Officer James Moody, Chief Officer Henry Wilde, Captain E.J. Smith and First Officer William Murdoch; and standing, left to right Chief Purser Hugh McElroy, Second Officer Charles Lightoller, Third Officer Herbert Pitman, Fourth Officer Joseph Boxhall and Fifth Officer Harold Lowe. However, Lowe had distinctive facial features, and the man in this photograph is not Fifth Officer Lowe, although he is wearing the sleeve stripes of a Junior Officer.[5] The man in this picture looks like *Titanic's* original Second Officer, David Blair.

When could *Titanic's* officers have assembled on the deck of *Olympic* for this picture? Charles Lightoller transferred to *Titanic* from the *Oceanic*, arriving in Belfast on 20 March 1912. Pitman, Boxhall, Lowe and Moody transferred from their old ship assignments, arriving in Belfast on 27 March. With these dates in mind, how did these men assemble on *Olympic* when she supposedly departed Belfast after her last recorded repairs on 7 March? Could this be a third piece of evidence indicating that *Olympic* was in Belfast at the very beginning of April, allowing enough time for a few photos of the new *Titanic* crew? Fig. 3, possibly taken on the same day, shows four of the same men, and, based on the previous photograph, they would be, from left to

Figure 3. This photo taken on the Navigating Bridge shows four of the officers from the previous photo.

right: Murdoch, Boxhall, Wilde and Smith. But again, where did Boxhall come from when he didn't arrive in Belfast until 27 March?

These photographs will be addressed further in chapter eight. In the meantime, we consider another question: how did Smith get here? The day that Pitman, Boxhall, Lowe and Moody signed on *Titanic* at Belfast, 27 March, was also the day the ship was registered. On the 'Agreement and Account of Voyages and Crew' recorded in Belfast, Captain Haddock is listed as the man who would command *Titanic* during her sea trials. Following this he would have transferred command to Smith, who would have still been in command aboard *Olympic* – at Southampton. If this photograph of *Titanic*'s officers shows Smith in command of *Titanic* at Belfast, what happened to Haddock?

One possible explanation is that Smith arrived at Belfast with *Olympic* following the 'minor collision' in the English Channel. With a window of opportunity now open to switch *Olympic* with her now-completed sister, a contrived collision would have given the company the excuse it needed to send *Olympic* back to Belfast for 'repairs' while *Titanic* happened to be there, nearly side by side, her sea trials having been conveniently delayed. The graving dock and the Fitting-Out Wharf were nearly opposite one another, and were located remotely from the main shipyard – it was the perfect location to carry out the final clandestine changes to both ships that would alter their appearance sufficiently to fool anyone familiar with them. Haddock would then sail the disguised *Titanic* back to Southampton as *Olympic* to meet that ship's 3 April departure date, and Smith would then assume command of *Olympic (now Titanic)* from Belfast.

Would the logistics of *Olympic*'s dash to Belfast and back have been possible? She would have had to depart Southampton on the afternoon of 30 March 1912, steam the required 570 miles to Belfast and arrive in the early hours of 1 April. Because of this extremely tight schedule, timing would have been essential. *Olympic* disguised as *Titanic* would then have been required to depart Belfast not long after dawn on the same day in order to make it back to Southampton in time for her scheduled departure on 3 April. Astronomical records show that *Olympic*'s passage up the Victoria Channel and the River Lagan to the shipyard would have been assisted by the light of a near-full moon. The moon on that date would have set at 5.53a.m., but the sky would already be light by then as sunrise was at 5.56a.m. On darkened waters a nearly full moon provides a great deal of illumination – more than enough to navigate by – so this move could conceivably have taken place providing one was willing to assume some risk.

However, navigation aside, it would not have been possible for *Olympic* to have safely negotiated the narrow confines of the channel without the assistance of four or five tugs. She also could not have been moved into her berth without tugs to guide here there. So where would the necessary tugs have come from? If these tugs had been sighted standing by at Belfast it would have been obvious to the casual observer that the arrival of a large ship was imminent.

Titanic's sea trials were scheduled for 10.00a.m. 1 April, and in preparation Harland & Wolff had engaged the Alexander Towing Company to supply four tugs[6] to assist *Titanic* out to Belfast Lough. Although it is recorded that these tugs were alongside *Titanic* at 9.00a.m. that morning, it would be reasonable to assume that the tugs, which had been sent from Liverpool, would have arrived at Belfast the evening before. If this was indeed the case, could not these same four tugs have also assisted *Olympic* up the channel and into her berth a few hours prior?

At the same time, *Titanic* would have had to steam up upon *Olympic*'s arrival in order for *Olympic* to take her place at the Fitting-Out Wharf. We know that *Titanic* was scheduled to depart for her sea trials on the morning of 1 April, so one can reasonably expect that if the tugs were expected alongside at 9.00a.m., the boilers would have been up to operating pressure with the fires slightly banked. Assuming that the fires would have been lit 8–12 hours earlier, as was the norm with Scotch boilers, the first shift of firemen and trimmers would have started work sometime between 9.00p.m. the previous night and 1.00a.m. that morning. Therefore, the ship would have been able to get underway as soon as required.

Up to this point, we have managed to get *Olympic* out of Southampton without raising any real suspicions and have found sufficient time to sail her to Belfast and back. We have also explained how she was able to sail into Belfast under cover of darkness, and managed to have the necessary tugs in place to assist her. Between the recollections of a Southampton dock worker and a caption on a postcard, we also know that *Olympic* left her berth at Southampton and returned to the same berth in time for her scheduled departure. There is one more factor to consider however: coal. A round trip of over 1,100 miles from Southampton to Belfast could not have been done on the coal remaining in her bunkers after a westbound crossing, and coaling twice over a three-day period at Southampton would certainly have raised questions.

When *Olympic* had departed New York on her prior eastbound trip, she took on additional coal, ostensibly to ensure that she would not be affected by the critical shortage in British ports. It has even been said that coal in canvas bags had been stored in the Third-Class Dining Saloon[7] and possibly in her reserve coal bunker. The additional coal would have provided the ship with sufficient fuel for the scheduled eastbound crossing plus 36 hours of additional steaming to Belfast and back.

There is still one more matter of timing to address however. Assuming that *Olympic* could have arrived in Belfast in the early morning hours of 1 April, *Titanic* was scheduled to depart that same day on her sea trials. It is known that there were high winds on that morning, and that has always been given as the reason that Harland & Wolff decided not to proceed, citing unnecessary risk. Could the cancellation of these trials have had anything to do with the fact that a 24-hour delay was required to complete the modifications necessary to carry off the deception? On *Titanic* – modified to be *Olympic* – they would have been virtually complete, except for a fast removal of the Promenade Deck weather screens which would have been left to the last minute. *Olympic*, on the other hand, would have had only a single day for conversion to *Titanic*, and this work would have consisted mainly of a hurried installation of the same weather screens removed from the other ship, painting on any missing portholes and changing the names on the bow and stern.

Delaying the sea trials would have also facilitated the deception in another way. With the time on sea trials cut by half, any manoeuvres and inspections would have been far more cursory. Many obvious examples of the ship being more than twelve months old, such as the boiler rooms, hull paintwork, lifeboats and their emergency equipment and so on, could have gone totally unnoticed. At the same time, the White Star Line might have decided that it could not afford to run the risk of full two-day sea trials, believing that the structurally compromised *Olympic* might have given indications of serious hull problems at some point.

It should be remembered that *Titanic* had been virtually completed by the evening of 31 March and that nearly all of the workers assigned to *Titanic*'s construction would have finished their assigned work on board by the end of their shift on Saturday 30 March. The following Monday they would have been reassigned to a different project in the yard and would never set foot on *Titanic* again. The only exception to this would have been a selected (and trusted) workforce that would have continued to make last-minute adjustments and provide a skeleton crew on board for the sea trials and the subsequent voyage from Belfast to Southampton.

The 31 March was a Sunday in the United Kingdom. If *Olympic* had been altered externally to look like *Titanic* by Monday morning, who among the yard's 14,000-strong workforce – apart from those who carried out the necessary alterations – would have ever realised that the ship sitting placidly at the Fitting-Out Wharf that morning was now *Olympic* masquerading as *Titanic*?

From the time *Titanic* arrived in Southampton to the time she sailed, very few people were allowed to come aboard her. She was never opened to public view. Her funnels were repainted over the weekend prior to sailing and the paint on her hull was touched up only on the port side – facing the dock. Why was this done to a new ship? Was someone trying to hide something before the throngs of passengers and officials arrived on sailing day, four and a half days hence?

By this point, it would seem that the White Star Line, with the cooperation of its shipbuilder, could have pulled off the greatest sleight of hand of all time. Still, not just a little work would have been involved to alter each ship to resemble the other. What exactly would have been involved? We begin to explore this in the next chapter.

7

PHOTOGRAPHIC ASSESSMENT

Possibilities and suppositions aside, photographs are the evidence that hold the key to determining whether or not a switch between *Olympic* and *Titanic* would have been possible. Unfortunately, far fewer images were taken of *Titanic*, as she was the second of her class and mirrored *Olympic* in many ways. Nonetheless, *Titanic's* progress during the construction and fitting-out process was documented in more photographs than most people realise. Copies of plans and construction drawings survive in various archives and many of the latter carry detailed notes as to the last-minute changes that were made to *Titanic* based on experience with *Olympic*. Taking these together with images of the wreck on the ocean floor, it should be fairly easy to establish whether or not a switch was possible or took place. However, photographs can be altered, and given that most images of the ship were taken by Harland & Wolff's official photographers, some conspiracy proponents have made this very claim.

We begin our investigation with a photograph of *Titanic's* port bow taken in May 1911, prior to her launch. The name *Titanic* appears in bold contrast to the light-coloured shell plating in the image. This photograph has been the centre of discussion for years, as some historians have asked 'were nameplates used, or weren't they?' At first glance, the name appears to be painted on. However, enlarging the photograph to show this area in greater detail reveals that the name '*Titanic*' was scratched or painted onto the original glass-plate negative. Altering photographs to improve their appearance or composition was a common practice, and there are several that have been widely reproduced in which entire people were carefully etched out because they were in the way of a key detail. Retouching glass-plate negatives by photographers of the time is a well-known practice.[1] Therefore no suspicions can necessarily be ascribed to the alteration of the name in the bow photo.

In this view, edited for contrast and brightness, the name '*Titanic*' has clearly been enhanced on the negative and is not painted on the side of the ship. Also note the rectangular outline around the letters in the shell plate.

Returning to the question of a nameplate, there certainly appears to be no evidence of one in the photograph of *Titanic*'s port bow. However, close examination under enlargement, reveals that the name is 95 per cent obscured by the scratched or painted-in letters on the negative. *Titanic*'s Rigging Plan states that the ship's name letters, 18in high, were to be 'cut in' to the plating, and divers to the wreck have verified that they were indeed fully cut in. This provided a guide for the painters and ensured that the edges of the letters would be crisp and straight when the paint was applied, regardless of how many successive coats were added over the years during the periodic repainting. When the photographs of *Titanic* under the gantry were taken (before she was launched) she had not received her final coats of paint yet, and thus the letters that form the name *Titanic* may not have been painted on at this early stage. Even if they had, the yellow chromate paint used at the time is notoriously difficult to see in black-and-white photographs and the photographer in this case no doubt wanted the name to stand out in the picture. Would the letters have eventually been painted on the sides by someone on a scaffold or bosun's chair? Absolutely, especially since more coats of paint still had to be applied to the hull.

The practice of painting the ship's name onto rectangular steel plates has been dismissed over the years in some reference books. The reason usually cited is the impracticality or difficulty of cutting letters that are perfectly aligned, perfectly proportioned and with straight edges, all done while working high on the sides of a ship. However, in examining a high-resolution version of the image the rectangular

In this enlargement of a picture very similar to the one opposite, and taken on the same day, the photographer's reference lines are readily visible. The letter 'C' incised into the shell plate is visible to the right. is not painted on the side of the ship. Again, note the rectangular outline around the letters in the shell plate.

outline of a seam can be seen around the letters. This same outline – and the grooves of the letters – can be seen in close-up pictures of *Olympic*'s bow. The letters were not incised to the steel plating once it had been riveted to the hull, they were incised instead into a separate steel plate or plates, and then riveted to the side of the ship. A close enlargement of picture H-1712 (overleaf), taken while *Titanic* was moored in the Fitting-Out Wharf in late September 1911, shows what appears to be a rectangular metal plate making up the name *Titanic*. Adding weight to this is the fact that vertical streaks of discolouration are visible on the plating, interrupted by the steel of the nameplate. No photographs are known to exist of a nameplate being installed, but since the two surfaces are flush, it is obvious that the larger shell plate was cut to accommodate the thickness of the nameplates.[2]

In order for the two sisters to be successfully switched, the most obvious starting point would have been to change their bow and stern names. Removing the plates with the incised letters and then re-riveting plates with the other ship's name in the same place would have been a difficult and time-consuming process. On the other hand, given that the letters were incised into the steel, simply applying black

Harland & Wolff photo H-1712 shows a rectangular outline in the steel plating around the letters. (*Authors' Collection/Harland & Wolff*)

hull paint over the existing letters and painting new names on top would not have worked either. The only solution would have been to either rivet new steel name-plates over the existing incised letters or to fill the letters with lead or vulcanite putty, sand and buff them smooth, and then eliminate all traces by applying hull paint. This would leave a new surface ready for re-lettering. This would have been relatively simple and achievable within the time available.

Our investigation inevitably takes us to the wreck of *Titanic* for further clues. Conspiracy theorists have stated that close examination of underwater video foot-age of *Titanic's* port bow shows that most of the letters that form the word *Titanic* have apparently disappeared. Since we know that letters on the bows were incised into the steel, it would have been impossible for any of the letters to have fallen off. To compound the mystery further, close examination of the area where the letters are missing from the hull reveals a mysterious area of light-blue paint. It is common for areas that have been filled with lead to turn blue as a result of a reaction with salt water. Could this blue colour have resulted from lead that was used to fill or cover *Olympic's* original letters? Unfortunately, when one turns to the starboard bow for further evidence, no photographs or video footage of this area are available. This is an area of the wreck subject to strong currents, and for that reason the port bow is the one usually photographed up close.

In examining video footage of the port bow area, another anomaly comes to light. The steel in the area where *Titanic's* name should be appears to be covered in light-grey paint. There are also areas of this light-grey paint showing in the area of the hawse port on the same side. There is no doubt that this paint has slowly been exposed over decades as the currents have worn away the top coats of black. Why is this significant?

In preparation for her launch, *Olympic* was painted a very light grey.[3] This was done at Lord Pirrie's direction to enhance her appearance for the press cameras. It was, after all, the launch of the largest vessel ever to be built at that time. Afterwards, the hull would be painted in a much darker graphite-grey primer. If the wreck is actually

In this image of *Titanic* (left) and *Olympic* (right) under the Arrol gantry, the difference in the colours of the primer used on the hull are clearly evident.

Titanic shouldn't dark-grey paint or bare metal be visible, not light-grey paint? This would certainly seem to cast doubt on the wreck's identity, and it adds weight to the argument that the two ships were indeed switched.

There is also another area that has raised suspicion. There are photographs taken of *Titanic* on 2 April in Belfast and on 10 April in Southampton that show shell plates that appear to be faded and discoloured, consistent with a ship that has been in service for over a year. Why should a newly painted ship have this appearance?

Next we turn to the subject of portholes,[4] the locations of which were not identical between the two ships. At the time of *Titanic*'s launch there were fourteen portholes in the shell plating on the port side of the ship just below the railing along the port bow. By late July of the same year two additional portholes were added to the same area for a total of sixteen. None of the existing portholes were changed or moved. Her starboard side had fifteen portholes in the equivalent area, and this number remained unchanged throughout her construction. *Olympic* had the same number and arrangement on the starboard side, but only fourteen on the port side – the additional two were not fitted until her conversion to a troopship during the war. The reason why and when they were fitted will be covered later, but for now this difference will be used as a means of distinguishing each ship.

Olympic just before on her maiden voyage at Southampton in June 1911, still with fourteen portholes along the sheer strake of the port bow.

By September 1911, *Titanic* would have sixteen portholes on the port side of the fo'c'sle.

From C Deck downwards, the porthole arrangements on both ships were almost identical. Where they differed was in the row of C Deck portholes; these were the lowest row of portholes in the white-painted area of the hull. On each ship there were periodic gaps (wider spaces) between the some of the large portholes. Whereas *Olympic* had a single smaller porthole in some of these gaps, on *Titanic* each of these gaps has two smaller portholes side by side. These additional portholes were never added to *Olympic*. In addition, the uppermost row of C-Deck portholes in the stern area on each ship (below the Poop Deck railing) is noticeably different in terms of grouping and spacing.

Recalling James Fenton's claim of seeing painted-on portholes, it would have not been much trouble to alter the appearance of these areas by doing just that. Notably, *Olympic* was seen with two newly acquired C-Deck portholes in the port bow area after her return to Belfast in March 1912. But in correspondence with the authors, Harland & Wolff stated that *Olympic* did not receive these additional two portholes until 1914. So why does *Olympic* appear with sixteen portholes in March 1912? In photograph H-1636, could the two additional portholes have been simply painted onto the plating? This would almost certainly indicate that something was going on with these two ships. Close examination of all photographs showing *Titanic*'s port bow after *Olympic*'s departure from Belfast reveal sixteen portholes.

Counting aft from the stem, there is some doubt regarding portholes three and five. The photographs available to us are not good enough to make out the sidelights within the portholes, as the portholes appear totally black in some cases. The only way to satisfactorily resolve this problem would be by close examination of this area of the wreck, which would conclusively determine whether these portholes were all genuine. If a close examination revealed sixteen, it would positively identify the wreck as *Titanic*.

Photograph H-1636 has already been referenced in the previous chapter as being key to ruling out a switch in early March. The ship in this photograph is, without a

On *Titanic*, the row of portholes at the C-Deck level included pairs of small windows between groups of larger portholes. One was for a bath room and the other for a WC.

Olympic's C-Deck portholes had a different configuration in that there was only one small porthole between the groups of larger portholes.

H-1636 – *Olympic* in the graving dock for propeller blade replacements in March 1912. (*Authors' Collection/Harland & Wolff*)

doubt, *Olympic*. She can be definitively identified by the fact that the Bridge wing cabs (the box-like structures outboard of the Navigating Bridge on either side) are flush with the side of the superstructure. One of the key differences between *Olympic* and *Titanic* when they were constructed is that *Titanic* was built with her wing cabs overhanging by 18in to afford greater visibility aft. Because this photograph was taken on 3 March 1912 – four days before she departed Belfast for Southampton – there would have been insufficient time to make such a major structural change.

The section of deck all the way forward at the bows, forward of the 'sunken' Well Deck, is the Forecastle Deck. From the No. 1 hatch in the centre of the deck, a steel breakwater angled outwards and back toward the railings on either side. This was fitted to divert excessive water from washing backward into the Well Deck when heavy seas came over the bows. It is here that one can find another minor difference between *Titanic* and *Olympic*. The top edge on *Titanic*'s breakwater, made of rolled steel, was painted white, but on *Olympic* it was painted brown. Photographs of *Titanic*'s Forecastle Deck at Southampton show a breakwater with a white edge; images of *Olympic* after docking in New York on her maiden voyage show one with a dark edge. However, the colour of the breakwater could have easily been altered with minimal effort. Could there be brown paint still intact on the upper edge of the breakwater on the wreck, exposed by the scouring of the ocean currents beneath an overcoat of white paint? Regrettably, available video footage shows the wreck's breakwater so corroded with rust that it is almost impossible to tell.

Visible in photographs of *Titanic*'s Forecastle Deck at Southampton was a large white cowl vent on the port side just forward of the breakwater. Yet in early photographs of her there is no visible cowl in this position. In early photographs of *Olympic* the cowl also is not fitted, but in a photograph taken of the two ships together in Belfast *Olympic* can be seen with the cowl in place. It should be explained that stand-alone cowl vents like these (with no motorised fan unit at their base) were easily removed so they could be stowed and capped in heavy seas. Otherwise, heavy seas breaking over the bows might carry them away and flood the spaces below. Because of this, little importance should be placed to the cowl vent in this area on either ship being present. But there are two additional details in the same general area that are key. One is the crew galley skylight. This was located on the after side of the breakwater almost directly in line with the cowl vent described above. A very few photographs of *Olympic*, studied carefully, show that she was not originally built with this skylight as *Titanic* was. This skylight does, however, suddenly appear in Harland & Wolff's photograph of *Olympic* after the sinking (see H-1827 on page 107). As our investigation delves deeper, an increasing number of inconsistencies continue to suggest the possibility that the two ships could have exchanged identities.

Next, we move aft to an area directly above *Olympic*'s Navigating Bridge. Immediately forward of the No. 1 funnel is a large forward-facing ventilator with a rectangular grille. This was one of six stokehold vents that provided the intake air to the boiler rooms deep in the bowels of the ship. On the starboard side of the vent forward of the No. 1 funnel is a large 'swan-neck' ventilator, named for its resemblance to the curved neck of a swan. On *Olympic* this vent was noticeably shorter in profile than the one fitted to *Titanic*; however, after *Olympic*'s return from Belfast in early March 1912, the height of this vent appears to be the same height as that fitted to *Titanic*. There is probably little significance to this, as it could easily be explained as a modification. But when *Titanic* departed Belfast a week later her vent in this position had been lowered. There had been a complete reversal in appearance of the ventilators on both ships. Why would the shipyard have taken the lower-profile vent off *Olympic* and replaced it with a higher profile one and do the opposite to *Titanic*? If Harland & Wolff officials believed that *Olympic* required a higher swan-neck vent in this area, why remove the existing vent on *Titanic* and replace it with a smaller one?

Moving further aft, in pictures taken of *Olympic* during her maiden voyage there is only one cowl vent visible on the top of the reciprocating engine casing on the port

Olympic at New York in June 1911, on her maiden voyage. Notice the lack of a large cowl vent and no Crew Galley skylight, and the upper edge of the breakwater is painted brown.

Titanic's Forecastle Deck photographed at Southampton. Notice the Crew Galley skylight, the large cowl, and the all-white breakwater.

H-1827 – *Olympic* at Harland & Wolff for her 1912–13 refit. Notice the additions of the large cowl and the Crew Galley skylight. The foul-weather vent seen at New York on her maiden voyage is still present.

This enlarged crop is from a photo of *Olympic* in New York on her maiden voyage. Notice the size of the swan-neck ventilation head to the left of the centre stokehold duct.

side.[5] In a later photograph showing both ships together, one can see that a cowl has been added to the starboard side of the roof on *Titanic*. At some point before March 1912, this cowl was added to *Olympic*, producing a configuration that now matched *Titanic's*.

Finally, we consider the appearance of the lifeboats. All photographs taken of *Olympic* on her first few voyages show her lifeboats to be painted completely white. When the ship returned to Belfast following her collision with the *Hawke*, the lifeboat gunwales[6] were all painted brown, as were *Titanic's*.

Why the White Star Line chose that point in time to change the colour scheme of *Olympic's* lifeboats remains a mystery. Changes such as this are not normally documented so we are left with speculation only. It would appear that the company wanted, for some reason, to make the lifeboats on both of the ships look exactly the same. At about the same time (when *Olympic* sailed from Belfast on 7 March), two additional portholes had been added to the port side shell plating below the Forecastle Deck and a cowl vent had been added forward of the breakwater on her port side – exactly like *Titanic*. In addition the swan-neck vents forward of the No. 1 funnel had been reversed, so with regard to this detail each ship looked like the other.

Titanic at the Fitting-Out Wharf having her new B–Deck windows added. (*R. Terrell-Wright collection*)

By the time this picture was taken of *Titanic* in Southampton, the swan-neck ventilation head was cut shorter.

To the casual observer, the ships were now virtually interchangeable except for the weather screens enclosing the forward end of the Promenade Deck and the windows along B Deck. As noted in chapter two, *Olympic* originally had a second open promenade on B Deck that was eliminated by extending the staterooms inboard of the promenade out to the side of the ship. This work was done while *Titanic* was fitting out. Work on changing these windows began in the weeks following her launch, and required the removal of almost all of the original external windows and framing on B Deck. The same conversion was done to *Olympic*, but because *Titanic* did not have a uniform series of identical rooms in this area as a result of the parlour suites and private promenades that were added, the pattern of windows was distinctly more irregular than on *Olympic*. If the ships were to be switched, *Titanic's* B Deck windows would have to be changed to match the arrangement of those on *Olympic*. In theory, this would be as simple as removing the existing windows, shifting the openings to match the other ship and refitting them with the frames that had originally been installed. After all, these frames would have probably been stored away somewhere in the yard when they were removed from the ship.

At this point, much like a murder mystery, we have both motive and opportunity. Our suspicions have been raised by a growing body of evidence pointing to the crime. The difference in our case, of course, is whether or not the 'crime' actually occurred. The time has come to consider all the evidence and present, in the spirit of Sherlock Holmes and Hercule Poirot, our analysis and conclusion.

The two great ships in echelon, *Titanic* in drydock and *Olympic* at the Fitting-Out Wharf on 1 March 1912.

Olympic now in dry dock with *Titanic* at the Fitting-Out Wharf on 2 March.

Titanic in March 1912. In this image as well as the first one, the swan-neck ventilation head is visible on the left side of the centre stokehold duct.

An enlarged crop from the picture above, taken on *Olympic*'s arrival at New York on her maiden voyage. The reciprocating engine casing has only one cowl.

In this enlarged crop from the top image, *Olympic* now has a second cowl over her reciprocating engine casing. The two sisters are starting to look very similar.

In this image from *Olympic*'s maiden voyage, her lifeboats have white-painted gunwales.

Lifeboats with brown gunwales on *Titanic*.

Olympic in the graving dock at Harland & Wolff, supposedly during her repairs after the *Hawke* incident. By the time of the collision, *Olympic*'s lifeboat gunwales were already painted brown.

THE FINAL VERDICT

One of the most common mistakes made in analysing historical events is to view them from a twenty-first-century perspective. Too often this leads us to flawed conclusions based on standards or practices that were very different from those of the period we are considering. Shipbuilding technology was very advanced in 1912, but was not based on the same knowledge available today. Practices at the time were based on what was known then. Hindsight often clouds our appraisal of events past, and for that reason we first turn to a discussion of the shipping industry and the maritime practices of the time.

The twentieth century saw almost daily advancements in science and technology. The explosive growth in mechanisation kindled by the Industrial Revolution was pushing shipbuilding and machinery further and further beyond existing limits. It was an age of innovation and daring, resulting in ships far larger than anyone had ever considered – or had experience in handling.

Nonetheless, it was also an age of conservatism. New technology was willingly embraced, but not relied on until it had been tried and tested. Electric arc welding is one example: it was available well before *Titanic's* time, but the shipbuilding industry was not yet willing to adopt it in place of riveting. The *Olympic*-class ships, far from utilising new and innovative technology, simply pushed existing technology to new limits in size and application. The basis of the ships' construction – steel hull plates riveted to a structure of built-up channel frames springing from a vertical keel with a double bottom – had been the standard for decades. In building *Titanic* and her sisters, Harland & Wolff simply used existing technology on a scale that had never been attempted. And, because her builders recognised that they were breaking new ground in terms of size, they were careful to err on the side of caution in terms of structural

HARLAND & WOLFF, LIMITED.

Builders of the "OLYMPIC" and "TITANIC," the largest steamers in the World, 45,000 tons each.

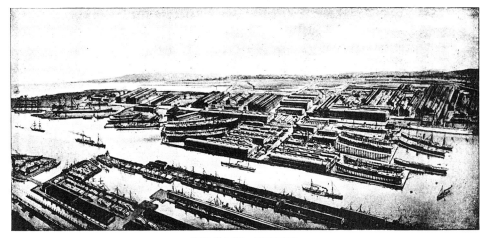

BELFAST WORKS.

SOUTHAMPTON WORKS.

Harland & Wolff, Ltd., have headed the returns for Shipbuilding twelve times in the last twenty years. They have often exceeded 80,000 and 90,000 tons in the year, and thrice their output has been over 100,000, viz.:—

1903	8 vessels	110,463 tons,	100,400 I.H.P.
1908	8 ,,	106,528 ,,	65,840 ,,
1910	8 ,,	115,861 ,,	100,130 ,,

In 1912, Harland & Wolff was shipbuilder to the world.

integrity and to build the *Olympic*-class ships far stronger than the minimum standards might have allowed.

In business, the Edwardian age was an era of very rich men and very poor immigrants. Antitrust laws were not yet in effect, so there was both an incentive and a drive to create business monopolies and financial conglomerates. The 'Atlantic Ferry' was very profitable, with the huge influx of emigrants flocking to America to fill the factories and streets of her cities with cheap labour. The White Star Line astutely recognised that it would pay handsome dividends to treat their Third-Class passengers well, as many single males or families would send for their relatives once they had found work and a place to live in New York or other gateway cities. Thus Third-Class passengers were given accommodations that might have been spartan by even Second-Class standards but positively palatial compared to what they were used to. Once aboard, Third-Class passengers slept on clean linens and were served by stewards at tables. The White Star Line confidently expected to recoup the cost of such accommodations tenfold as relatives arriving in the New World extolled the virtues of taking passage aboard a White Star Line ship to friends and family at home.

The passenger steamship trade in 1912 was a hard-hitting competition with vast sums of money at stake. It was also an era of peace throughout the western world, and millionaires and those who were well-to-do regularly travelled between America, England and the Continent. To make money, a steamship company had to appeal to emigrant and millionaire alike. To succeed they needed speedy ships and luxurious ones. Even though the *Olympic*-class liners had no chance of breaking the records set by their Cunard counterparts, they still had to cross the Atlantic in a reasonable amount of time or else their customers would find passage with a competitor. At the same time, they had to set new standards of living aboard that would entice those with the means to travel First Class. And set new standards they did. It is no exaggeration to state that the wealthy were cosseted in luxury no less substantial than they could enjoy at the finest hotels in the world.

By *Titanic*'s time the competition for passengers – at least the First-Class ones – had stabilised to a few major competitors. One result of the company's drive to win passengers over is that many passengers devoted a following to not only a particular line, but a particular ship or captain. One such captain was Edward J. Smith. He was a true 'salty dog', well respected by his peers and immensely popular with his passengers. He is repeatedly accused of driving his ship recklessly through an ocean with known sightings of ice, yet he was doing nothing more than what any other captain would have done, as was reaffirmed repeatedly during testimony after the sinking: maintaining course and speed in the firm expectation that any danger large enough to endanger the ship would be seen in time to avoid it. In short, they sailed as fast as possible, assigned men to the lookout, and carried on until someone sighted something. At that point, if ice were seen, they would take the appropriate action. Statistically, the chances of a ship *Titanic*'s size colliding with an iceberg large enough to sink it were slim to none. This is why, on a course that would take them through thousands of square miles of ocean, individual ice sightings were of little concern. *Titanic's* Second Officer Charles Lightoller affirmed this when he said: '[you can] cross the Atlantic for years and have ice reported and never see it.'

Did knowledge of these ships' safety features and advanced technology lull her captain and officers into a false sense of security? Certainly the thought of a ship like *Titanic* sinking outright was unthinkable. Whether this belief caused her officers to be overconfident to the point of complacency has been suggested more than once. However, the White Star Line was extremely strict in its regulations for officers. Anyone who commanded a White Star ship would never have dared to relax their vigilance or risk any event that might result in their dismissal, nor would any officer who aspired to command. For that reason a careful watch was kept for icebergs, and the lookouts were enjoined to be alert for them. *Titanic's* officers also maintained a constant watch on the Bridge, no less vigilant than that of the lookouts, and knew they were entering an area of ice regardless of whether any ice warnings were given to them. A watch was kept with the naked eye, never binoculars. Binoculars were only for examining an object once spotted. Advanced optics and lens coatings, scan-and-search techniques – these were all years away, not present or practised in *Titanic's* time. As Lightoller stated: 'I have never seen ice through glasses first, never in my experience. Always whenever I have seen a berg I have seen it first with my eyes and then examined it through glasses.' Despite assumptions to the contrary, binoculars do not amplify light and would have been of little use to the lookouts that night.[1]

Once the collision occurred, there was nothing that could have been done to save the ship. The entire ship's pumping power combined was substantial – 1,700 tons per hour – but had no hope of keeping up with the incoming flow of water, estimated at 24,000 tons in the first hour.[2] Flooding compartments further aft would have only hastened the ship's end and put the ship's main electrical generation plant out of commission sooner. Occasionally one also reads of opinions that the crew could or should have attempted to put some sort of canvas over the opening to stem the inflow of water. This is another example of an opinion that is tendered out of ignorance. While collision mats existed – the *Hawke* deployed them after her collision with *Olympic* – they were not carried aboard *Titanic*, nor would it have been within the realm of possibility to get lines under such a huge liner to the deck on the other side preparatory to working any such mat into place.

The *Olympic–Hawke* Collision

The collision between HMS *Hawke* and *Olympic* on 20 September 1911 is certainly an area that deserves scrutiny. It must be stated, and reiterated throughout, that these *Olympic*-class ships were a new frontier – not in technology, but in size. *Olympic* was far larger and longer than any ship that anyone had ever seen or handled. There were several accidents that happened to her in her first few voyages based on this, despite those involved having experience on very large ships.

On *Olympic's* maiden arrival at New York, an accident occurred while was being guided by tugs into her berth at Pier 59 in New York. The pilot attempted to assist the tugs by giving the ship a nudge into her slip: he gave the order for 'Dead Slow', followed by an immediate 'Stop'. However, the 103ft tug *O.L. Hallenbeck* was too close to *Olympic's* side and the suction of her propellers pulled the tug under *Olympic's* stern and into the hull. Her decks awash, the tug was able to right herself and limp to a nearby pier. Her stern frame had been smashed and her rudder and propeller shaft had been disabled.

The phenomenon of suction forces caused by the displacement of water from a very large ship moving through the water – or, in close confines, from her propeller wash – were only beginning to be recognised by the time of the *Olympic*-class ships. The hydrodynamic forces at work are well known today and involve a body of specialised knowledge all of its own. In 1912 ships' captains were only starting to become aware of the forces at work, and the *Hawke* collision resulted partially from ignorance of those forces. While the failure of the warship's steering gear was no doubt responsible for the severity of the damage, the proximity of the two ships was a major factor. Perhaps no better example of suction can be given than *Titanic's* near-collision with the *New York* upon departing Southampton, when the suction caused by *Titanic's* passing caused the *New York's* wire rope hawsers to snap like twine as her stern was drawn in towards *Titanic*.

There are plenty of pictures that show the damage inflicted on *Olympic's* starboard quarter by the *Hawke* and they are impressive in conveying the severity of the damage. The initial point where the ram bow of the *Hawke* penetrated *Olympic's* hull can be clearly identified. The impact crumpled the warship's bow and tore off her cement-reinforced ram. Because *Olympic* was still in forward motion, the *Hawke* was pulled backwards as her bow tore free and either her hull or the ram was responsible for damaging *Olympic's* starboard propeller blades, shaft and shaft boss plating. The damaged section of the shaft itself was located directly beneath the shaft boss, and was most likely bent along with the plating as a direct result of the collision rather than from *Olympic's* propeller making contact with any portion of the *Hawke*.

There are pictures that show *Olympic* in Southampton after the collision, and the stern is noticeably down in the water. The bow is up and shows no sign of damage and certainly no breach in the plating. Some theorists believe that the damage may have been more extensive than what was disclosed at the time; however *Olympic* was required to offload most of her coal, all her cargo, baggage and mail and all her perishable food stores. Prior to repairs the damage had to be inspected as thoroughly as was possible at Southampton, as did the surrounding structural components of the hull that were not readily accessible. The starboard engine had to be given at least a preliminary inspection, temporary repairs had to be made to the hull and the

The collision with HMS *Hawke* damaged *Olympic* both above and below the waterline. This is the damage above the waterline resulting from the *Hawke*'s prow. The damage from her bow ram is much further down.

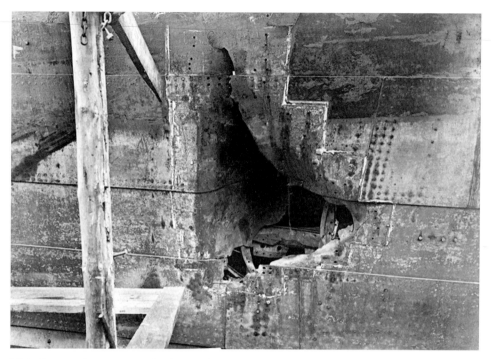

This close-up image shows the damage beneath the waterline resulting from the *Hawke*'s cement-reinforced bow ram.

This dramatic photo shows the damage to *Olympic*'s starboard propeller boss. The propeller shaft is exposed here after removal of some of the shell plating.

compartments had to be pumped dry. Therefore, two weeks would not have been an excessive amount of time to spend at Southampton. In addition, Harland & Wolff would undoubtedly have required some lead time to make the necessary arrangements for her arrival, the time spend in transit notwithstanding.

As discussed in chapter three, *Olympic* sailed to Belfast with only the port reciprocating engine in operation – not the damaged starboard engine, nor the centre turbine. Conspiracy theorists claim that the centre turbine was not engaged because vibration from its use would have increased the risk of exacerbating an already damaged keel or bottom. However, the ship made the return trip to Belfast at half-speed on the port engine, and it is a certainty that the reduced quantity of steam required to drive her at that speed would have resulted in an insufficient volume of exhaust steam to operate the turbine. Sufficient steam to operate the turbine was only available when running at a minimum of 50 per cent on both reciprocating engines, or when running full-ahead on one or the other. This *Olympic* did more than once when making a crossing at reduced speed after dropping or breaking a blade on one of her wing propellers. In either case, doing so required the idle (non-operating) engine on that side (and most likely the condenser, as well) to be isolated from the turbine.

Even if the port engine could supply sufficient steam to run the turbine at low power, there was another problem to overcome. The turbine was engaged by means of a changeover valve that diverted the steam from the condensers to the turbine. This changeover valve was linked to two separate valves, one connected to the exhaust manifold of each reciprocating engine. Both the port and starboard valves were worked in tandem. When one was in the 'operate' (open) position, so was the other. If the valves feeding steam to the turbine were open on both the operating and idle (non-operating) reciprocating engines, steam from the turbine case – where it first entered from the reciprocating engines – would have fed back into the idle starboard engine's manifold and condensed due to the cooler temperatures there, and then the condensed water would have run back into the turbine. There were strainers located at the bottom of the main turbine inlets to deal with this sort of runoff, but from minor condensation only. It is unlikely that they would have been able to deal with the volume of condensed water that would have resulted from large volumes of steam backing up into the idle engine's manifold. The strainers were there primarily to break up small water droplets that tended to form in the low-pressure steam coming from the reciprocating engine exhaust, as even tiny droplets of water are capable of causing severe damage to the blading inside a rotating turbine. In short, these strainers weren't designed to deal with what would have been a small stream of water pouring back out of that pipe.

Had it been necessary to return the ship to Belfast over a very long distance such as from New York, the turbine could have been configured to run at reduced power from the steam of one reciprocating engine being run at full revolutions. This could have been done by disengaging the linkage to the changeover valves and manually jacking the valve from the exhaust manifold of the starboard engine into the closed position. But the work involved just to gain an extra several knots' speed would have been impractical given the short distance from Southampton back to Belfast. It must be remembered that the turbine engine was employed simply to make use of residual steam pressure and as such did not materially add to the ship's speed. In addition, the turbine engine, by virtue of its rotary motion, created minimal if any vibration, so any claims of the turbine engine putting a damaged keel at risk are completely baseless.

Did *Olympic* suffer damage to her shell plating further forward on her hull? The drawings acquired from Harland & Wolff for this book do show damage forward of the bridge on the starboard side. However, it is jumping to conclusions to assume that this damage resulted from the *Hawke* collision. In addition, it should be remembered that neither the pilot nor any of the officers aboard *Olympic*, nor a witness who observed the event from out on the water, believed that the *Hawke's* bow had advanced further than the Navigating Bridge before the liner began to pull ahead. The most significant evidence in this regard comes from the pilot, George Bowyer, who testified that he saw the stem of the *Hawke* through the window of the Bridge wing cab. As Bowyer was most likely standing on the Bridge itself at the time, this gives us a line-of-sight reference directly abeam to starboard and neither forward or abaft the Bridge.

So where did the damage come from? There is no doubt that when *Olympic* was brought in for the extensive repairs to her stern Harland & Wolff would have made maximum use of the time to repair any minor damage caused from earlier incidents which did not require immediate attention at the time. These same types of small repairs were generally addressed at the end of each season when a ship was brought in for annual maintenance, as it was not economically feasible to bring in a ship for repairs after every minor dent and ding.

All ships were prone to bent and dented plating, especially very large ocean liners. Channels dredged in the late nineteenth and early twentieth centuries were often inadequate in many places to safely manoeuvre these ships in proximity to other vessels. Though shipbuilding was advancing in great strides, the port authorities were generally slow in making the improvements to waterways necessary to safely manoeuvre these giant liners. Compounding the situation, the captains of other vessels operating within these same waters were often unfamiliar with what constituted a safe degree of separation from these huge vessels, and as a result there were quite a few groundings and collisions in those days.

Problems also resulted from having to learn the handling characteristics of a completely new class of ship when docking. Tug captains were frequently caught by surprise when the huge ships under their charge simply would not move until much more power had been applied from the tug's engines. At New York, docking at the Hudson River piers presented some particularly difficult challenges. The

Olympic moving into her berth at the White Star Line pier in New York.

Hudson River has more than a 2-knot current at full ebb, and while that may not seem particularly fast, with its full force acting on the liner attempting to berth at a pier that is perpendicular to the river can be very difficult. The usual technique was to first position the liner's bows partly in the slip, and guide her forward as she turned the corner – not unlike trying to turn into one's garage from the side instead of by pulling straight in. On her maiden arrival in New York in June 1911, *Olympic* caught the corner of the dock at Pier 59 and scraped her hull for a good distance along the starboard side. It must be remembered that the mass of the ship was also at work, exerting enormous force against the heavy pilings of the pier and with the relatively thin shell plating of the hull making the contact. Examination of a photograph from this incident shows a long, deep scrape approximately 15ft above the water and extending as far aft as her No. 3 funnel.[3]

   There is absolutely no evidence that the damage to the forward shell plating in the Harland & Wolff drawing resulted from the collision with the *Hawke*. When the tide was on the flood in the Hudson River (with the current moving upriver at that location) a well-known fact is that some captains would purposely position the forward portion of the hull against the corner pilings of the pier and let the current swing the

When *Olympic* was being berthed at New York on her maiden voyage, she scraped along the corner pilings of the dock and sustained damage to the shell plating along an extended length of her starboard side.

stern around straight. This made it easier for the tugs, but it certainly created problems with the shell plates sooner or later. The incident in the photograph shown was not the last time *Olympic* would get a scrape from the pier, and the forward area of damaged plating that was replaced as shown on the Harland & Wolff drawing could have very likely resulted from the June incident described above.

Next we address the claim of conspiracy theorists that the *Hawke* collision resulted in damage to the keel or double bottom. The idea that the damage was either irreparable or not economically feasible to repair is central to the theory of a conspiracy to switch the two ships. When looking at the damage to *Olympic*'s hull after the *Hawke* collision, it can be clearly seen that there was no damage anywhere near the keel, nor could there have been. *Olympic*'s keel was over 34ft below the waterline, whereas the *Hawke* only drew 24ft. The top of *Olympic*'s keel and double bottom was about 29ft below the waterline, so it would have been a physical impossibility for any part of the *Hawke* to make contact with either. As for the damaged frames, they were of built-up construction, meaning that they were riveted together from separate components. They were not cast in one piece like the stern frame. Any of the damaged frames could readily be exposed and their damaged sections replaced without having to remove the shell plating from the uppermost strake all the way down to the keel.

Claims that the keel or double bottom might have been damaged when the rotating starboard propeller made contact with the *Hawke* fail as well. The theory of torsional shock or vibration from a bent shaft having caused material damage to the engine mountings or keel simply does not stand up to close scrutiny. The mass of the ship's structure alone was more than sufficient to absorb such vibration before any meaningful amount of shock could be transmitted directly to the keel. None of the engines were mounted directly to the double bottom or the keel itself. Instead, they were mounted to bedplates on the Tank Top plating, which in this area was some 6ft above the keel plate. The weight of the machinery was supported by the vertical steel plates called 'floors' which essentially joined the keel to the frames. 'Intercostals', or vertical steel plates running in a fore-and-aft direction, joined the floors with one another, thereby creating the cellular bottom structure. This was an incredibly strong and resilient structure well able to absorb shocks and vibration.

In addition, the propeller shaft itself would have absorbed a great deal of the shock from the blade impacts before it could be transmitted to the propulsion machinery. An explanation of how the propeller shafts and engines were constructed will make this clear.

First, the wing propellers, which were driven by the reciprocating engines, were composed of manganese-bronze blades bolted to a steel hub. This hub was keyed and locked onto the tail shaft, the last segment of the propeller shaft. The tail shaft was bolted to a series of hollow tubular segments of shafting supported on a series of large bearings called plummer blocks. Propeller shafts were made in segments for ease of manufacture and to facilitate installation and removal aboard ship. Each segment

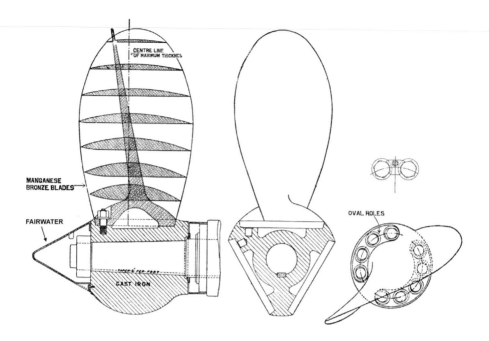

A three-bladed propeller of the same type as on the *Olympic*-class ships, having separate blades and a hub. The flange at the base of each manganese-bronze blade was seated within a circular depression and was fastened by nuts and locking pins to studs threaded into the steel hub. (*Scott Andrews collection*)

was held to the other by a series of bolts passed through flanges. Near its forward end was a solid, forged segment called the thrust shaft, which contained a series of large annular rings that acted against bearing surfaces within what is called the thrust block assembly. The thrust block assembly was bolted securely to the double bottom and is what transmitted the thrust created by the propellers to the hull. Without it, the thrust of the propellers pushing on the shafts, combined with the terrific inertia of the huge hull resisting movement through the water, would have transmitted this force directly to the crankshafts. The crankshafts rotated in simple bearings that were not designed to absorb fore-and-aft movement or transmit the driving force of the propellers to the hull. Without the interceding thrust blocks, the thrust of the propellers would have instead been transmitted directly to the crankshafts, pushing the engines hard against the bedplates and quickly resulting in irreparable damage. The thrust block assembly also insulated the engines from shock created by any fore-and-aft movement of the shafting. Torsional loading, which is created by the torque of the engines working against the resistance of the propeller cutting through the water, is dissipated.

The propeller shafts were also designed in a way that prevented the ship's vital propulsion machinery from being damaged if the propellers struck a solid object. Torsional loading, which is created by the torque of the engines working against the

Olympic's thrust shaft being manufactured in the lathe at Harland & Wolff. The annular rings around the shaft are what made contact with the bearings in the thrust blocks. (Engineering/*Authors' Collection*)

resistance of the propeller cutting through the water, is dissipated largely through the normal twisting of the propeller shaft as it is put under load. In extreme cases, such as that created by a propeller striking a solid object, the blades of the propeller, being of a softer material, would yield first, bending or breaking off from the hub. Should even this have failed to dissipate all of the shock, the bolts coupling the shafting segments would have been broken somewhere along its length. As a matter of design, these bolts were made to a specific strength that would have ensured that they broke before causing damage to the shaft. All this was specifically designed to ensure that the ship's vital propulsion machinery would not be affected by damage to the propellers.

Even if the keel and double bottom had been damaged, regardless of how badly, Harland & Wolff could have repaired it. It was not unknown for ships to run aground and tear their bottoms wide open, completely exposing the compartments within and even inflicting severe damage to the keel in the process. Damage of this type was routinely repaired and the ships placed back in service, ships that earned far less revenue than the express ocean liners of the day. One example is the Atlantic Line's *China*. This ship went aground and suffered major damage to both the exterior plating and the structural portions of its double bottom. The *China* was so badly damaged that two thirds of her bottom had to be replaced. Yet Harland & Wolff rebuilt her and returned her to service.

This dramatic photograph shows the damage to the SS *China* of the Peninsular & Oriental Steam Navigation Company, which ran aground and tore her bottom open on 24 March 1889, near the entrance to the Red Sea. She was initially regarded as a total wreck, but by 11 August salvage crews began blasting beneath her hull to free her from the bottom. Salvors then filled the damaged area with wood and concrete and successfully refloated her by 9 February 1890. She was made more watertight and then had a temporary bottom of wood and concrete built into her hull. Six days later her long journey to Belfast began, and she finally arrived on 20 March after being towed a distance of over 4,000 miles. She was placed in the Alexandra Graving Dock where shipyard workers set about building her a new keel and bottom. In this image workers can be seen removing the damaged sections of the hull, surrounded by mounds of concrete removed from her bottom. The *China* was fully repaired and remained in service for another twenty-seven years. This would hardly have been possible had Harland & Wolff not been able to build a new section of keel *and* a double bottom.

Harland & Wolff was a shipbuilder's shipbuilder. The firm was a pioneer in lengthening ships by cutting them in half and fitting in new sections. A case in point is the 12,000-ton White Star liner *Suevic*, which grounded on the rocks of the Lizard[4] on 17 March 1907. Harland & Wolff built a whole new bow section to fit on this vessel after wreckers had to blast the ship in two in order to free the after section containing the boilers and propulsion machinery.

Another demonstration of Harland & Wolff's impressive repair capabilities took place in *Olympic*'s 1924–5 refit, when shipyard workers removed her cracked stern frame and replaced it with a new one. All of these tasks required work on and around the keel. It is an undeniable fact that Harland & Wolff had the expertise to repair a keel if it were necessary. The old idea of a ship being permanently weakened because she had a 'broken back' came from the days of wooden sailing vessels, and was not relevant to steel ships whose keels were assembled from separate plates.

The famous *Baltic*, one of the White Star Line's original 'Big Four', was launched by Harland & Wolff on 12 November 1903, and was also accorded the term 'practically unsinkable'. She was the largest ship in the world at the time, partly due to an early modification that increased her size. Her construction had already begun when her owners gave the orders to enlarge her. Harland & Wolff proceeded to cut the already-completed keel in half amidships, moved the after portion 28ft,

The wreck of the *Suevic*.

The after section of the *Suevic* entering the Trafalgar Dock in Southampton, 4 April 1907.

The new bow of the *Suevic* photographed in the River Lagan under tow for Southampton. Is this evidence of a shipbuilder who couldn't repair keel damage?

and then inserted a new connecting piece. For its day, it was an amazing piece of surgery.

Titanic did not break into two pieces while sinking as is commonly believed. Technically, she broke into four sections. The two much smaller middle sections were found a distance from the two larger segments of the wreck and were overlooked for a long time. One of these middle sections was a short segment of the double bottom that was found lying upside down. The keel was exposed and found to be twisted at the breaking point. This indicates that the keel was the last part of the structure to tear apart as the ship was foundering; in fact it was probably the last thing connecting the pieces together as the ship was falling to the bottom. *Titanic* certainly did not break in two because of any inherent weakness in her keel.

The paint shade differences observed on *Titanic* while at Southampton and Belfast were nothing out of the ordinary. The varying shades of black could have been brought on by a different batch of paint or could indicate an area that required a move of the painter's platform; it could be lighter or darker depending on whether this area was painted in the dry dock or in the Fitting-Out Wharf. Then, too, the paint used in shipyards in the early part of the twentieth century and even years later did not come from commercial paint manufacturers. Though commercial paints were available, Harland & Wolff mixed their own paint in barrels using lead powders, linseed oil and other materials. There was a Paint Shop in the yard specifically for this purpose.

Mystery or History?

Former boatswain James Fenton, in his conversation with fellow sailor Dennis Finch, made some extraordinary claims as outlined in Chapter 4; chief among these claims was that he was a survivor from *Titanic*'s crew. As noted in that chapter, it is entirely possible that he was on the ship, given the incomplete and inaccurate system of recording crew names. However, several circumstantial factors point to his story being a false claim. Detailed analysis of lifeboat loadings and lowerings by historians who specialise in that aspect of the sinking have put a name to every single crewman who entered a lifeboat. It is certainly possible that Fenton was recorded under the wrong name, but as historian George Behe points out, it was highly unlikely that any crew member, regardless of how traumatic he found the event to be, would have foregone the pay he had coming to him, and no pay was ever claimed by a crewman named James Fenton.

Fenton also claimed that some portholes had been painted on the ship. This claim holds little water, as there would have been no need to paint portholes on a ship if a few needed to be added for the purposes of a switch. The process of cutting out a porthole is relatively simple: a pneumatic cutting device is positioned against the side of the hull, and the porthole is simply carved out through a rotary cutting action.

Afterwards, bolt-holes for mounting the sidelight are drilled around the periphery of the opening, and the sidelight is bolted in place. This process is relatively straightforward, can be performed from either outside or inside the hull, and can be undertaken at any time. With the proof in the photographs of *Olympic* having the added two portholes by March 1912, any idea of the painted holes should be laid to rest. It is important to mention that according to the *Olympic*'s Drawing Office Notebook, a ledger kept by Harland & Wolff to outline the changes made to *Olympic* through 1913, the portholes along the port bow were added by 23 January 1912.

The second half of Chapter 4 addresses the testimony from some passengers regarding a severe vibration on the starboard side of the ship in the area above and around the Reciprocating Engine Room. As discussed earlier, there was little to no possibility of damage to the starboard engine in the *Hawke* collision as they specifically had features that prevented any torsional shock from being transmitted to the engines as part of their design requirements. It is impossible to gauge the truth of the passengers' claims or to know to what degree any vibration was felt. It was also *Titanic*'s maiden voyage, and some vibration in a new engine was not unusual. For that matter, some vibration would have been expected under the best of conditions and was quite common in those days. In fact, some ships had vibration problems so severe that they required changes in propellers or other work to reduce the severity of the problem. The *Olympic*-class liners, although built in a way to avoid unnecessary vibration, were still vulnerable to some vibration. There is no evidence to suggest that dam-

A pneumatic porthole-cutting tool, shown in use on the construction of the Cunard liner *Aquitania*. (Engineering/*Authors' Collection*)

aged engine components caused these vibrations. A ship is highly complex machine with equally complex hydrodynamic forces acting against its hull, and these factors along with others can cause vibration to varying degrees. Frequently issues of this nature were largely perceptual – the vast majority of comments regarding vibration on *Titanic* were in reference to how remarkably free she was from this particular problem!

Could this vibration have come from 'mismatched' propeller blades from *Titanic* being used on *Olympic*? Nowhere is it recorded that during repairs following the *Hawke* incident that Harland & Wolff used one of *Titanic*'s propeller blades as a replacement on *Olympic*, because there *were* no spares. The publications available only mention the requisition of a few segments of *Titanic*'s propeller shafting to replace the ones on *Olympic* that had been damaged in the collision. This was understandable, as it was the most expedient way to return *Olympic* to service. As *Titanic* was still months away from completion, there would be more than adequate time to fabricate replacements for the donated shaft segments. There is no reason to believe that spare propeller blades were not put aside for *Olympic*. We know that there were spare blades made for *Titanic*, because after *Titanic*'s loss Harland & Wolff donated several to be melted down to make some of the many monuments to those who were lost. Spare blades were made in sets for each ship, because they needed to be balanced to one another and they all had to have the same overall diameter and pitch. Each was lettered to indicate port and starboard, and numbered to indicate its position on the propeller boss. Unlike with a mass-produced automobile, most parts were not usually interchangeable from one ship to another even when they are made from the same drawings.

The damage sustained to *Olympic*'s starboard propeller off Newfoundland on 24 February 1912 has raised questions by those skeptical of how a ship could strike a wreck in water over 2 miles deep. What many people fail to realise is that period news accounts that said the ship 'hit a wreck' did not refer to a wreck on the bottom in shallow water. *Olympic*'s officers later believed that they hit a derelict, not a submerged wreck. Derelicts are ships that have foundered but stubbornly remain afloat. Wooden sailing vessels – still very common in 1912 – did not sink immediately, but floated at the surface or just awash beneath it and hidden from view. It is quite likely that *Olympic* passed close alongside one, just barely striking it with her starboard propeller.

Fenton also claimed that the ship 'sailed in a great hurry from Belfast'. *Titanic*'s sea trials had been scheduled for the morning of 1 April; however, because of high winds and treacherous conditions in the Victoria Channel the trials had been first postponed and later rescheduled until the following morning. This 24-hour delay would have thrown *Titanic*'s planned two-day sea trial schedule into disarray. There is no doubt that *Titanic*'s departure from Belfast had been planned for the evening of 2 April, because if she had departed any earlier she would not have had berthing space at the already-crowded Southampton Docks due to the coal strike that laid up so many ships. It should also be noted that prior to *Titanic*'s arrival at Southampton, the White Star Line's Pier 44 had been occupied by *Olympic* until just after midday on 3 April.

Although there is no written record to confirm this, it is worth considering that the trials may have been scheduled for completion in only one day and not two as history records, especially if the ship had originally been scheduled to stop at Liverpool first.

In light of the above, *Titanic* would not have departed Belfast in 'a great hurry'. The only apparent rush would have been caused by the fact that the date planned for her sea trials had been set back because of the unfavourable conditions. Therefore, the only burden of pressure would have been among the ship's officers and management to complete the required sea and acceptance trials in the limited time available. However, in defence of Fenton's claim, the delay may have caused an air of tension aboard ship. The crew would have without doubt realised that if the inclement weather continued the following day it would have likely forced another postponement. As it turned out, the morning of 2 April dawned clear, and *Titanic* apparently performed flawlessly during the trials. A Board of Trade certificate of seaworthiness, valid for twelve months, was issued and the ship was then formally handed over from builder to owner.

The Coal Bunker Fire

Titanic's famous coal bunker fire, mentioned by James Fenton, is a staple for many conspiracy theorists. Coal bunker fires were not uncommon aboard ships carrying thousands of tons of coal, and testimony by surviving crew members established that there was indeed one burning aboard *Titanic* in the starboard bunker in the after corner of Boiler Room No. 6.

Coal is, in essence, compressed organic matter, and can spontaneously combust when large quantities are stored for any period of time. As the US Department of Energy stated in a bulletin of May 1993: 'Spontaneous combustion has long been recognised as a fire hazard in stored coal. Spontaneous combustion fires usually begin as "hot spots" deep within the reserve of coal. The hot spots appear when coal absorbs oxygen from the air. Heat generated by the oxidation then initiates the fire. Such fires can be very stubborn to extinguish because of the amount of coal involved (often hundreds of tons) and the difficulty of getting to the seat of the problem.'[5]

However, a coal bunker fire should not be confused with a raging fire as when a wooden structure burns. It produces great amounts of heat and toxic gases, but can be easily contained within the steel bulkheads of the bunker. It is quite possible the Board of Trade surveyor, either at Belfast or Southampton, knew of the fire but let it go, considering that this type of incident was not uncommon.

The process used to extinguish a coal bunker fire is quite straightforward: a number of men are detailed to remove the coal from the bunker as the top layers are sprayed with water to contain the hot embers at the bottom. This is what was done on *Titanic*. It is quite possible that the stokehold crew believed they had the fire out before arriving at Southampton but, after bunkering the new coal, they found it was still active. At this point, extra men were assigned to the task of shifting the coal and extinguishing the fire once again. If the crew had failed to extinguish the fire by the time *Titanic* arrived in New York, it is possible that a New York City fireboat would have been called out to extinguish the smouldering coal by closing the internal access doors in the affected bunker, opening the coal chute from the outside, and simply dumping water down the chute into the bunker. However, testimony established that the fire was out by the following Saturday.

James Fenton claimed that water coming into contact with the coal fire caused an explosion. This could not have happened, as coal is not explosive when it is heated or even when combusting coal is suddenly cooled. In any event, as noted, the fire was out by then. However it is frequently claimed by conspiracy proponents and others that the fire-damaged bulkhead later failed at a crucial time, adding to the flooding of Boiler Room 5, and that up to that point the ship appeared to be maintaining its precarious trim, aided by the pumps. The claim is always that the bulkhead, weakened by the fire, gave way because of the force of the water in the adjoining flooded boiler room, No. 6, thereby sealing the ship's fate. It is probable that the heat damaged the bulkhead, but analysis by marine forensic experts tells us that the damaged bulkhead had little or no bearing on *Titanic*'s fate.

Coal fires were far more common than coal dust explosions. The theory that a coal dust explosion was responsible for blowing a hole in the starboard side of *Titanic*'s hull is based on misinformation and is not supported by the facts. In order for such an explosion to occur, two requirements must be met. First, there must be a certain amount of airborne coal dust present in the surrounding air. Second, there must be a source of ignition present. The presence of a fire smouldering within a bunker would seem to satisfy the second requirement. However, while fighting a coal bunker fire, water is continually sprayed over the top of the coal pile being worked as the burned material is raked out. This continual wetting of the surrounding coal would have precluded any dust being created within the immediate vicinity of the fire. Even had the proper conditions existed to create a coal dust explosion, the odds of this occurring at the very moment *Titanic* just happened to be passing an iceberg would have to be astronomical. An occurrence of this type would be just too coincidental, and an explosion of this magnitude could not have taken place without anyone's notice. The later 'explosions' heard by the survivors while *Titanic* foundered would have been the steel tearing and the rupture of the main steam pipes or boilers that were still in use at the end. The amount of force caused by the sudden release of steam is immense. The term 'boiler explosion' does not refer to a boiler blowing itself to pieces, it refers to a breach in a pressurised device. In rare instances where a pressurised boiler actually blew apart, the cause was nearly always old equipment and/or improper upkeep or operation.

The Lifeboat Evidence

Why Captain Rostron of the *Carpathia* elected not to recover lifeboat Nos. 4, 14 and 15 is anyone's guess. We know that some of the boats were partially flooded, and the added weight of the water inside of a boat may have mitigated against their retrieval. Apparently lifeboats were considered expendable at the time, or else Rostron would have made more of an effort to bring the three boats aboard. If it were necessary, no doubt he would have found room to stow them on the deck of the *Carpathia*. It must be remembered that as the recovery continued, he found himself with a ship crowded with wet, freezing survivors and he may simply have decided that it was not worth the additional delay to recover a few more boats.

The White Star Line and Harland & Wolff truly didn't believe that anything could ever sink their new liners (nor did anybody else for that matter). It is probably because of this belief that the oil lamps were not kept in instant readiness. In addition, the reason why many of the lifeboats had no lamps was because the White Star Line was not required by law to keep them in the boats. By the time Lamp Trimmer Samuel Hemming had been roused from his berth and had been to the Lamp Room, filled the lamps and brought them up to the Boat Deck to distribute them, many of the boats had already been launched.

Mrs Frederick Spedden's reference to the wrong number being on her lifeboat, as detailed in Chapter 5, may or may not be accurate. However, if it is true, it is possible that it was a simple mistake, especially with the outboard numbers. With the fact that *Titanic* was hurried through the process of her final fitting out, it is possible that the numbers were mismatched on the outboard sides of the lifeboats.

Any instance of the falls being jammed while the lifeboats were being lowered had to do with an inherent design problem called 'toppling'. With large multiple-sheave (multiple roller) blocks, the lines that run between the upper block hanging from the davit and the lower block holding the boat are not evenly distributed across the block from one side to the other, and lowering great weights can cause them to tilt sideways, or 'topple'. This twisting motion can result in the falls jamming with tangled rope. After *Titanic's* demise many new patents for non-toppling davit blocks were issued.

Some claim that the Engelhardt collapsibles were not new based solely on the difficulty in raising their canvas sides and getting them locked into position. Here, the twenty-first-century perspective must be put aside. There were no lifeboat drills that required any of the crew to uncover these boats and make them ready in regular drills, and as there were a number of different types of collapsible boats on the market, it was highly likely that the crew had no experience with them. Perhaps the hardware was stiff or the joints were not properly oiled or possibly even faulty, but more than likely there was simply no time to try and figure out how to manipulate the gear as the boat was practically brought down with the ship. The people aboard this half-sunk collapsible appeared not to know how to pull up the frame, or perhaps were just too cold to try and figure it out in the dark.

It is true that Captain Rostron thought that one of the collapsibles went down with the ship. Second Officer Lightoller is said to have stated that he did not think Collapsible A made it off the ship. It is possible that he never saw it leave the roof of the Officers' Quarters deckhouse. Lightoller may have been the one who passed this on to Rostron while onboard the *Carpathia*, which would explain why Rostron thought that one of the collapsibles went down with the ship. Rostron did testify that this information was relayed to him on the *Carpathia*. In fact Collapsible A was never launched from *Titanic* in the true sense of the term, but instead floated off. Rostron also did not know exactly what type of supplemental lifeboats *Titanic* was carrying. He thought she was fitted with Berthon collapsibles. In retrospect it is entirely understandable that neither Rostron nor the crew were familiar with the Engelhardt collapsibles. They were relatively knew and not well known, and testimony of the surviving crew confirms this. Berthons, on the other hand, were well known among mariners with naval experience because they were commonly seen on naval ships. A Berthon was a true collapsible boat, as it literally folded longitudinally along its whole length. An Engelhardt collapsible was really a raft constructed with airtight divisions within its hull and with collapsible canvas bulwarks. Many of the crewmen of *Titanic* rightfully called them 'rafts', because that is what they technically were. This is what Seaman Scarrott and passenger George Sloper were referring to when they testified to seeing people on a raft. As for the overturned boat that Mrs Thayer stated she saw, her recollection was put forth in a piece written years after the sinking. There are numerous cases where the identical event or fact was recalled differently by different people, and given the passage of time Mrs Thayer's recollection becomes suspect.

Did Captain Rostron testify to seeing an overturned 30ft lifeboat, suggesting a mysterious twenty-first boat from another ship? No. Part of his testimony appears to indicate this, but when read in its entirety one sees that he did not make that statement. The record of Rostron's testimony at the British inquiry reads as follows, starting from line 25476:

The Attorney General: Altogether how many boats did you pick up?
Rostron: We got 13 lifeboats alongside, two emergency boats, two Berthon boats. There was one lifeboat which we saw was abandoned, and one of the Berthon boats, of course, was not launched from the ship, I understand. That made twenty altogether.
The Attorney General: My impression is there is one collapsible still unaccounted for in that?
Rostron: Oh, yes; I beg your pardon, one bottom up; one that was capsized. That was in the wreckage. That was the twenty.
The Attorney General: You picked up and actually took on board the Carpathia 13 of Titanic's lifeboats?
Rostron: Precisely.

The Attorney General: One of them you saw; the occupants of the boat were rescued and taken on your boat, but the boat was left in the water?

Rostron: Yes, she was damaged.

The Attorney General: You did not bother any more about her?

Rostron: No.

The Attorney General: That made the 14 lifeboats. Then there were the two emergency boats; were they taken on board the Carpathia, or abandoned?

Rostron: I cannot say which were the boats we took up. I took them as they came along, and after the whole thing was over we got as many boats as we could. I did not notice which they were.

The Attorney General: There were two emergency boats, and besides that there were –?

Rostron: The two Berthon boats.

The Attorney General: The two collapsibles?

Rostron: Yes; and there is one Berthon boat which we saw amongst the wreckage bottom up. It was reported to me that there was another Berthon boat still on board the ship.

The Attorney General: That makes 19 out of the 20?

Rostron: No, excuse me. It makes the 20 if you reckon the one still left, but I am not reckoning that. It comes to the same thing. If you reckon that one in, of course it accounts for the lot.

The Commissioner: The one collapsible boat was not launched in the proper sense of the word; it got into the water, very likely?

Starting at Line 25568 Rostron is questioned by Sir Robert Finlay in an attempt to clarify his lifeboat testimony:

Finlay: I wish you would tell us again what you know about the collapsible boats. There were four collapsible boats on board the 'Titanic'?

Rostron: Yes.

Finlay: How many came alongside your ship, or did you get alongside of?

Rostron: Two.

Finlay: Did you see any collapsible boat adrift?

Rostron: We saw one adrift bottom up amongst the wreckage of Titanic.

Finlay: Then you only know of three boats?

Rostron: We only know of three collapsible boats.

Finlay: As to what became of the other boat you know nothing?

Rostron: Nothing whatever, my Lord.

Nowhere in Rostron's testimony does he state that he saw a capsized standard 30ft lifeboat. In fact, Rostron describes nineteen boats, and cannot account for the fourth collapsible. This was probably Collapsible A, which was abandoned during the morning some time before the *Carpathia* arrived.

It is also important to also address erroneous statements regarding flooded lifeboats. There is no evidence to support the claim that any of the boats flooded because they were older boats of the same age as *Olympic*'s. Any rapid inflow of water would not have come from plank seams that were loose as a result of age or drying out. In the dark, the unknowing passengers simply assumed that their boats were leaking, when in reality the drain plugs – which were left out in order that rainwater would not accumulate in the boats under the davits – were not in place.

Some people testified to not having bailers, and others testified that there was no water or biscuit tins. In nearly all cases, it was merely a case of not being able to find these items in crowded lifeboats or even knowing where to look. The inventory of equipment performed on *Titanic*'s surviving lifeboats in New York lists at least one water keg and 'provision tank' for each boat except for the two cutters, which apparently carried no provisions. On the 30ft boats, the provisions were stored in a locker beneath the gangboard at the far end of each boat, and no one apparently knew the lockers were there. As to compasses, they were never stored aboard the boats as they were subject to theft. They were no doubt stored in a secure place and simply never made it to the boats – either because no one seriously thought they would be needed, or because it never occurred to anyone in charge.

It is evident that the White Star Line wanted to downplay their liability in the sinking as much as possible. When company officials ordered the boats to be removed from the water at the White Star Line pier in New York and placed in the loft, protecting them from souvenir hunters was no doubt a concern. However, the real reason they were stored was most likely to keep them from the eyes of the public and the press.

The fate of the lifeboats has never been determined. However, a photograph exists that shows what some believe to be *Titanic*'s lifeboats tied up at a Southampton pier a few weeks later, with *Olympic* clearly visible in the background. This would lead us to believe that the lifeboats had been shipped back to England aboard *Olympic*, eventually to be reconditioned and fitted to another White Star Line ship. However, current research indicates that it is highly probable that the lifeboats were sold in New York and never left the United States.

Photographic Assessment

Our discussion on photographic assessment opened with several questions as to the names on the bows of the ship and whether they could have been, or were, altered. Wreck footage clearly shows the letters 'TITANIC' on the port bow, and they are correct and evenly spaced. Some of the video footage does not show them as such at first glance, until one realises that the wide-angle lens artificially distorts them.

The letters themselves are incised into the steel plating, just as they should be. However, they are hard to see because in most cases the letters are darker than the

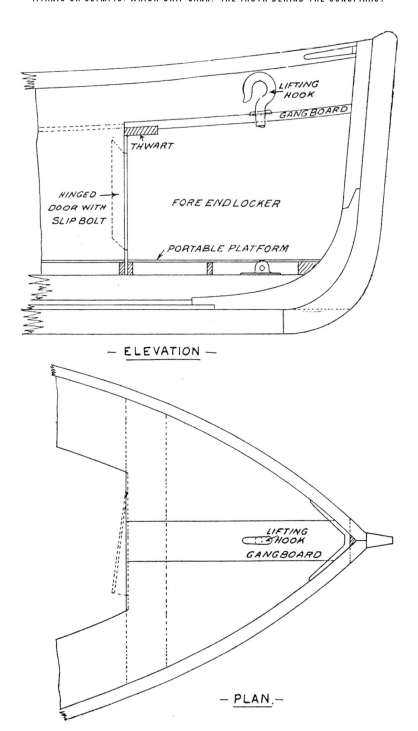

LIFTING HOOK

GANGBOARD

THWART

HINGED DOOR WITH SLIP BOLT

FORE END LOCKER

PORTABLE PLATFORM

— ELEVATION —

LIFTING HOOK

GANGBOARD

— PLAN.—

Beneath the gangboard of the lifeboats at each end was a locker where the water kegs and the provision tanks were stored. It is easy to see how these escaped notice in the dark.

steel that surrounds them. In the case of a few of the letters there is what appears to be light-coloured paint exposed beneath the black hull paint. One expedition used a robotic arm on the dive submersible to scrub the steel surface surrounding the letters on the port side to clean off the rusticles to make the letters readable. The black paint came off in the areas where it was not strong enough to withstand the scrubbing. The light-coloured paint beneath, when this footage was released, gave fuel to the conspiracy theorists' fire; they claimed that because *Olympic* wore light-coloured paint when she was launched and *Titanic* was never painted that colour, it proves that the ship is not *Titanic*. However, the primer used on these ships was nowhere near as dark in colour as it appears in old black-and-white photographs. Camera film of the era was notorious for not reproducing shading accurately – some colours reproduced much darker than they appeared in life. The primer used on the *Olympic*-class ships was a medium grey. Given the fact that these paints were simply chemical compositions, with many of the materials organic, and the fact that they have been immersed in what is essentially a chemical (salt water) bath for the better part of a century, it is not hard to understand how this medium grey could have altered in colour over time. The colour in wreck images also appears artificially lighter owing to the high-intensity lights used, which tend to wash out colours up close.

On 14 April 2000, Ralph White, a cameraman on Dr Robert Ballard's 1985 expedition that discovered the location of the wreck, was personally interviewed by one of the authors. By then White had been down to the wreck no fewer than twenty-eight times and substantiated all his information by sharing his personal slides of the wreck. In the interview, he was asked about the name on the starboard side of the hull. White advised us that the letters of the name on the bow of *Titanic* are in fact incised. He went on to state that the reason why the starboard side name is never seen in any video footage is because of the severe current running over the bow on that side of the wreck. He stated that it is very difficult to navigate the camera in place to video the starboard name letters. He also stated that he was not able to find the stern name and port of registry letters.[6] Owing to the strong currents it is dangerous to manoeuvre the submarine under the counter of the wreck, so it is entirely possible that he just didn't get close enough.

The wreck of *Titanic* will show the astute observer that many of the fittings that made *Titanic* different than *Olympic* are still visible, even after many years under the cold Atlantic water. The teak sill of the Wheelhouse is still present, showing the different configuration from what *Olympic* originally had; and even the round skid lights that were specific to *Titanic* are still visible.

When referring to videotape footage of the propeller on the ocean floor, it has been said that the blades and hub had been originally buried in the silt, then suddenly uncovered to expose the number 401 on one of the blades. The truth of the matter is that Ballard simply missed the propellers when he searched for them back in 1986. He was in the wrong place when he searched the side of the hull. It must

In this image of *Titanic* (left) and *Olympic* (right) under the Arrol gantry, the difference in the colours of the primer used on the hull are clearly evident.

be remembered that *Titanic* was huge, and the visibility was not good at that point. These problems are compounded by the difficulty of trying to manoeuvre the submarine in the unstable current.

Is the number 401 incised on propeller blades as is seen in wreck photos? Yes. Yard numbers were generally indicated on propeller blades. Each blade also had an incised port and starboard designation, and a position number indicated at the base where the blade attached to the hub. In fact *Titanic's* exposed starboard propeller also shows a position number for placement on the hub on the face of the blade. These numbers were cast or etched into the blades for identification purposes. The number 401 seen on the thrust side of the propeller blade of *Titanic* is the remnants of a founder's handiwork, and would not have worn off as a result of the blade pushing through the water.

The later addition of items such as cowl vents and skylights that were initially fitted only to *Titanic* was not out of the ordinary. *Olympic* underwent constant changes from 1911 to 1913, all based on trial and error. Some may even have been decided upon based on experience with *Olympic*, but added to *Titanic* first simply because it was not practical to pull *Olympic* out of service for every minor change that was needed. Therefore it is not surprising that *Olympic* would turn out looking like *Titanic* at some point, as *Titanic* was fitted with upgraded parts as she was being built, just as *Olympic* was. The starboard-side swan-neck duct seen ahead of the forward funnel is an example of this. *Olympic* did have a much smaller swan-neck duct and fan housing during her first voyages, but this was changed to a different diameter fan and a larger duct by January 1912. However, her duct in this area never matched *Titanic*'s; they were close, but never the same size. This was a constant throughout both ships' careers.

The lifeboats on *Olympic* were in fact painted all white, including their gunwales. Why the White Star Line painted them all white is not known, as brown gunwales were the usual colour for White Star boats (and those of other shipping lines, for that matter). It is not odd that *Olympic* had her lifeboat gunwales repainted brown at some point. What is odd is that they were painted white to start with. It is possible – and this is only a guess – that the White Star Line wanted to emphasise the immense size of the ship by painting the lifeboats all white. If so they would have intended to

Olympic's starboard propeller blades damaged in the *Hawke* collision. The large identification numbers 'S1, S2, and S3' have been written on with chalk for the benefit of the photograph. These identification markings were cast into the base of each blade, and were used to identify which position on the propeller hub the blade was to be bolted to.

repaint the gunwales brown at a later date to match the brown trim along the deck-house and deck edges.

The Belfast Switch

The possibilities of a switch occurring in October 1911 during the *Hawke* repairs, or in March 1912 during the propeller repairs have been addressed in detail and appear to hold promise. The writings that speak of *Olympic* being 'laid up' prior to the 3 April voyage from Southampton certainly suggest this. Was it true? Certainly 2nd Officer Lightoller, by all accounts a no-nonsense, reliable officer, had to get this information from somewhere. The story of *Olympic* being involved in a minor collision in the English Channel may very well be true; however, it is never mentioned what is meant by the term 'laid up'. One cannot assume it to mean that *Olympic* had to return to Belfast to have her hull checked for damage. In fact, if *Olympic* was required to depart Southampton on 3 April under the command of Captain Haddock, she would not possibly have had time to return to Belfast for repairs. *Olympic* was just coming in from a westbound rip and had to disembark the passengers; unload the baggage, mails and cargo; offload the dirty linen and take on fresh supplies; clean all the rooms and public spaces; take on several thousand tons of coal; and so on. Then on the day of departure they had to provision with all the perishable foodstuffs, as well as begin loading passengers, baggage, mail and cargo, beginning early in the morning. One must also understand that these ships were not returned back to dry dock after every bump and dent. After whatever 'collision' *Olympic* had in the Channel, Harland & Wolff would, without a doubt, have sent a diver down to inspect the hull and the propellers while she was at Southampton.

Captain Smith was indeed at Belfast, but he travelled aboard a transport from Southampton prior to taking over his new command. It is true that Haddock signed on as the original commander to take *Titanic* on her sea trials and thence to Southampton, but for whatever reason Smith was written in at the end papers of the registration document as taking over the command from Haddock at the last minute. Thus his presence resulted from nothing more than a change of mind on the part of White Star Line management.

The picture of '*Titanic*'s officers' shown in Chapter 6, and reproduced again here, is quite possibly the most frequently mislabelled photograph in *Titanic* history. Although some of the men shown did indeed go to serve aboard *Titanic*, at the time this photo was taken they were all officers of *Olympic*. The man always identified as 2nd Officer Charles Lightoller (standing, second from left) is not him, though he bears a resemblance to Lightoller. Nor is the older man with the moustache next to Captain Smith actually Chief Officer Wilde. The picture was taken on 28 May 1911, while *Olympic* was at Harland & Wolff in Belfast, and these same officers would serve aboard her for her maiden voyage in June 1911. The officers in the picture are, standing, left to right:

CAPTAIN SMITH & OFFICERS OF THE TITANIC

This image is not of *Titanic*'s officers, but *Olympic*'s. It was properly captioned on the postcard where it appeared at the time but has been mislabelled ever since. (*George Behe collection*)

Purser Hugh McElroy (later of *Titanic*), 3rd Officer Henry Cater, 2nd Officer R. Hume, 4th Officer David Alexander and 6th Officer Harold Holehouse. Seated from left to right are: 5th Officer A. Tullock, Chief Officer Joseph Evans, Captain Edward Smith (later of *Titanic*) and 1st Officer William Murdoch (later of *Titanic*). The other photograph of some of the officers on the Bridge, reproduced again on the following page, shows (left to right): Murdoch, Evans, Alexander and Smith. This information came from the collection of George Behe, who owns a copy of the original postcard on which the mystery picture was printed, and which accurately captions the men as *Titanic*'s officers. Somehow, an error down through the decades has resulted in this photograph being consistently misidentified from that point onward.

Further confirmation of these men being *Olympic*'s officers from the June 1911 voyage can be found in a detail that is obvious yet nearly always overlooked: the colour of their uniform hats. The hats in these pictures are white. The white hats were part of the transition to the summer uniforms; eventually the navy blue coats would be traded for white ones. The hats worn on *Titanic* were navy blue, as the uniforms being worn at that point in the year were still for the winter–spring season.

The Belfast switch sounds tempting, but it is a far stretch at best. Even if the White Star Line was able to get *Olympic* back to Belfast and send a disguised *Titanic* back in time for the 3 April voyage to New York, there would not have possibly been time to perform the necessary work to alter the outward appearance of the ships to resemble each other. Removal and installation of window screens along the promenade, alter-

Four of *Olympic's* officers shown here on her Bridge on 28 May 1911. Left to right are
1st Officer William Murdoch, Chief Officer Joseph Evans, 4th Officer David Alexander and
Captain Edward Smith.

ing the B-Deck windows – this work alone would have taken weeks as it involves
cutting and drilling steel, installing frames and so on. A workforce of a thousand
would have been lucky to accomplish it in under a week.

Then there is the reality of the crew who served aboard *Titanic*. Many of them
came from *Olympic*, and it would have been absolutely impossible to fool any of
them for any length of time as to which ship they were on, as most knew *Olympic*
intimately. Ships of a class, despite theoretically being identical, differ in a thousand
different ways – the location of a coat hook, the orientation of a carpet pattern –
any single detail can alert the observer that something is not right. Then there are
the known changes that were made. In her memoirs Violet Jessop, a stewardess who
served aboard *Olympic* and would go on to survive the sinking of *Titanic* and *Britannic*,
mentions that there were changes in accommodations made to *Titanic*. She wrote of
the admiration for 'Tommy' Andrews and how he paid attention to the needs of
the Victualling Department. Jessop described how Andrews would walk around the
working areas of the ship and listen to the suggestions of the crew. She described how
she was very pleased to see that she had a private wardrobe in her room, which she
shared with another stewardess. This was a problem on *Olympic*, according to her, as

she had to share her accommodations and wardrobe with her roommate. A direct quote from Jessop's memoirs tells it best:

> Eagerly we joined the new ship — hundreds of curious eyes, each looking for what interested them most. Yes, there was my bunk placed the way I had suggested for privacy and there was the separate, though small, wardrobe for my companion and myself, one of the immeasurable blessings when two people of absolutely different tastes have to live together in a confined space. No longer would there be anxiety as to whether a companion's clothes bore testimony of her devotion to whiskey and smoke.

Jessop went on to write about a social call she made while on board *Titanic* to a friend who was a Second-Class bartender who had come from *Olympic*:

> It was not strange, therefore, that I should seek him out to exchange opinions about our new venture. He alone knew I did not like big ships, that I was secretly afraid; however we drank a toast to his happiness and *Titanic*. Then he proudly showed me all his new improvements to make his bar work easier and chaffingley added that we women were not the only ones with something to show off about.

Would Jessop have been fooled? Hardly. If anyone would recognise a switch, she would, as she had just been transferred from *Olympic* after serving aboard her since the maiden voyage.

The Collision with the Rescue Ship

It has been alleged that *Titanic* hit a waiting rescue ship that was darkened out. The theory is that *Titanic's* planned sinking was not supposed to involve loss of life, and that all aboard were to be rescued while *Titanic* — actually *Olympic* — slowly sank. (This rescue ship is where the mysterious 'rafts' and extra lifeboat supposedly came from, although as we have seen these did not exist.) The concept of *Titanic* running over another large vessel with no one noticing does not even make believable fiction. There is also no collision imaginable with a vessel of any size that could puncture and distort plates beneath the waterline without doing any damage to any part of the vessel above the water. The wreck on the ocean floor has been thoroughly examined and photographed in detail, and shows no evidence of any damage to the upper part of her hull.

Conspiracy theorists steadfastly insist that the flooding in a passageway along the Tank Top called the Firemen's tunnel[7] — which should have been far below any iceberg damage — was caused by colliding with and running over the darkened rescue ship. The Firemen's tunnel was 3½ft inside the hull at its furthest forward point, and was located at the centreline of the ship above the double bottom. The impact of

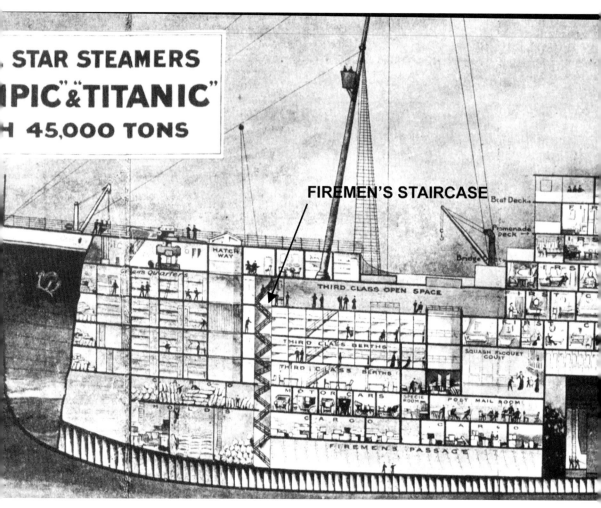

In this crop from a period illustration, the Firemen's tunnel (Firemen's passage) can be seen running along the Tank Top between the Firemen's staircase and Boiler Room No. 6.

anything that could penetrate that far in to cause flooding would be felt by many people. In fact, when *Olympic* struck an attacking U-boat in the First World War, the shock was enough to nearly jolt *Olympic's* Captain off his feet. The only damage sustained by *Olympic* in that deliberate collision was a bent stem. Consider the force that would have to be delivered to penetrate *Titanic* some 3 to 5ft into her hull, and any idea of a ship-on-ship collision enters the realm of fantasy.

However, if the Firemen's tunnel could not, as a result of its location, be damaged in a collision with another ship, how could it have flooded? Some researchers have suggested that the flooding in the passage resulted from *Titanic* grounding on an underwater shelf of ice extending out from the berg, resulting in the bottom plating being breached and the floors of the inner bottom becoming loose enough to allow water through their watertight caulking. Though this theory is certainly more believable than a rescue ship tearing a hole in the side of *Titanic*'s hull, it does not coincide with the testimony of Fireman Charles Hendrickson.

In Hendrickson's earlier testimony at the British inquiry he stated that the water was 'falling' in. This would indicate that it was coming from on top of the Firemen's tunnel on the starboard side. Later on Hendrickson is questioned by Sidney Rowlatt, appearing as counsel on behalf of the Board of Trade. Starting at line 4,890 of the transcript:

> Rowlatt: But what I want to get from you is this. You said you saw the water coming from the ship's side; do you mean that you saw it coming through the ship's side?
> Hendrickson: No, coming from the ship's side.
> Rowlatt: That was merely the direction from which you saw it travelling?
> Hendrickson: Yes.
> Rowlatt: That is, into the space into which the spiral staircase is descending?
> Hendrickson: Yes.
> Rowlatt: You could not tell whether the water was coming through the fore and aft bulkhead at the bottom of the staircase, could you?
> Hendrickson: No, I could only see the direction it came from.
> Rowlatt: Was it coming hard?
> Hendrickson: Yes, it was more than rushing in; it was falling in.

This leads us to a more plausible conclusion as to the source of the water. There was a freshwater tank near the forward end of the ship, 6ft wide and extending clear across the beam of the ship, but only as far up as the Orlop Deck level. It was referred to by some as a 'saddle tank' because the Firemen's tunnel was built through this tank. As the tank had reinforced framing, it is quite conceivable that a side impact – such as from the iceberg – could have pushed the internal framing of this tank against the watertight plates of the Firemen's tunnel, breaching its integrity and flooding it with fresh water.

One last piece of evidence must be presented, and by itself it is enough to discount any theory of *Olympic* having been switched with *Titanic*: the hidden numbers throughout the ship that identify *Olympic* as such over and over. That number is '400', and it will be remembered that 400 was Harland & Wolff's yard number for *Olympic*. Nearly every piece of woodwork on the ship had '400' painted or stamped on its reverse side, along with its designated location aboard the ship. A large amount of the wood fittings and pieces of panelling from *Olympic* survive to this day, having been sold through auction when the ship was scrapped, and continue to adorn hotels, other businesses and private homes throughout the United Kingdom. Pro-conspiracy theorists will state that during *Olympic*'s service during the First World War, all of her internal woodwork was removed and stored until the end of the war. Then, when the wood was reinstalled during her 1919–20 refit, the identification numbers were changed to 400 prior to their reinstallation aboard ship. However, like many other pro-conspiracy claims, this one does not survive the scrutiny of evidence. There is no

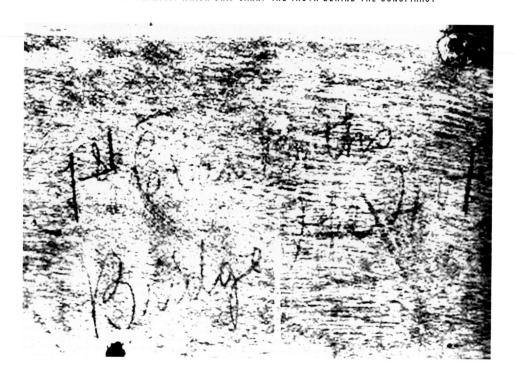

This wall cabinet was found floating at the wreck site in 1912. The stencilling on the back reads '1st Class Baths – Bridge Dk. 401'. The front of the piece is shown below. (*Stewart Kelly Collection*)

The back of a panel from one of *Olympic*'s sitting rooms from C Deck. (*Stewart Kelly Collection*)

The backside of a piece of *Olympic*'s wooden panelling indicating the position on deck and the yard number of '400'. (*Stewart Kelly Collection*)

TITANIC OR OLYMPIC: WHICH SHIP SANK? THE TRUTH BEHIND THE CONSPIRACY

evidence of number tampering on these pieces of wood, nor any evidence of new replacement pieces manufactured to replace the wood panels and trim that were supposedly branded with '401' originally. In addition, when *Olympic* was readied for service as a troopship, Harland & Wolff did not remove all of the decorative wood throughout the ship: the First-Class staterooms, for example, remained as they were during peacetime service.

Having examined the evidence in our 'murder mystery', it becomes evident that there was no crime at all – no switch would have been possible. There were too many differences in the two ships, and too many passengers and crew who had travelled aboard both and would have known the difference immediately. It is plausible only on the surface, and does not stand up to any real scrutiny once all the facts become known.

CONCLUSION

Since 2002 there have been many informative dives done on *Titanic*, the most revealing of those undertaken by film director James Cameron in preparation for his movie *Titanic*. Even after the blockbuster movie was released in 1997, he continued to pursue his interest in the wreck by returning in 2002 and 2005. Though the B Deck private promenade – a *Titanic*-only feature – had been filmed in the past by RMS *Titanic* Inc., Cameron filmed it in better clarity than ever before, his cameras even penetrating the stateroom that was once occupied by White Star Line Managing Director J. Bruce Ismay. Cameron was able to penetrate as far down as F Deck into the Turkish Baths, and proved once again the subtle differences between *Olympic* and her sister. His use of high-definition cameras allowed the world to view the interior of *Titanic* right in their homes, and with this, the death knell to the conspiracy theory had been rung. One would assume that after Cameron's in-depth studies of *Titanic*'s wreck that the conspiracy theories would disappear – but they did not.

Proponents of a conspiracy to switch the two ships will state that this book contains only circumstantial evidence, and that comparison photographs and plans are not enough to prove that a switch did not occur. However, photos and plans are all that exist. The wreck of *Titanic* lies too deep to be raised and *Olympic* was scrapped decades ago. Photographs do not lie, and they show innumerable instances where details differ between the two ships. Many of these differences never changed throughout *Olympic*'s career. Some of the dissimilarities were minor and are not obvious to the casual observer, but involve changes not easily made for appearance's sake. In the appendix that follows, these have been detailed so that the reader can appreciate for himself just how different the ships really were.

The dynamics of a switch would have been enormously complex, involving the cooperation, complicity and coercion of thousands of individuals. At the time the press of the western world was focused on *Olympic* and her new running mate, and every one of their moves and every step of *Titanic's* progress was closely followed. Proponents of a conspiracy will readily claim that workers and crewmen were either silenced or suborned by management and that records were altered. Records and even photographs can be altered, and Harland & Wolff could have conceivably done this with the ones in their archives. But photographs taken by press photographers, passengers, and later, aircraft pilots, could not have been altered or suppressed. Any switch theory must stand up to technical scrutiny, and this one fails on multiple counts. Many switch theorists have never researched basic principles of ship construction nor have they taken the time to carefully analyse photographs.

Perhaps the best proof that a switch did not happen lies in the argument used by the conspiracy theorists – that it was done to cash in on an insurance claim. That in itself makes the theory illogical, because the fact remains that *Titanic* was seriously underinsured once fully furnished and fitted out. Both ships, in fact, were insured for considerably less than their build costs. Each vessel, fully equipped, cost £1,500,000. At the time of the accident the vessel carried insurance of £1,000,000, with the remaining risk being carried by the company's insurance fund. There simply was no profit in sinking *Titanic* on purpose, and even if there were, an elaborate switch scheme would have been unnecessary. One man, one box of matches and a drum of lamp oil is all that would have been needed. Imagine this scenario: on 30 February 1912, while en route to Belfast for replacement of a propeller blade with a limited crew aboard, *Olympic* catches fire. Uncontained, the fire becomes a raging inferno fuelled by the vast amounts of furniture and joinery aboard. The crew is forced to abandon ship – this time with no loss of life, as there are plenty of lifeboats to go around. The fire burns for several days unabated, totally gutting the ship. The hulk is then towed back to Belfast and later declared a total write-off. The newspaper headlines read '*Olympic* lost to fire; investigation underway to determine cause'. The insurance companies pay out and the hulk is scrapped. End of story. But as we have learned, even this scenario is untenable, as the ships were vastly uninsured.

There will always be proponents of a conspiracy theory, ready to ardently defend their claim that a switch really did happen. This book has presented the possibility of a switch from the viewpoint of those promoting it, presenting the evidence for a switch and then putting forth other evidence along with analysis to show that it could not have occurred. Perhaps it is human nature to find fascination in the idea that secret deceptions exist and that certain events are not what they seem. In the end, they make entertaining reading but not much more.

Weigh the evidence, and decide for yourself.

APPENDIX I

ALMOST IDENTICAL SISTERS

S ince before *Titanic* sank, photographs of *Olympic* have been misidentified as her sister and vice versa. In some cases this is understandable, as the two sisters appeared nearly identical to the general public at a casual glance. The White Star Line regularly substituted pictures of *Olympic* for *Titanic* in early postcards and promotional brochures, even when it came to photos of *Titanic's* internal room arrangements. With *Olympic* being the first build of the class, there were many more pictures taken of her construction than *Titanic's*. Management deliberately used *Olympic* photos for *Titanic* because they already had the photos and they were essentially representative of what *Titanic* would, or did, look like. In fact, only ten photos were taken of *Titanic's* interiors.

Of the photos of *Titanic* that exist today, only some were taken by Harland & Wolff's principal photographer, Robert Welch. Many others were taken by amateur photographers, and some were taken by the press immediately before or during her maiden voyage, at least as far as Queenstown. To these photographers we are indebted for leaving a photographic record for comparison to *Olympic*, of which hundreds of photographs survive.

One must remember that the main structural components of the first two *Olympic*-class liners were built from the same set of plans. Some of the original builder's drawings for yard Nos. 400 and 401 still survive. When viewing the plans, the common notations of 400 and 401 are always present at the top of the drawings. In instances where upgrades or changes were made to *Titanic* based on experience with *Olympic*, there are notations drawn in pencil, usually also indicating a date. A case in point is the forward bulkheads on *Titanic's* Promenade Deck, which closed off the Promenade Deck on each side from the area at the forward end of the ship. This bulkhead, which *Olympic* never had, is noted in pencil with a date of 14 February 1912

Titanic in 1912.

Olympic in 1911.

as being drawn on a supplemental plan. A change would not necessarily be pencilled in on a main drawing but instead would have been drawn up on a supplementary sheet. Other additions may have been carried out as afterthoughts and may never have even made it to paper. Because few of these supplemental plans for *Titanic* exist, we will probably never know just how numerous they were.

Olympic was a ship in evolution while on her earlier voyages, at least up until 1913. What was learned from *Olympic* was applied to *Titanic*, and then on *Olympic* herself as soon as they could be incorporated. Because *Olympic* and *Titanic* were so similar in appearance, at least from a distance, conspiracy theorists are quick to make claims about how easy it would have been to switch the two ships. A close examination will show many differences resulting from ongoing changes in the ships' evolution, including the most minute details. Many can be found in even in *Olympic*'s hull and were never changed throughout her long and successful career.

When comparing *Olympic* and *Titanic* in this appendix, it is only practical to present that which can be seen in photographs. Although there were differences below decks that are known from testimony or from technical journals and plans of the period, we present here only those that can be proven without debate.

THE ILL-FATED "TITANIC" NEARING COMPLETION. DOCKED IN THE LARGEST GRAVING DOCK IN THE   No.
WORLD, BELFAST, FEBRUARY, 1912.   LOST WITH 1,500 SOULS, APRIL 15th, 1912.

THE ILL-FATED WHITE STAR LINER "TITANIC"
Struck an iceberg off the coast of Newfoundland on her maiden voyage, & sunk
with over One Thousand Six Hundred of her Passengers & Crew,
Monday morning April 15 TH 1912.

Two postcards of *Olympic* labelled as *Titanic*. This was not a mistake, but done intentionally as most people would not notice the difference in the two ships.

Manufacturer's plate from a Sirocco fan unit.

Cowl ventilation head.

The fittings that were the most visible as being different on the two ships were the many fan units and air intakes serving the ship's ventilation system. The fan units with attached ventilators seen on the Boat Deck of the *Olympic*-class liners were referred to as Sirocco fans. Sirocco was a brand name of the company[1] that built the devices. These Sirocco fan units came in many sizes and had many different configurations with regard to the ducting and intakes. For this reason they are a useful tool for distinguishing *Titanic* from *Olympic*, and an explanation of the various Sirocco vents and other vents is necessary.

The commonly recognised Sirocco attachment was the cowl vent. These cowls were attachments that were secured to the tops of the Sirocco fan housings and looked like the bell of a sousaphone. Cowl vents were attached to the fan housings and serviced 10in, 20in, 30in and 35in diameter fans located within the base unit. Cowls were used to assist the fans in drawing air out of the ship by positioning the cowl opening to face aft, thereby assisting the motor by creating a negative pressure inside the cowl while the ship was underway and air was blowing past the aft-facing opening. The cowls could be rotated to adjust the amount of natural suction that they produced, or rotated away from strong following or quartering winds to prevent reversed flow. When attached to an intake ventilator, the cowl could be positioned to face forward. There are a few examples of this on *Olympic* later in her career; cowls positioned with their openings facing the direction of the wind acted as wind scoops to create a positive pressure at the fan's intake opening. These were only seen in use on *Olympic* after the 1913 refit. This configuration was an exception to the original design and was presumably done to increase the volume of air intake at specific locations.

In most cases the intake in the centre of a Sirocco fan unit was covered by a heavy mesh grille to prevent personal injury, but in a few cases one can see these Siroccos tucked into corners of the deck with the intake holes hidden or fenced off. In a few cases, where it was not practical to position the intake hole out of reach of the passengers or to fence it off, one sees a swan-neck attachment or straight duct installed on the fan opening.

Another ventilator unit where the Sirocco fans were used was the thermotank, a self-contained heating device consisting of a drum or tank containing steam-heated coils and a Sirocco mounted on one side to supply the air. The fan, usually 30in in diameter, would draw in air, force it through the thermotank, and then send it

Thermotank and Sirocco fan.

Stokehold ventilation duct on *Olympic* forward of the No. 1 funnel.

through an insulated duct system to distribute heated air to the spaces below. There were also many other smaller ducts and ventilating devices seen on the deckhouse roofs and in the well decks. Many of these were the same on the two ships. However, the most numerous were the large Sirocco ventilators.

Located above the Officers' Quarters deckhouse (the structure on the Boat Deck extending back from the Navigating Bridge) were several examples of what some call a curl duct, or swan-neck ventilator. This type of attachment was rectangular in shape as seen from the front or back. It connected to one side of the Sirocco fan housing, extended upward, and then curled back down. The opening would usually face outward or downward. These attachments were fitted with a protective screen to keep debris out of the fan below. In a few cases the duct attachment would just project upward, having a simple screened rectangular opening, eliminating the 'curl'. For the purposes of this discussion, they will be termed a straight duct.

To ensure that the stokeholds[2] deep in the ship received the large volumes of air needed for the furnaces and ventilation, huge stokehold ducts were located on both the forward and after sides of the first three funnels (there were no stokeholds beneath the No. 4 funnel). Within each stokehold duct at the F Deck level there were large Sirocco fans of 40in, 50in and 55in diameter to pull air in. The stokehold ducts were wide, quarter-circle ducts, sometimes referred to as whaleback ventilating ducts owing to their appearance, with the rectangular openings again covered with protective grilles. It was against the stokehold duct forward of the No. 1 funnel that 2nd Officer Lightoller found himself pinned as the water flooded into the submerged duct as the ship went under. Lightoller also testified that he was freed from the

A Sirocco with a straight duct.

A Sirocco ventilator attached to the corner of a funnel casing.

stokehold duct by a backblast of hot water or air coming up from below. However, Lightoller then found himself trapped against a foot grate by an inrush of water pouring into it. This was a Fidley grate, servicing boiler room No. 6 below. 'Fidley' is a term used to describe an air space and service shaft on the forward and after sides of the first three funnels, and served as a means for heat to escape from the boiler rooms below. These shafts contained ladders that led all the way from the stokeholds to the tops of the funnel casings on the Boat Deck and were topped off with a foot grating. This is what Lightoller was briefly pinned against after being freed from his first predicament.

Swan-neck ventilator head.

Galley flue pipe on *Olympic*, 1911.

Lastly, there were two galley flue pipes that serve to differentiate the two ships. There was one located directly to the port side of the foremast, used to service the ovens and stoves of the Crew Galley, which was located under the forecastle. The second chimney flue was located above the fireplace in the First-Class Smoking Room. The flue pipe rose out of the raised roof aft of the fan room on the Boat Deck, bent forward at a 90 degree angle, and then entered the base of the No. 4 funnel horizontally.

The Forecastle Deck

When *Olympic* left on her maiden voyage, her No. 1 hatch cover (in the centre of the breakwater) had a cover with squared-off sides fore and aft. It is highly probable that the configuration of the forward side of this cover changed because of an incident that happened during a transatlantic crossing on 14 January 1912. On that day the ship encountered tremendous seas with gale-force winds and blinding snow. One particularly heavy sea broke over the bows and tore off the hatch cover, hurling it backwards into the Well Deck. (The same wave also tore a steam winch and anchor

Olympic's No. 1 hatch cover in 1911.

Olympic's No. 1 hatch cover in late 1912.

windlass from their mountings while carrying away the forward port-side railing.) Although there are no photographs that clearly reveal the configuration of *Titanic's* No. 1 hatch cover, there is a set of plans that refer to 'alterations made to the forward watertight hatch cover over the No. 1 hold.' *Titanic's* hatch differed in that it had a forward face that was angled at more than 45 degrees. This would create less resistance when hit with green water sweeping the deck. To add to this, *Titanic* had an added steel plate breakwater angled at 45 degrees and mounted to the deck against

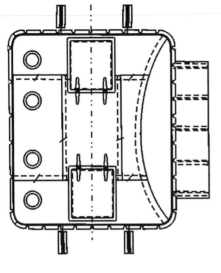

A tracing from the original plan of *Titanic*'s No.1 hatch cover.

Titanic's No.1 hatch coaming as it appears today. (*Bernhard Funk Collection*)

the hatch coaming. *Olympic* would be seen with a cover much like *Titanic*'s when she was photographed in 1913 during the post-disaster refit, with *Olympic* also gaining several round skylights located on the forward angled face. *Titanic* did not have these same windows according to the plans. Photographs of *Olympic* also show that the angled steel breakwater had still not been added to the forward side of the hatch coaming by 1913. However, this breakwater does appear later in aerial photographs taken in the early 1920s.

Olympic's main breakwater running the width of the forecastle had an upper lip that was originally painted brown. *Titanic*'s breakwater was painted completely white, as is seen in photographs. *Olympic* would show the brown upper lip even after the disaster.

In a photo of *Olympic*'s Forecastle Deck taken while the ship was in New York on her first voyage, one can see that there is no Crew Galley skylight located aft of the breakwater on the port side. Curiously, there is a foul weather vent located in this

Olympic's Forecastle Deck as seen at New York on her maiden voyage. In this image can be seen a number of details that differed from those on *Titanic*:

1. The top edge of the breakwater is painted brown.
2. There is a foul-weather vent but no Crew Galley skylight and no cowl vent.
3. The Crew Galley flue pipe is straight for its the entire length and has a distinctive head.

All of these features, though small, play a part in identifying the two sisters from each other. Harland & Wolff utilised the time *Olympic* spent in dry dock for repairs and to make improvements, whereas *Titanic* incorporated them from the beginning. However, there are some things *Olympic* had that *Titanic* would never see.

area instead. There also is no large cowl vent forward of the port-side breakwater. The large cowl vent here would appear on *Olympic* in pictures taken in March of 1912, when she entered the graving dock for replacement propeller blades. Also appearing for the first time in the pictures of *Olympic* taken in March of 1912 is a small cowl vent located at the far port side of the Forecastle Deck aft of the breakwater near the railings. It appears, after looking at the photo of *Olympic*'s Forecastle Deck in 1913, that by then the Crew Galley skylight had been added like the one *Titanic* had. Surprisingly, the small cowl and foul weather vent were never removed; *Titanic* never had these two additional features.

Titanic's Forecastle Deck as photographed at Southampton. Some fittings were different to those on *Olympic*:

1. The top edge of the breakwater is painted white.
2. There is a Crew Galley skylight.
3. There is a large cowl vent forward of the Breakwater.
4. The base of the Crew Galley flue pipe is curved at deck level. *Titanic*'s Galley flue pipe also had a different type of head at the top, although it cannot be seen here. *Olympic* was never fitted with the same head.

In this photo of *Titanic* taken at Southampton, details can be seen that were unique to her:

1. The bulkhead of the B Deck promenade with a window for an added stateroom. This was an upgrade that *Olympic* would not see until her 1928 refit.
2. The weather screen for the A Deck promenade containing a door and window. *Olympic* would never have this fitted.
3. Round windows in doors that were exclusive to *Titanic*. *Olympic* had no doors in this location but a continuation of the rectangular windows. This feature would never change on her.
4. The Bridge wing cabs have been moved out to overhang the sides of the ship by about 18 inches. *Olympic* would not see this until her post-sinking refit.

H-1826 – *Olympic* during her post-sinking refit on 1 December 1912:

1. A small cowl was added – an *Olympic*-specific fitting.
2. The rectangular foul-weather duct was retained as originally fitted.
3. A Crew Galley skylight has been added as on *Titanic*.
4. A large cowl has been added as on *Titanic*.
5. The top edge of the breakwater is still painted brown.
6. The forward end of the hatch cover is slanted, but the forward-fitted windows were not on *Titanic*.
7. Notice the bell is mounted to the forward side of the mast. *Titanic*'s bell was mounted on the after side.
8. This weather screen along *Olympic*'s B Deck promenade was essentially the same as the one that *Titanic* had along her A Deck promenade. If the right side of the photo is studied carefully, daylight can be seen through the promenade windows.
9. *Olympic* never had weather screens enclosing the forward end of her A Deck promenade as did *Titanic*, but would later have a canvas screen at the forward end of the deck to act as a wind and spray barrier.
10. Here a rectangular window is in place where doors with round windows were on *Titanic*. This never changed on *Olympic*.
11. In this image Harland & Wolff workers have removed the Bridge wing cab roofs in preparation to extend these structures outboard, as *Titanic*'s had been all along.

A Deck (Promenade Deck)

Olympic was never fitted with the weather screens enclosing the forward end of the Promenade Deck as was *Titanic*. Although they were effective in keeping windblown spray from blowing back onto the deck, the post-sinking installation of additional Welin davits and lifeboats mitigated against the screens. (On *Titanic* there had been problems attempting to load passengers through the windows when some of the boats were lowered to the level of the Promenade Deck.) It seems that the spray problem was partially reduced in any case, as *Olympic* would be fitted with a canvas splash shield extending from the forward corner of the crew staircase enclosure and attaching aft to an outboard stanchion. On *Titanic*, at the forward end of the enclosed deck on each side was a bulkhead extending across the deck. This was the exact type of bulkhead that *Olympic* had on her B Deck promenade. Only crew members were permitted forward of this, with a crew-only door giving access. Next to the door on each side was a window.

The internal windows and doorways along the A Deck promenade (on the deck-house structure) were much the same on the two sisters, except for a few room configuration changes that are evident only on deck plans and not in photographs.

B Deck

As is well known, *Olympic* had an open promenade extending the length of B Deck. It would not be until the 1912–13 refit that the Café Parisien and *à la carte* Restaurant would be extended out to the sides of the ship. Looking aft from the Forecastle Deck to B Deck, the noticeable difference between *Olympic* and *Titanic* in this area is that *Olympic* had bulkheads fitted on either side, each with a door and a window, seen aft of the crew stairs. These were the entrances to the open B Deck promenades. *Titanic*, which had staterooms in this area, was fitted with a single window on a solid bulkhead on either side. These windows are visible in photographs.

The forward-facing bulkhead on B Deck differed on the two ships in that *Titanic* had two doors with round windows among the row of rectangular stateroom windows, providing access to the corridors inside. *Olympic* did not have doors in this area, only a row of rectangular glass windows servicing the rooms. *Olympic* would never have doors fitted in this area.

The sides of the hull along B Deck were different on *Titanic*, but not at first. Looking at launch photographs, one will notice that the windows along the length of B Deck are uniform, just as seen on *Olympic*. With the later addition of the staterooms and private promenades on *Titanic*, the windows would be reconfigured in a manner to accommodate the various rooms. The windows on *Titanic*, commonly known as 'Utley sliding glass windows', were much narrower on the forward area of the deck, and were spaced differently as is evident in photographs taken as early as September 1911.

This image of *Olympic* is claimed by some to have been taken in March 1912, and for that reason is cited as proof that her B Deck windows had been altered by then. In fact, this image was taken after her post-sinking refit when she was opened to the public for inspection.

Officers' Quarters Deckhouse

The Wheelhouse on *Olympic* underwent three different design changes during her career. When one looks at the earliest plans for her, one sees that the Wheelhouse had a forward bulkhead that was straight and not curved. The plans show the bulkheads (walls) of the Wheelhouse extending all the way out to the roof line above and with a recessed door on either side. However, before the Wheelhouse was built on *Olympic*, the forward bulkhead was changed to a curved configuration. This is the way it is seen in photographs taken during the ship's construction and later during her maiden voyage. It appears that this configuration was not practical, as *Titanic*'s Wheelhouse would have a flat forward bulkhead, a reversion to *Olympic*'s original design plans. *Titanic* would also have the port and starboard bulkheads recessed well inside the roof line with flush-mounted doors, the width of *Titanic*'s Wheelhouse being only as wide as the funnel casing further aft.

During the refit that *Olympic* underwent post-sinking, her Wheelhouse was greatly transformed so that it eventually matched *Titanic*'s to some degree. Unknown to many *Titanic* historians is the fact that the Officers' Quarters deckhouse on *Olympic* was approximately 9ft shorter than *Titanic*'s. It would not be until her 1912–13 refit that *Olympic* would have her deckhouse extended forward like *Titanic*'s. With the

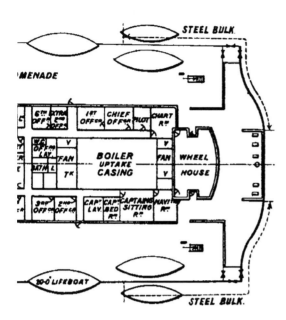

Partial plan of *Olympic*'s Officers' Quarters deckhouse as originally built:

1. The Wheelhouse extends all the way out to the edge of the roof, and the doors are recessed.
2. The forward bulkhead of the Wheelhouse is curved.
3. The Officers' Quarters deckhouse itself (not including the Wheelhouse) terminates immediately forward of the fan trunk casing.
4. The Bridge wing cabs are flush with the sides of the ship.

After the 1912–13 refit, nearly the whole of the internal deckhouse arrangement would change. With the forward extension of the deckhouse, there would be room to add First-Class staterooms aft of the officers' accommodations.

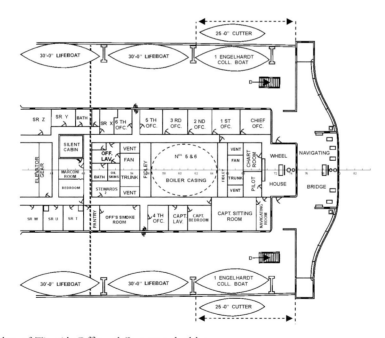

Partial plan of *Titanic*'s Officers' Quarters deckhouse.

The differences are quite apparent between the two ships in these plans. *Titanic* was an improvement over *Olympic* in many ways. But *Olympic* would not be left out, as she would see the majority of these upgrades after her 1912–13 refit.

Captain Smith on *Titanic*. A round skid light is visible behind his feet.

addition of First-Class staterooms on each side at the after end of this deckhouse, the whole of *Titanic's* Officers' Quarters was pushed forward past the edge of the forward funnel casing. This is probably the main reason for the forward bulkhead of the Wheelhouse having a straight-line front, as there was less space for a curved one. Reducing this space beyond a certain point would have been inadvisable as officers on the Bridge had to be able to see across the ship from one wing to another for manoeuvring and docking purposes.

When comparing pictures of *Olympic's* Officers' Quarters deckhouse windows with those of *Titanic*, one can see a different window spacing as the result of the added rooms. In addition, the skid lights at the base of the deckhouse on either side were different. These skid lights transmitted light into the inside row of First-Class staterooms below on A Deck, the ones that were not contiguous with the sides of the deckhouse structure at that level. *Olympic* was fitted with oval skid lights, much like those on the *Oceanic*, whereas those on *Titanic* were round. Because of the different room configuration and deckhouse length configuration, *Titanic's* skid lights would have a different spacing than that of her older sister. Finally, to add to the window differences of this deckhouse, *Olympic* had a window on the forward port bulkhead abreast of the Wheelhouse; *Titanic* did not.

Olympic during construction, showing the curved wooden footing for the Wheelhouse, complete with recessed doors and curved bulkhead. Another difference between the two sisters was the addition of a forward-facing window on the port side of the deckhouse. Inside was the Chart Room. *Titanic* lacked this window altogether.

Titanic's Bridge roof at Southampton. Note that the roof of the Navigating Bridge is overhanging the outboard bulkhead of the Wheelhouse by a considerable margin. In fact, the Wheelhouse bulkhead cannot even be seen here. A Chart Room window is also not present, which is a difference between *Olympic* and *Titanic*. *Titanic's* Chart Room was not located in this part of the deckhouse. The large starboard swan-neck ventilation head is seen here, along with the large cowl on the port side. Here, the motor is facing longitudinally and the fan housing is athwartship. The large Sirocco ventilator aft of the cowl was another fitting *Olympic* would never have, at least not in this form. *Olympic* would see a ventilation fan in this position but with a large swan-neck duct attached. On *Titanic*, this fan had an intake opening facing forward with the top visually obstructed by a hood.

The Sirocco ventilators and stokehold duct over the Bridge, ahead of the No. 1 funnel, differed on the two liners in the beginning but would later start to look very similar, as *Olympic* was continuously being updated even before 14 April 1912. *Olympic* sported a 30in cowled Sirocco on the port side of the stokehold duct above the Wheelhouse. This lone Sirocco was mounted to the side of the stokehold duct, parallel to the centreline of the ship. *Titanic* had the same 30in Sirocco cowl in this area, but the fan housing was mounted athwartship. This is a distinct difference clearly seen in photographs prior to, and after, 14 April 1912.

Olympic at New York on her maiden voyage in June, 1911. Note the following details:

1. A swan-neck ventilation duct that was an original *Olympic* fitting, but later replaced before April of 1912.
2. The height of this water main. The top is about centred between the two ladder support brackets.
3. *Olympic's* No. 6 stokehold ventilation duct. The screen is divided by reinforcing mullions creating a visual appearance of (from starboard to port) one narrow and three evenly spaced rectangles.
4. A Sirocco ventilation fan with a cowl head. The housing is positioned longitudinally, and the motor is athwartship.
5. Window facing forward from the Chart Room, a window *Titanic* did not have.
6. The outboard bulkhead of the Wheelhouse is seen here flush with the roof line, and the door is recessed.

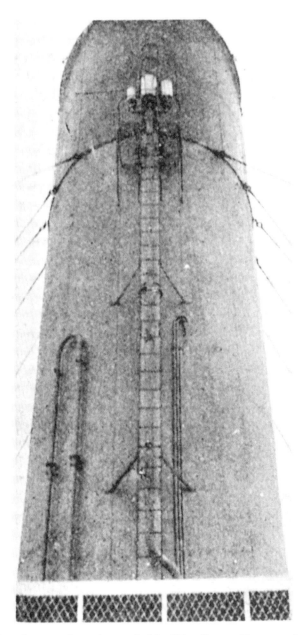

Titanic's No. 1 funnel as seen from the roof of the Wheelhouse. Compare the height of the water pipe to the left of the ladder with the one in the image of *Olympic* at New York – it extends higher up. Also note the divisions of the grille on the front of the stokehold duct. They are different to *Olympic's.* (*Eaton and Haas Collection*)

The protective grille on the face of the stokehold duct forward of the No. 1 funnel had three vertical metal strips that divided the screen into four rectangular sections. In the case of *Olympic* these columns appeared, from starboard to port: narrow, wide, wide, wide. *Titanic's* grille divisions were completely opposite: wide, wide, wide, narrow.

On the port side forward of the No. 1 funnel *Titanic* was fitted with a large 35in Sirocco with a swan-neck duct. *Olympic* was originally fitted with a smaller 30in Sirocco with a duct that was unique in shape. It is apparent that this duct did not provide enough air flow, as it was replaced with the same type of 35in Sirocco as *Titanic* had, also before March of 1912. However, it should be noted that *Titanic's* swan-neck duct in this location was shorter than the one later fitted to *Olympic*. *Titanic's* shorter swan-neck duct did not match the original Sirocco fitted to *Olympic*. They did not look alike and were of a slightly different design.

Aft of the No. 1 funnel, *Olympic* originally had a small 30in Sirocco connected to the stokehold duct on its starboard side. This too was upgraded to a 35in fan with a larger swan-neck duct, just like *Titanic*. The port-side roof over the Officers' Quarters deckhouse aft of the funnel was the home of a thermotank and its accompanying Sirocco fan housing. Both ships had the same size of thermotank and fan at this location; however, *Titanic's* was installed so that the fan housing was perpendicular to the centreline of the ship, and *Olympic's* was installed so that the fan housing was parallel. This configuration never changed on *Olympic* and remained the same until the end of her career.

Just forward of the port-side thermotank was another configuration of Sirocco vent. The one on *Titanic* consisted of a 35in fan housing and a large swan-neck duct, exactly as was seen on the starboard side. *Olympic* had a smaller Sirocco fan housing, probably a 30in unit, minus the ventilation head. The pictures show a simple intake opening on the opposite side of the motor. This was updated prior to the sinking to include a swan-neck duct.

Located on the starboard side aft of the No. 2 funnel and over the First-Class Gymnasium was another air intake fan. As with the other air intakes originally seen on *Olympic*, Harland & Wolff upgraded this Sirocco with a larger fan and swan-neck duct. This was done before March 1912.

It is more than apparent from early documented reports that *Olympic's* ventilating system was inadequate at first. With the process of trial and experiment, *Olympic's* ventilation system evolved as time went on. As previously stated, what was learned from experience with *Olympic* was applied to *Titanic*, and it certainly is evident in the photographs of the period.

A major structure that helps any White Star Line enthusiast identify *Titanic* from *Olympic* is the dome cover over the Grand Staircase forward of the No. 2 funnel. *Olympic* had sidelights installed on all four sides of the structure. Attached to the sidelights were sliding screens to cover the windows and protect them from the weather and to close out the glare of the light from inside at night. These appear as square boxes when looking at the sides of the dome cover. *Titanic* never had these sidelights and associated screens on her dome cover. Instead, *Titanic's* dome cover was plain, with only two sidelights located on the after side.

Just forward of the dome covers on each ship was a Gibbs extractor vent situated over the forward elevator motor room. A Gibbs extractor vent resembles a large

Olympic during her sea trials in 1911:

1. The grand staircase dome cover has sidelights and rectangular screens fitted. *Titanic* did not.
2. The awning rafter runs from the top of the No. 5 stokehold duct over the Gibbs ventilation head and connects to the edge of the dome cover. *Titanic's* awning rafter ended on the Gibbs ventilation head and did not pass over it.
3. This water tank did not last long on *Olympic*, and would never be fitted to *Titanic*.

Olympic photographed at Southampton shortly after *Titanic* sank. It should be noted that though there are some vent size increases, the fittings that were present in her pre-sinking era are still there:

1. The cover over the grand staircase dome still has the sidelights and the rectangular screens.
2. The motor for the cowl ventilator is still facing athwartship, and the fan housing is still longitudinal.
3. The outboard bulkhead of the Wheelhouse is still extended out to the roof line.
4. The screen divisions in the stokehold duct are still the same as in 1911.
5. This upgraded swan-neck ventilating head is new, but taller than *Titanic's* was.
6. These two sets of lowering tackle for the collapsibles on the Officers' Quarters deckhouse roof are one way to identify pictures of *Olympic* post-sinking and pre-refit. In the emphasis to provide lifeboats for all and to make the existing equipment safer, these sets of tackle were permanently left in place on the rigging attachments in the funnel shrouds. *Titanic* had these, but they were stored somewhere below on the night of the sinking.

Titanic in Belfast, 1 April 1912. Among other differences, *Titanic* had no sidelights in the dome cover of the grand staircase.

Titanic above, and *Olympic* (1911) below. It is rather obvious that there were more differences between these two sisters than just the A Deck promenade screen windows. The majority of upgrades made to *Olympic* which resembled *Titanic* would not be done until the 1912–13 refit.

upside-down can with a rounded bottom and open slots in the side. Seen in many pictures of the two ships is a pipe, which on *Titanic* extended horizontally from the top of the Gibbs extractor vent to the top of the stokehold duct aft of the No. 1 funnel. This pipe was not part of the ventilating apparatus. It was merely a pipe that was fastened to the top of the Gibbs vent to provide support for a canvas awning that kept the Marconi rooms inside cooler on hot summer days.[3] *Olympic's* support pipe differed in that it mounted onto the forward edge of the dome cover, passed over the Gibbs vent, and then connected to the centre of the stokehold duct, aft of the forward funnel. This is the way the configuration remained on *Olympic* throughout her career, the difference with *Titanic* again being that the pipe was mounted to the top of the Gibbs extractor vent and then extended forward.

Very few of *Titanic's* interior spaces were captured on film, but a notable exception is the First-Class Gymnasium. Several images were taken of this room, and an examination of them reveals the presence of a rowing machine, whereas *Olympic* had different exercise apparatus. Less obvious, but important just the same, is the large glass-fronted map on the inboard bulkhead of each ship. If one compares the shades of grey in the countries on each map, one will notice that the countries on *Titanic's* map had light colours painted within, while those on *Olympic's* map had darker colours. The illustrations of the ships to the right of each map were also different. Adding to the differences in the two gymnasiums was the furniture: *Olympic* had wicker furniture and no wooden bench, whereas *Titanic* had a bench and leather furniture.

The illuminated displays in *Titanic's* gymnasium. Notice the colour shading of the map and the illustration to the right showing a cut-away of the ship.

Olympic's illuminated displays in 1911.

Olympic's illuminated displays in the 1920s. Notice the absence of *Titanic's* name on the illustration, and lighter colours of the countries on the map.

Olympic on her maiden voyage (left) and post-sinking (right). Notice the window just forward of the door. This was the captain's lavatory window on *Olympic*. Lavatory windows in this deckhouse were unique in that they did not have the round mechanism at the bottom of the frame. It can be seen in the same position in both pictures. Not only is this evidence that the deckhouse remained the same through these periods of *Olympic's* history, but also illustrates a different window configuration than *Titanic*. *Olympic's* Officers' Quarters deckhouse, though later modified, would never have exactly the same internal configuration of rooms as *Titanic*. Also note the elliptical skid lights at the base of the bulkhead – *Titanic's* were round.

Chief Purser Hugh McElroy and Captain Edward Smith on *Titanic*. The left-most window in this picture had a round locking mechanism and was for the 4th Officer's cabin. The window just forward of this was for the Captain's lavatory. Note the round skidlights at the base of the deckhouse behind the men.

Olympic later in her career looking aft from the starboard side on the Boat Deck. The Officers' Quarters deckhouse windows would never change, as this photo indicates.

Raised Roof over the First-Class Lounge and Reading and Writing Room

This is the raised roof that sits between the Nos. 2 and 3 funnels and which has the compass tower prominently standing in the centre. This area of the ship was photographed on *Olympic* both before and after 14 April 1912. As with many of the Sirocco fan configurations elsewhere, there were changes and enlargements to those on *Titanic*. On *Olympic*, the edge of this raised roof followed the outline of the bulkheads of the rooms below with its many 'ins and outs' resulting from the recessed bays. Because of this, there was an alcove on both sides of the raised roof that corresponded with the bay windows of the First-Class Lounge on A Deck. On *Titanic*, the raised roof was not 'notched out' for the alcove; instead, the roof edge bridged the alcove. The alcoves on each side were still there, but they were now recessed beneath the straight edge of the roof. This little bit of extra deck space on *Titanic*'s raised roof was utilised for 20in Siroccos with cowls, one above each alcove. *Olympic*, on the other hand, with her exposed alcoves, had only one cowl vent in position on the port side. This configuration remained throughout *Olympic*'s career, because a 20in Sirocco was never added to the starboard side. Also, located just forward of *Titanic*'s raised roof on the port side was a 20in Sirocco and cowl. *Olympic* never had a ventilator in this position.

H-1543 – *Olympic*'s port side raised roof, pictured in May 1911:

1. *Titanic* would have a 20in Sirocco fan and cowl in this position.
2. This swan-neck ventilation head would be replaced on *Olympic* in the months to come to match *Titanic*'s.
3. 20in fan with cowl attachment. This had a mate in the exact same position on the other side on *Titanic*, but *Olympic* would only have a port side cowl here, and this configuration never changed throughout her career.
4. The divisions of the screen of the stokehold duct were different on *Titanic*.

Titanic's raised roof-port side:

1. The ventilation head that can be seen just behind the cowl was an upgrade.
2. The divisions of the stokehold duct screen were different than on *Olympic*.
3. A 20in fan and cowl is added just forward of the roof over the Reading & Writing room. *Olympic* was never fitted with this ventilator.

Left: *Olympic* 1911. Right: *Titanic* 1912.

Observe the alcove on the Boat Deck formed by the bay windows extending up from A Deck:

1. On *Olympic,* the decking of the raised roof was cut around the perimeter of the alcove. On *Titanic,* the same space was decked over. These photos also uncover another difference.
2. *Olympic* did not have a cowl on the starboard side of the raised roof, but *Titanic* did.
3. Note the large swan-neck ventilation duct on the roof of the tank room. This was another *Titanic*-only feature.

Titanic's raised roof ventilators. A 20in cowl Sirocco ventilator can be seen on the starboard side of the roof, matching another one on the port side. This was a *Titanic*-only feature.

No. 3 Funnel Deckhouse

The No. 3 funnel deckhouse on both ships contained the Officers' Mess, stairwells, pantry, a storeroom for deck chairs and a machinery room for the motor that operated an electric hoist serving the pantry. There were no significant differences in this deckhouse between the two ships except for the configuration of the Siroccos that served the heating elements inside the corners of the funnel casing. As mentioned before, these Siroccos differed in size and configuration in regard to their swan-neck ducts and air-intake apparatus. As with the many Siroccos on the roof of the Officers' Quarters deckhouse, Harland & Wolff felt it necessary to enlarge or upgrade them on *Titanic* to increase airflow, resulting in slightly different fan housings and attachments.

At the very aft end of the No. 3 funnel deckhouse, along the face of the stokehold duct built into the casing at this location was a crew stairwell. Pictures show that *Olympic* did not have this stairwell after construction whereas *Titanic* did. The original builder's plans showing the addition of this stairwell to *Titanic* are dated 26 September 1911. The stairwell is not seen in pictures of *Olympic* until the 1920s, but it is known to have been added by the date of her 1912–13 refit. It is not known if *Olympic* had the stairwell added before this refit, as it does not appear in the Drawing Office notebook.

Olympic, 1911:

1. Notice the position of the window for comparison to the next photo.
2. This water pipe arrangement was particular to *Olympic* in this stage of her career.

Titanic, 1912:

1. Notice the position of the window relative to the ladder in comparison to the previous photo.
2. The water pipes on *Titanic* were much different and ran higher up than *Olympic*'s. *Olympic* would see a similar arrangement after her post-sinking refit, but the pipes would never look exactly the same as *Titanic*'s.

You will also notice a few differences in ventilators between these two pictures.

Titanic, 1912:

1. Notice the position of the deck lamp relative to the window for comparison to the next photo.
2. This large swan-neck ventilation head was particular to *Titanic*.

Olympic, 1911:

This photo is frequently mislabelled as *Titanic*. Besides the white-painted gunwales on the lifeboats in the background we can see:

1. No large swan-neck ventilation head.
2. The deck lamp is slightly more inboard than on *Titanic* in the previous image.

(to copies)

Signal Letters (if any) _____

Transcript of Register ~~for Transmission to Registrar-General~~ ~~of Shipping and Seamen.~~

Official Number	Name of Ship	No., Date, and Port of Registry
131346	*Olympic*	39 / 1911 *Liverpool*

No., Date, and Port of previous Registry (if any)	*new vessel*		
Whether British or Foreign Built	Whether a Sailing or Steam Ship; and if a Steam Ship, how propelled	Where Built	When Built	Name and Address of Builders
British	*Steam ship triple screw*	*Belfast*	*1911*	*Harland & Wolff &c. Belfast*

				Feet	Tenths
Number of Decks	...	*Five + two partial*	Length from fore part of stem, under the bowsprit, to the aft side of the head of the stern post	852	5
Number of Masts	...	*two*	Length at quarter of depth from top of weather deck at side amidships to bottom of keel	849	2
Rigged	...	*Schooner*	Main breadth to outside of plank	92	5
Stern	...	*Elliptical*	Depth in hold from tonnage deck to ceiling at midships	31	5.8
Build	...	*clencher*			
Galleries	...	–	Depth in hold from upper deck to ceiling at midships, in the case of three decks and upwards	59	5.8
Head	...	–	Depth from top of beam amidships to top of keel	64	9.1
Framework and description of vessel	*Steel*	Depth from top of deck at side amidships to bottom of keel	65	3.3
Number of Bulkheads ...	*fifteen*	Round of beam		2.5
Number of water ballast tanks, and their capacity in tons	*seventeen = 5426 tons*	Length of engine room, if any	123	–

PARTICULARS OF DISPLACEMENT.

Total to quarter the depth from weather deck at side amidships to bottom of keel	*47,780* Tons.	Ratio per inch immersion at same depth	150 Tons.

PARTICULARS OF PROPELLING ENGINES, &c. (if any).

No. of sets of Engines	Description of Engines.	Whether British or Foreign made.	When made.	Name and address of makers	Reciprocating Engines. No. and Diameter of Cylinders in each set.	Length of Stroke.	Rotary Engines. No. of Cylinders in each set.	S.H.P. I.H.P. Speed of Ship.
2 reciprocating *1 turbine*	*4 cylinder triple expansion crank inverted vertical direct acting surface condensing one turbine*		Engines. *4*	Engines. *Harland & Wolff &c. Belfast*	1 · 54" 1 · 84" 1 · 97" 1 · 97"	*75*	*one turbine*	6 906 50,000 21 knots
No. of Shafts. *three*	Particulars of Boilers. Number ... *24 (D.E.) & 5 (S.E.)* Description *single & double ended* Iron or Steel *Steel* Loaded Pressure *215 lb.*	*British*	Boilers. *1911*	Boilers. *Harland & Wolff &c. Belfast*				

PARTICULARS OF TONNAGE.

GROSS TONNAGE.	No. of Tons	DEDUCTIONS ALLOWED.	No. of Tons
Under Tonnage Deck ...	14,640·64	On account of space required for propelling power ...	21,695·68
Space or spaces between Decks (*saloon, upper + middle*)	14,142·81	On account of spaces occupied by Seamen or Apprentices, and appropriated to their use, and kept free from Goods or Stores of every kind, not being the personal property of the Crew ... These spaces are the following, viz.: *In lower, middle, upper + saloon tween decks and in houses on deck*	2553·85
Turret or Trunk ...			
Forecastle ...	269·76		
Bridge space ...	3,653·54		
Poop ~~or Break~~ ...	297·99		
Side Houses ...			
Deck Houses ...	4,873·82		
Chart House ...			
Spaces for machinery, and light, and air, under Section 78 (2) of the Merchant Shipping Act, 1894 ...	1185·21	Deductions under Section 79 of the Merchant Shipping Act, 1894, and Section 54 of the Merchant Shipping Act, 1906, as follows:— Cubic Metres. *Master's accommodation 20·12 Boatswain's stores 45·00 Chart Room 9·59 Fore peak ballast tank 46·43 after – 30·95 Total ...*	180·09
Excess of Hatchways ...			
Gross Tonnage ...	45,323·82 128,266·41		
Deductions, as per Contra ...	24,429·62 69,135·87		24,429·62
Register Tonnage ...	20,894·20 59,130·5?		

NOTE.—1. The tonnage of the engine room spaces below the upper deck is 11,212·32 tons, and the tonnage of the total spaces framed in above the upper deck for propelling machinery and for light and air is 1185·21 tons.

NOTE.—2. The undermentioned spaces above the upper deck are not included in the cubical contents forming the ship's register tonnage:

Open space in front of poop 16·0 ft long = 65·72
Open spaces port + starboard on bridge deck in way of windows = 357 ft long = 751·68 tons

Name of Master		Certificate of { Service No. Competency No. }

Names, Residence, and Description of the Owners, and Number of Sixty-fourth Shares held by each ...} viz.,
Oceanic Steam Navigation Company Limited. Sixty-four shares no encumbrances

Dated 15 June 1911

I certify the ...

Dated _____ Registrar.

NOTE.—Registrars in the Colonies are requested to distinguish the Managing Owner by placing the letters "M.O." against his name.

N.B.—To be sent in an envelope addressed to the Registrar-General of Shipping and Seamen, Tower Hill, London, E.

20002 10,000 10—10 H W V 9 28 9   No. 345. Instructions to Registrars of British Ships, para. 26.—Sec. 23445. 1910

Original Transcript of Register document for *Olympic*. (*Courtesy John White*)

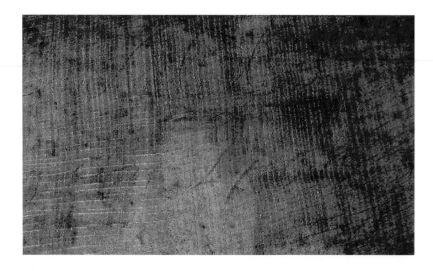

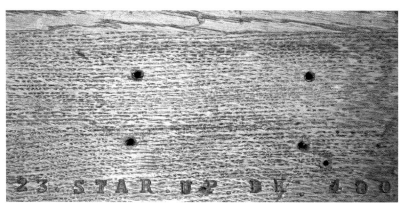

This group of images shows the markings on the rear of woodwork from *Olympic* ('S.S. 400')

Top: a section of corridor panelling with the number '400' written in pencil.

Middle: a skirting board marked '23 STAR. UP. DK. 400' identifies it as being from Stateroom E-23 on E Deck (Upper Deck).

Bottom: a skirting board marked, in part, 'SALOON DK PORT 400'.

(All images courtesy John White)

A corner panelling segment marked 'SITTING RM 3 SHELTER DECK SS 400 PORT SIDE'. This came from one of the Parlour Suites on C Deck. (*Courtesy John White*)

A bed from Stateroom E-23. As with the skirting board shown opposite, centre, the headboard below is marked '23. STAR. UP. DK. 400'. (*Courtesy John White*)

RMS OLYMPIC

RMS Olympic. (Drawing by Cyril Codus)

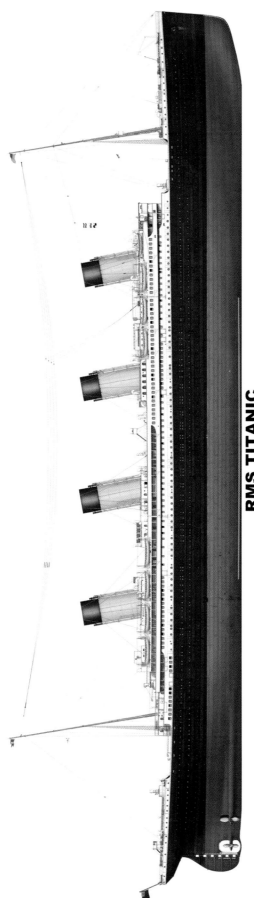

RMS TITANIC

RMS *Titanic*. (Drawing by *Cyril Codus*)

An oak board from Louis XIV Stateroom C-62 on *Olympic* stenciled 'S S 400 PORT SIDE' on the rear. (*Steve Hall collection*)

A section of panelling from *Olympic* with the writing '1st Cl Rms Shel Dk 400'. (*John White*)

A panelling section from *Olympic*'s forward First Class main stircase between the Saloon and Upper Decks (D Deck and E Deck). (*Courtesy John White*)

A panelling section marked 'No 1 Frame 1st Class Fore & Aft State Room Passage Forward Prom. Dk S.S. Olympic'. (*Courtesy John White*)

RMS OLYMPIC HULL PLATE
Piece Of Damaged Plate Removed In October 1911

A section of shell plating (hull plating) removed from *Olympic* during repairs in October 1911. (*Steve Hall collection*)

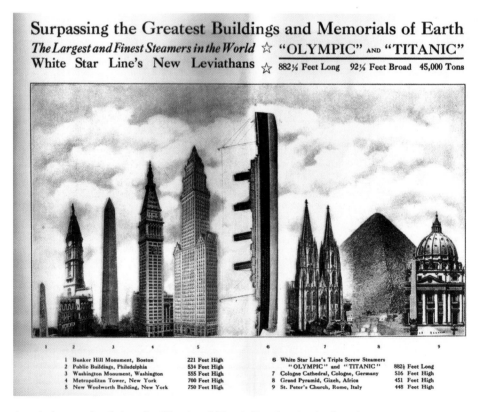

Surpassing the Greatest Buildings and Memorials of Earth

The Largest and Finest Steamers in the World ☆ "OLYMPIC" AND "TITANIC"
White Star Line's New Leviathans ☆ 882½ Feet Long   92½ Feet Broad   45,000 Tons

1 Bunker Hill Monument, Boston	221 Feet High	
2 Public Buildings, Philadelphia	534 Feet High	
3 Washington Monument, Washington	555 Feet High	
4 Metropolitan Tower, New York	700 Feet High	
5 New Woolworth Building, New York	750 Feet High	
6 White Star Line's Triple Screw Steamers "OLYMPIC" and "TITANIC"	882½ Feet Long	
7 Cologne Cathedral, Cologne, Germany	516 Feet High	
8 Grand Pyramid, Gizeh, Africa	451 Feet High	
9 St. Peter's Church, Rome, Italy	448 Feet High	

A period promotional piece for *Olympic* and *Titanic*. (*Jonathan Smith collection*)

Reciprocating Engine Casing, Tank Room and after Skylight Dome Cover

This deckhouse, traditionally termed the 'Tank Room', was located aft of the No. 3 funnel and is readily identifiable by the four large skylight hatches on each side that are always seen propped open. This structure, although termed a room in the singular, contained several rooms and it is here that many of the openly visible differences in the two ships other than Sirocco vent configurations can be seen (see overleaf). The primary purpose of the deckhouse structure on either side of the reciprocating engine casing was to house water-supply tanks for the passenger and crew accommodations – specifically, the fresh water, washing water, and salt water used for baths. The tanks were located on the highest deck of the ship as a simple gravity process supplied water to the many outlets throughout the ship. These tanks were housed in two different rooms flanked by the reciprocating engine casing, which was in effect an open shaft extending upward from the Reciprocating Engine Room far below. The skylight referenced earlier sat atop the casing. A narrow catwalk spanned the open shaft and was accessed by a door inside each room.

Located on the after side of the No. 3 funnel just forward of the Tank Room was a series of large water supply pipes that went up the funnel and looped back down.[4] These pipes appear in photographs as an elongated upside-down U. On the starboard side was an even smaller series of pipes with the loop at the top resembling the letter P. At the base of the funnel these pipes made a 90-degree bend and ran nearly horizontally across the gap between the two deckhouses, across the roofs of the Tank Room on either side of the skylight and then via a 90-degree bend on each pipe down through the roofs. On the funnel, *Olympic* had a very simple arrangement of pipes in that she had only one set of loops on each side of the funnel which turned and passed down through the Tank Room roof on either side near the forward edge of the deckhouse. However, *Titanic*'s Tank Room differed from *Olympic*'s in that there was an Engineer's Smoke Room added on the starboard side. This occupied more than half of the forward end of the deckhouse on that side with the water supply tanks relocated to a smaller room further aft. Consequently, *Titanic*'s water pipes extended further aft along the roof on that side. The port-side Tank Room on *Titanic* also differed in that the pipes extended further aft along the roof to accommodate a different arrangement of the tanks inside. *Olympic* would not see the addition of the Engineer's Smoke Room until her 1912–13 refit, and the locations where the water pipes entered the roofs of the Tank Room on the port side would always remain different.

With regard to the water supply pipes on the funnels, even though the loops at the top of the pipes on *Olympic*'s funnel would later look much like those on *Titanic*, they never became exactly the same. One example is the P-shaped overflow on the starboard side the funnel on each ship: *Olympic*'s and *Titanic*'s were opposite of each other - *Titanic*'s looked like a reversed letter P. Another example of how the pipes

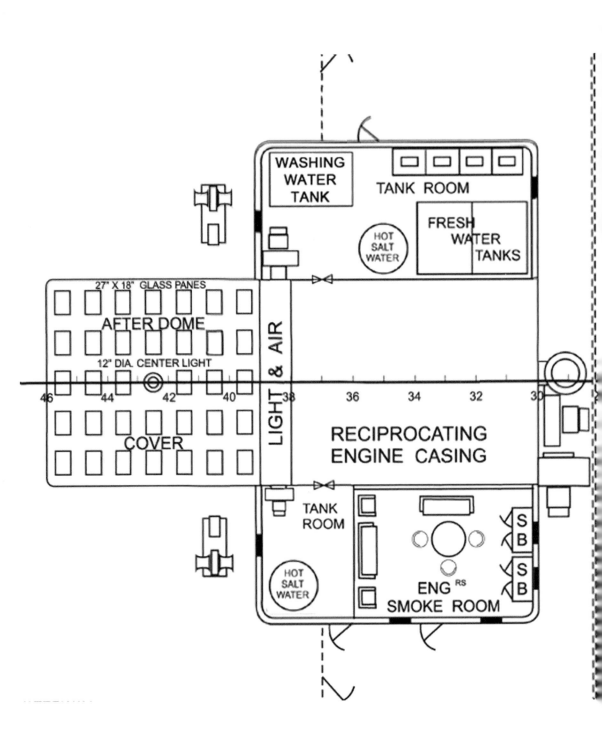

General arrangement of Tank Room. (*Drawing by Bruce Beveridge*)

This image was taken in New York after *Olympic*'s return to service in 1913. Several details have changed:

1. The water pipes extend further up the No. 3, but do not match *Titanic*'s.
2. The loop at the top of the smaller pipe still resembles a backwards P, whereas *Titanic*'s was the opposite.
3. The 20in cowl has not been added to the starboard side of the raised roof, nor have the alcoves been decked over.

differed is that *Titanic* had an extra set of loops on the port side of the funnel, giving her two on that side, whereas *Olympic* had only one prior to the sinking.

The addition of the Engineer's Smoke Room to *Titanic* also resulted in a difference in the bulkhead on that side. When looking at pictures of the starboard side of *Titanic's* Tank Room one can see the water pipes above extending further aft, and two doors, one for the room with the water tanks and one for the Engineer's Smoke Room. The forward bulkhead of the deckhouse also showed a difference, with *Olympic* having only one window per side but *Titanic* having an additional window on the starboard side. Although *Olympic* was later fitted with the Engineer's Smoke Room, the window configuration on this forward bulkhead never changed throughout her career.

From the beginning, *Titanic* had a set of cowls located on the after section of her Tank Room, one per side (the associated Sirocco fans were located inside). *Olympic* would start out with just the port-side cowl, with the starboard one added by March 1912.

The aft-facing bulkhead of the Tank Room and reciprocating engine casing on *Titanic* had a ladder and a window on each side flanking the after First-Class stairwell dome cover. On the starboard side, the positions of the window and ladder on *Olympic* were reversed.

Examining the skylight dome cover on the after side of the Tank Room, *Olympic* had sidelights on all three exposed sides of this cover and would have them throughout her life. *Titanic* did not have any on the port and starboard sides. It is not known whether *Titanic* had any on the after side because there are no pictures that show this area.

No. 4 Funnel Deckhouse and Raised Roof

The No. 4 funnel deckhouse is commonly known as the fan room, because the deckhouse largely contained Sirocco fans for the ventilation of the galleys, the Turbine Engine Room and other areas. Because the No. 4 funnel was essentially a large ventilating shaft rather than being used to vent the gases from the boiler furnaces as with the other three funnels, the surrounding deckhouse could be used to contain a large number of Sirocco fans that ducted into it.

When examining the roof of the fan room on *Olympic* as she was originally configured, one will see a long rectangular duct on the port side which exited the roof at its forward edge and then ran horizontally aft, connecting to the base of the funnel itself. *Titanic* had two of these, one on each side of the roof. *Titanic* also had, in the centre of the roof near its forward end, a huge 35in Sirocco fan and a swan-neck duct with an opening that faced to starboard. Instead of a single long horizontal rectangular duct on the starboard side like that on *Olympic*, *Titanic* had one on each side. Both of these ducts ran up from the Siroccos in the fan room and ran along the roof horizontally and connected to the base of the funnel.

The port and starboard sides of the fan room on each ship differed in several aspects. These are enumerated below:

Starboard side bulkhead:

Olympic: two doors.

Titanic: three doors and a 20in Sirocco with a cowl vent located forward of the thermo-tank.

Port side bulkhead:

Titanic: a series of teak-framed air intake screens

Olympic: one fewer air intake screen, and all were recessed and not teak framed.

Olympic was fitted with a different configuration on her fan room roof by March of 1912. Pictures of her entering the graving dock for her propeller blade replacement show that the rectangular duct with the louvres on the starboard side was replaced by a 20in Sirocco and cowl. A large 35in Sirocco and cowl were installed in the centre of the roof on the forward section. This configuration would remain with *Olympic* throughout her career and would always be different than the configuration of *Titanic*. Because of this slightly different design on *Olympic*, there was room to mount a railing around the forward roof of the fan room. *Titanic* did not have a railing in the same location.

After the 1912–13 refit the ventilating apparatus for *Olympic's* fan room would see a Sirocco added forward of the thermotank on the starboard side, in the same place where *Titanic* was fitted with the 20in Sirocco and cowl. In the case of *Olympic*, a wider fan housing would be fitted with a large swan-neck duct that faced forward.

A point of confusion for structural researchers of *Olympic* and *Titanic* is the presence of what was originally thought to be a Gibbs extractor vent located aft of the No. 4 funnel deckhouse, rising out of the raised roof over the First-Class Smoke Room. It was commonly thought that a pipe exited the top of this Gibbs vent, angled forward and then entered the after side of the No. 4 funnel. In actuality there was no Gibbs extractor vent in this location at all. The object in this position was a chimney flue from the fireplace located at the very aft of the Smoke Room. The pipe exited the deck vertically, angled forward and then ran to the funnel. The base of this flue pipe had a protective sleeve fastened around it as far up as the point where it angled forward. This sleeve was probably made of asbestos and protected passengers from heat. Because of its width, it was mistaken for a Gibbs extractor vent in early photo studies.

On *Olympic*, there was no flue pipe running to the funnel – only a simple vertical flue that stood a bit higher than the Second-Class entrance deckhouse located just aft. This flue had a flapper valve at the top that opened when hot gases from the fire were rising and closed when not in use. *Olympic* would not see a flue pipe like *Titanic's* until after her 1912–13 refit.

One final difference can be found at the after entrance of the raised roof here. When Dr Robert Ballard photographed the stern section of *Titanic's* wreck, little did he know that his images would capture another difference in the two sisters, one

Olympic on her maiden voyage (compare with the image on the following page):

1. The First-Class Smoke Room fireplace flue with veined damper.
2. A single door. The general arrangement of the after end of this deckhouse was different than on *Titanic*.
3. A large louvred ventilation duct that was soon to be removed, but never fitted to *Titanic*.
4. These windows appear to be framed out in teak.

that is certainly missed by many people and that shows up in very few photographs of either ship. One of Ballard's photographs showing the remains of the after Second-Class entrance also shows the remains of the short bulkhead that supported the raised roof of the Smoking Room. In this image there are three skid lights, just like the ones along the base of the Officers' Quarters deckhouse. In the wreck photo, the steel aft end of the raised roof has been bent back, exposing the skid lights from the inside. Pictures of *Olympic* from both before and after the sinking show that she never had these three round windows.

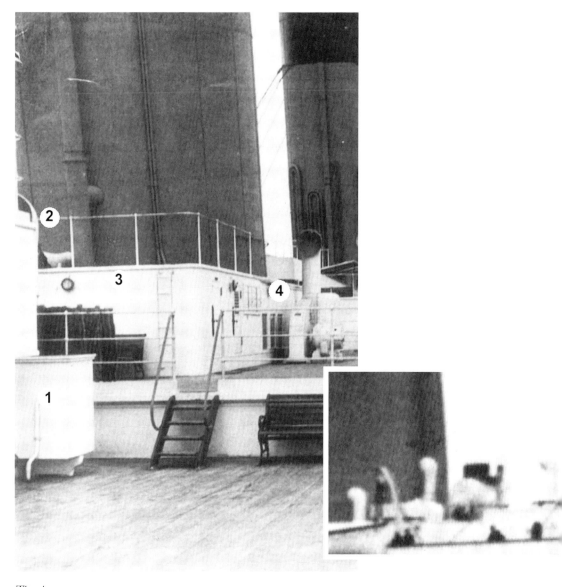

Titanic, 1912:

1. A mystery box that was never on *Olympic*. As of the writing of this book the purpose of this box has yet to be identified.

2. The Smoke Room fireplace flue exhausted to the base of the No. 4 funnel. This feature would be added to *Olympic* later.

3. The after end of the deckhouse is a bit different to *Olympic* and had an extra door to starboard.

4. The windows were not trimmed in teak. They are merely set into the steel. The ventilation ducting above was different on *Olympic*, as can be seen in the smaller picture on the right. The large swan-neck ventilator is plainly visible.

Olympic some time before 15 April 1912.

This is a transition picture, probably taken during the propeller blade replacement in March 1912:

1. One of the sidelights in the aft dome cover. *Titanic* did not have these fittings.
2. Teak trimmed windows.
3. A large cowl has been added by the time of this photo, and the louvred duct on the starboard side has been replaced with a 20in cowl and fan.
4. The chimney flue standpipe is present.

Olympic arriving in New York on her maiden voyage. In this photo one can clearly see the starboard louvred duct on the top of the No. 4 funnel deckhouse. As stated above, this was removed in place of a cowl prior to *Titanic*'s demise.

Titanic at Queenstown:

1. After dome cover with no sidelights.
2. The outward curve of the fan housing for a 20in Sirocco and cowl.
3. Windows minus the teak framing.
4. The chimney flue leading into the base of the funnel.

The After Well Deck

The after Well Decks of *Olympic* and *Titanic* appear to be nearly identical but there are a few differences. On *Titanic*, on the after bulkhead beneath the Poop Deck, are two large propeller spanners – one on each side – that resemble giant wrenches (which, in fact, they were). Although there are no pictures of *Olympic*'s after Well Deck showing a starboard spanner before *Titanic* sank, there are pictures of both spanners after the disaster. It is believed that the starboard spanner was added after the propeller repair was undertaken in March 1912, or after the *Hawke* collision in October 1911. The main point of this find is that pictures do exist showing the positions of *Titanic*'s

Olympic in New York on her maiden voyage:

1. This bulkhead is where a propeller spanner was fitted on *Titanic*. It is absent here on *Olympic*. There is, however, a spanner on the corresponding port bulkhead. *Titanic* would have a spanner on the port side also, but mounted at a different position.
2. Special attention should be given to the location of the doors on the crane platforms, as this is a certain way to identify one sister from the other. Many *Titanic* historians have labelled *Olympic* as *Titanic* based on cropped photos of this area which show the doors facing forward. *Titanic*'s doors faced outboard.
3. In the lower right corner of this picture a Gibbs extractor vent can be partially seen. The one here was particular to the original configuration of *Olympic*, but would be replaced by a 10in fan and a tall cowl. *Titanic* followed suit with the 10in fan from time of construction, never having the Gibbs extractor.

Titanic at Queenstown:

1. The propeller spanner on the starboard side. The object just to the left is a water fountain for Third Class, another fitting *Olympic* would do without.
2. The doors of the crane platforms faced outboard. There was another door on each platform which is not seen in this picture. All crane platforms had two doors.
3. The docking bridge is extended over the side of the hull permanently by about 2ft – a *Titanic*-only feature. Also, the location of the life rings on the rail are different to *Olympic*.

propeller spanners mounted on the bulkhead and, when one compares the positions with later photos of *Olympic*, one can see that they are mounted at different heights and angles.

The Poop Deck

The most prominent feature of the Poop Deck is the elevated Docking Bridge, sometimes referred to by the crew as the 'after bridge'. The Docking Bridge had telegraphs for relaying steering and line handling commands to and from the Navigating Bridge at the other end of the ship. The ship could also be steered from here in the event of a breakdown of the steering mechanism on the Navigating Bridge.

Titanic's after Well Deck on the port side with spanner and water fountain circled. The spanner is hung at an angle.

The Docking Bridges on the *Olympic* and *Titanic* have what is probably the most noticeable difference at the stern area, this being the width of the structure itself. *Olympic's* Docking Bridge did not extend over the sides of the hull but ended right at the supports at the edge of the deck on either side. A hinged platform with chain supports could be folded down to overhang the edge of the deck. *Titanic's* was upgraded in that the permanent structure extended beyond the sides of the ship by a number of feet. This change to *Titanic* was made in September 1911. An additional difference is the placement of the life rings mounted on the Docking Bridges of the two sisters. Readers will notice that they are positioned in slightly different areas on the railing.

Below the overhangs of the Docking Bridge, just inboard of the supports, were goose-neck ventilation pipes – one on each side of the ship. These pipes resembled candy canes. *Olympic's* faced forward, whereas *Titanic's* faced aft.

Directly forward of the Docking Bridge are two rectangular box-like structures that were skylights for the steering engine compartment below. Just forward of these skylights were two cowl ventilators. These two cowls were mounted differently on the two ships. In the case of *Olympic*, they were mounted further forward and outboard of the skylights, whereas *Titanic's* were mounted considerably inboard and further aft.

Two different views showing *Olympic*'s docking bridge. The top one was taken immediately after the *Hawke* collision and the bottom one on her maiden voyage. *Olympic*'s docking bridge was unique in that the sides were flush with the hull of the ship. A teak platform was extended over the side for taking soundings and to improve visibility. This feature was upgraded on *Titanic* to a permanent extension of the bridge. This is another identification point commonly missed by *Titanic* researchers. The configuration on *Olympic* never changed throughout her career.

Olympic in the 1930s. The position of the crane platform doors have remained the same since 1911 and the propeller spanners are placed on the bulkhead in positions unique to this ship.

The cylindrical bases of the cranes located on the Poop Deck differed in the location of the watertight doors used to service the internal motors. *Olympic*'s doors faced forward, whereas *Titanic*'s faced outboard.

The Hull

Located on the shell plating all the way forward on the bows and just below the railing were horizontal steel bars called jackstays. These were mounted horizontally against the plating with numerous brackets. When it was necessary to fasten a canvas splash shield on the forepeak railing to provide protection for the anchor watch or lookouts stationed here, the jackstays provided a means to secure the lower end of the canvas. When viewing *Olympic*'s port-side jackstay, one will notice that it is in three separate sections because of a door in the shell plating that was removable to permit swinging the heavy centre anchor out from its well. On *Olympic*, the division of the brackets on the port side show, from forward to aft, groups of three, nine and three. When one looks at *Titanic* for purposes of comparison, one notices that the grouping consists of four, eight, and three. Looking at the starboard side of the ships, one will notice that *Titanic* had fifteen mounting brackets for the continuous jackstay, and *Olympic* had fourteen. This is a minor detail, but still a difference, one that never changed on *Olympic* throughout her years of service.

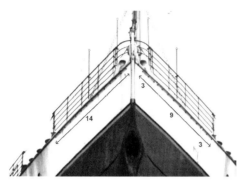 

Olympic, 1913.   *Titanic*, 1912.

When one looks at the original builder's Shell Plating Plan for *Olympic* and *Titanic* one finds a notation at the doubler forward at the bower anchors. The plans indicate an overlap of the plates, or strakes, for *Olympic*. A notation for '401' (*Titanic*) shows a change here in that the strake butted up against the doubler and did not overlap it. One can see an overlap in pictures of *Olympic* prior to the disaster and after. Pictures of *Titanic*'s bow show that the strake does, in fact, butt up to the doubler with a flush joint between them.

The gangway entrance doors to the First-Class entrances on D Deck present another difference: *Olympic*'s doors had round portholes, whereas *Titanic* had rectangular windows. The doors visible on the wreck today still retain these rectangular windows, as does the door that was retrieved from the wreck. *Olympic*'s remained round throughout her career.

Photographs of *Titanic*'s hull with the clarity necessary to fully count each of the strakes (rows of shell plates) and rivets are not known to exist; however, there are enough photographs that show the bow and stern well enough to discern subtle differences. As is noted in chapter seven, the C-Deck portholes below the Poop Deck railing in the stern area differed between the two ships. *Olympic*'s portholes were positioned in a different order to *Titanic*'s and remained different throughout her career.

At the stern, on the stern frame casting surrounding the centre propeller, at about the 23–24ft draft mark was a small plate. This plate differs between the two ships in the number of bolts on each. *Olympic* shows eight bolts in her plate both before and after the sinking, whereas *Titanic* shows five bolts at the time of her launch. Unfortunately, if one wanted to look for this plate on the wreck today one would have to dig some 6ft into the sediment.

Along the sides of the hull at the C Deck level[5] can be seen large portholes that have a semi-rectangular appearance, almost like vertical rectangles with very rounded corners. Interspersed with these are a number of small portholes. These small portholes were for the lavatories. On *Olympic* one can see only single small portholes within the line of large squared-off portholes. On *Titanic* one will notice that wherever there is one small porthole there is always a second, creating a pair of small portholes at every interval where they appear. This configuration never changed on *Olympic*. The 'Big Piece', which was raised from the wreck, is a part of the hull that included a set of these small portholes.

Olympic and *Titanic* were much the same in the big picture, but when one knows what to look for, the ships were very different indeed.

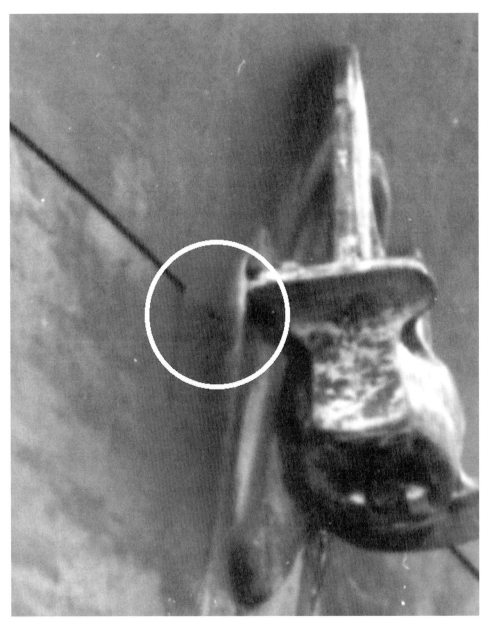

Olympic, December 1912. Though the overlapped doubler is hidden behind the stowed anchor, the shadow of the butt lap is still discernible.

Olympic in dry dock, 1911. An overlapping doubler just forward of the anchors was a specific feature to this ship.

Titanic prior to launch, 1911. There was no overlap of plates on *Titanic* because they were butted flush with each other. This change was specified in the original Shell Plating Plan of these two ships.

D-Deck gangway doors on *Olympic*, 1911.   D-Deck gangway doors on *Titanic*, 1912.

D-Deck gangway doors from *Olympic* at the beginning of the First
World War. The round windows never changed.

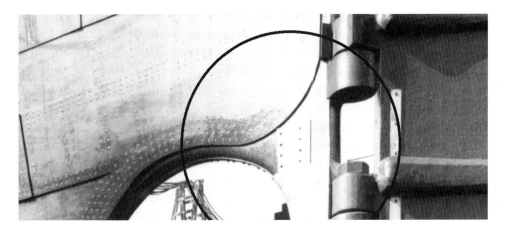

Top: *Olympic*, 1911; middle: *Titanic*; and bottom: *Olympic*, 1924. This zinc plate on *Olympic* had eight bolts whereas the matching plate on *Titanic* had five. Even up until 1924, the count and alignment of the bolts did not change on *Olympic*.

Olympic during her sea trials in 1911. Note the position of the portholes along the sheer strake of the Poop Deck.

Titanic at Belfast. Note the position of the portholes in the sheer strake of the Poop Deck, and how they differed from *Olympic*.

Olympic in the 1920s. Note that the position of the portholes along the Poop Deck sheer strake have not changed since 1911.

OLYMPIC: THE LAST GRAND LADY

The White Star Line started a new era in Atlantic travel with the building of the *Olympic*-class liners. Little did they know when the first of the trio launched that *Olympic* would be the last 'grand lady' built for the White Star Line. The company would go on to have other large ships, some obtained through war reparations, but none as grand as *Olympic*. The two younger sisters of 'No. 400' were intended to be her running mates in order to guarantee weekly departures across the Atlantic in each direction. Their lives would be cut short as victims of circumstance, but *Olympic* would go on to serve so long and well that she would earn the nickname 'Old Reliable'.

The beginning of *Olympic*'s career has been well covered in almost all the *Titanic* books that have been published since 1912. Within the circles of ocean liner historians one question has been frequently debated: would *Olympic* ever have gained the fame she did if *Titanic* had not sunk – or would she have just been another entry on the list of White Star Line ships?

Without *Titanic*'s demise *Olympic* might not have become as famous as she did, but her record stands on its own and she was both well known and had a loyal following of passengers and crew for many years. She holds her own place in history: not only was she the beginning of an era, but she was also the first at a number of other events in history as well. *Olympic* is at the top of nearly every ocean liner collector's priority list. Her postcards, furniture, china, menus, and other surviving memorabilia command top dollar. In all likelihood, *Titanic*'s sinking was what really cemented *Olympic*'s place in history. Therefore, we begin our discussion of *Olympic*'s history just before 15 April 1912.

At 3.00p.m. on 13 April 1912, *Olympic* left New York on the start of a routine eastbound trip. *Titanic* had left Southampton three days before on her maiden voyage.

Olympic after the *Titanic* disaster but prior to the refit that would add more lifeboats and other safety arrangements.

On the evening of 14 April 1912, the passengers on both ships turned in for the night as another day of ocean travel wound to an end. There was talk that the two ships might pass within sight of each other on 15 April but those on *Olympic* would wake on the morning of 15 April to be stunned with the news that *Titanic* had sunk. During the time that *Titanic* was desperately calling for assistance, *Olympic*'s captain, Herbert James Haddock, found that he could do very little, because his ship was more than 500 miles away. At 1.40a.m. he sent to *Titanic*: 'AM LIGHTING UP ALL POS-SIBLE BOILERS AS FAST AS CAN'.

Before *Olympic* arrived, Haddock was informed that *Titanic* had sunk, the news having been relayed from Bruce Ismay via Marconi transmissions from the *Carpathia*. The only assistance *Olympic* could give was to relay the list of survivors to Cape Race. For a time afterwards Haddock continued his ship to the scene, but it was soon decided that the sight of *Olympic* might be too much for the survivors to take, and so she was kept away. Out of respect for *Titanic*, all festivities on board *Olympic* were cancelled. Crew and passengers alike were struck hard with the news, especially the crew, as many of them had friends and family on *Titanic*. *Olympic* arrived at Southampton early on Sunday 21 April to find the entire city in a state of mourning. All of Southampton appeared to be affected by the disaster.

Olympic had to be made ready to depart again on 24 April but, because of what had just occurred some fast modifications to her lifesaving apparatus had to be made. Under the watchful eye of Captain Maurice Clarke, the Board of Trade surveyor who had cleared *Titanic* less than two weeks earlier, forty extra Berthon collapsible lifeboats were added to *Olympic*'s Boat Deck. Originally, the White Star Line had stated that only twenty-four extra boats had to be fitted, but because more boats were brought in than was necessary, rumours started to circulate that some of these collapsibles had been rejected by Clarke as not being fit for use. The extra boats were not new – they had been borrowed from naval vessels in the area. By the morning of Wednesday 24 April, the boats had all been fitted, and extra hands were signed on to crew them. Extra wire falls were installed to ensure that the boats could be launched quickly in case of an emergency. These extra wire falls would include a set attached to the middle shrouds of the No. 1 funnel to accommodate the Engelhardt collapsibles stored on the roof of the Officers' Quarters deckhouse on either side. (Titanic had fittings to accommodate wire falls at the same locations, but these were never used.)

On the morning of 24 April with Olympic's departure only hours away, trouble was in the air. At 7.00a.m. Clarke came aboard Olympic to inspect the boats. He was a strict inspector under any circumstances, but this time he was even more rigorous in his requirements. As passengers began to arrive, Clarke had various boat crews muster on deck and then had them uncover and lower a number of different boats to make sure that they could be lowered properly and without delay. He estimated that it took an average of 12½ minutes to lower each boat. At 11.50a.m., Clarke was just about to hand Captain Haddock his certificate of clearance when a message came to the Bridge that the stokehold crew (the Firemen and Trimmers) were leaving the ship. A meeting was arranged between officials from the White Star Line and the Firemen, in which the men claimed that the boats were unsafe. Clarke insisted that everything was in order and that the boats were safe, but the men refused to board the ship unless regular open wood lifeboats were installed.

Because of the mass desertions, Olympic's journey had to be postponed for a day until new crewmen could be signed on. It was decided to move the ship out of her berth and into the Solent, with her remaining at anchor at Spithead. This ensured that there would be no more desertions, because the ship was now in the open water. Meanwhile, 2nd Engineer Charles McKimm remained on shore to muster a replacement crew. By the early morning of 25 April the situation on board had not changed much. Maurice Clarke, the Board of Trade surveyor, had remained on board in order that the ship could be given its clearance the moment the new crew was in place. Wasting no time, Clarke again had some of the crew mustered on the Boat Deck to practice lowering the boats. This time the drill did not run as smoothly as the one the day before – it took almost 2 hours to prepare and lower the boats. By 8.00a.m. some of the passengers were starting to roam the decks, and Clarke had the drill stopped so as not to alarm anyone. Later that morning a delegation from the union came on board to negotiate a settlement. During the discussions, six of the collapsibles were lowered to the water and kept afloat for 2 hours. On examination, it was found that five were completely dry inside, although the sixth had some seepage. With the little amount of water that came in during the two-hour period, it was agreed that less than 3 minutes of bailing would empty it. After a quick conference in the captain's

Above and below: Berthon collapsibles put aboard *Olympic*.

Firemen leave *Olympic* on 24 April 1912 in protest over the conditions of the lifeboats.

cabin, the union delegates agreed to advise their members that the lifeboats were safe as long as this one faulty boat was replaced.

At 10.00p.m. the tender finally arrived with a replacement stokehold crew of 168. More men than necessary were included to allow *Olympic* to achieve a faster speed so that she could make up the 36 hours she had lost. All of this effort would be to no avail, because at midnight another message came to the Bridge. This time fifty-three men were deserting the ship. Among the men were thirty-five Able Seamen, five Quartermasters, five Lookouts, two Lamp Trimmers, four Greasers and two other engine room personnel. These men were boarding the same tender that brought the replacement crew from shore. This time, the source of grievance was not the lifeboats but the replacement crew. The men now deserting refused to sail with men whom they considered the 'dregs of Portsmouth'. Many had no experience on ships of this size, and some did not even have pay books. It transpired that the 2nd Engineer had, literally, taken any man he could find to replace the first round of deserters, and this new group of deserters refused to sail with them. Captain Haddock twice ordered them back to their posts, but the men refused. Expressing their respect for the captain, they said they just would not work with men who were unfit to operate *Olympic*. A spokesman for the deserters stated that they wholly agreed that what the Firemen did when they deserted at the dock was 'a dirty low down trick', but they felt that going to sea with these new men would be dangerous.

Haddock had reached the limits of his patience, and signalled for the assistance of HMS *Cochrane* lying at anchor nearby. Within half an hour the *Cochrane*'s captain,

Testing a Berthon collapsible from *Olympic* on 26 April 1912.

Commander William E. Goodenough, came aboard to mediate the dispute and to try to convince the men to return to their stations. Goodenough found that even though there were still concerns about the lifeboats, many of the men were more concerned with the abilities of the replacement crew to carry out their assignments. They objected to the fact that many were not union members, which probably was the real underlying issue. Having heard this statement, Commander Goodenough decided that the men's refusal to work was based more on their concern that they would get into trouble with their union than on issues of safety. He ordered them back to work, threatening them with mutiny if they refused. The men were respectful but unyielding, and short of physical force, they could not be compelled to comply.

If *Olympic* was to sail, another group of replacements had to be found. By 11.00a.m. the next day a tender arrived with more than thirty new men, although Captain Clarke refused to pass some as fit for duty. About an hour later, Clarke received orders from his office to clear the ship as soon as he felt she was sufficiently crewed. However, as *Olympic* was already two days behind schedule, it was becoming increasingly doubtful that she would be able to sail. At 3.00p.m. the news arrived from the White Star Line office that the voyage was cancelled. No doubt there was a mixture of relief and resentment on board as *Olympic* returned to her berth at Southampton to disembark passengers. It was here that she would remain, being fitted with union-approved crewmen and boats, until her next scheduled voyage on 15 May.

The embarrassing incident was over, but the White Star Line was not about to let the offenders off quite so easily. The fifty-four crewmen who deserted while *Olympic* was anchored at Spithead were arrested on charges of mutiny. They were arraigned on Tuesday 30 April in Portsmouth Police Court and the case was remanded to 4 May. On that date the accused were brought before the magistrates and required to answer to the charge that 'they were guilty of willful disobedience to the lawful commands of Captain Haddock, the Master of the steamship *Olympic*, contrary to Section 225 of the Merchant Shipping Act of 1894.'

The lawyers for their defence argued, on the basis of Article 458 of the same act, that the owners of the White Star Line were required to ensure the seaworthiness of their ships. Allowing *Olympic* to sail with a crew that was not competent, they argued, would be nearly as bad as allowing her to go to sea with a hole in her hull. The legal representative for the White Star Line, Norman Raebarn, called Captain Benjamin Steele, the White Star Marine Superintendent at Southampton, to the stand. Steele testified that the lifeboats were adequate and that there were enough crewmen to handle them. The 2nd Engineer, Charles McKimm, who had recruited the second group of replacements ashore, admitted that some of the men he picked were Yorkshire miners who had no experience at sea (although presumably they were familiar with coal). McKimm did not consider the job of Fireman to require that much skill,[1] but in a statement that amused the court, he did acknowledge that it was hard work.

The magistrates ruled in favour of the White Star Line and found the men guilty of mutiny. Instead of fining or imprisoning the mutineers however, the judge decided not to impose any form of punishment because he believed that the men had most likely been stricken with a case of nerves over of the recent loss of *Titanic*. In the end, the mutiny ended up fading into the background because the British Board of Trade Inquiry on *Titanic's* sinking was commencing. The case came up again only once more, on 14 May, when a question was tabled in Parliament as to what action would be taken against the British Seafarers Union which had, in effect, prevented *Olympic* from departing with the Royal Mail. The question was referred to the Board of Trade, who decided that on the basis of the outcome of the court's decision at Portsmouth, no prosecution would be undertaken.

On 6 May, Lord Mersey, chairman of the British Wreck Commissioner's Inquiry on the loss of *Titanic*, boarded *Olympic* at Southampton. He came in order to witness a lifeboat drill and to see for himself the ship's lifesaving apparatus. Boat No. 9 on the starboard side was dutifully lowered, after which Lord Mersey returned to London after lunching aboard with Harold Sanderson, General Manager of the White Star Line. *Olympic* slipped her mooring lines on 15 May and sailed without incident, arriving in New York seven days later. It was the first time she had crossed the Atlantic since *Titanic* sank.

Given the circumstances of her sister ship's loss, it was not surprising that that *Olympic* received quite a bit of attention when she arrived in New York. However, it *was* a complete surprise to Captain Haddock when on Saturday 25 May, Senator William Smith, chairman of the Senate Congressional Committee investigating

Lord Mersey and his assessors testing one of *Olympic*'s lifeboats.

the loss of *Titanic*, appeared on the ship without notice only hours before she was scheduled to sail. The White Star Line's Vice President in New York, Philip Franklin, rushed over from the International Mercantile Marine offices at 9 Broadway. Captain Haddock was advised to accord Senator Smith every courtesy and comply with any request he might make. The senator, escorted by Chief Engineer Robert Fleming, was then taken down to the working areas of the ship to see the watertight bulkheads and other safety arrangements. Fireman Frederick Barrett was on hand for questioning as he had been on *Titanic* in Boiler Room No. 6 on the night of the collision. Barrett recounted what he had testified to in the inquiry, after which a watertight door was lowered for a demonstration. Smith left that afternoon satisfied with what he had seen and *Olympic* returned to England one week later.

Olympic berthed at Southampton after *Titanic's* sinking. In the foreground are lifeboats, possibly waiting to be fitted aboard a ship.

Titanic's loss resulted in the travelling public being far less assured of the invincibility of ships at sea, and the provision of additional lifeboats was not enough to restore their faith. The White Star Line had to build up confidence in *Olympic*, and some permanent modifications would be necessary. These would also be incorporated into her sister ship *Britannic*, which was still being built. *Olympic* remained in service for only six more journeys before this work was undertaken. By the end of the summer season it was decided to bring her back to Belfast for what would be the first of four major refits that the ship would see throughout her career. She returned on 9 October 1912 and would be out of service for the better part of six months. The refit would cost approximately £156,500 (about $625,000) for the safety-related changes alone and would incorporate all of the lessons learned from *Titanic's* sinking. An extra transverse bulkhead dividing the Electric Engine Room in two was added, and many of the remaining transverse bulkheads were raised much higher above the waterline, some as far up as B Deck. However the biggest feature of this refit would be the addition of an inner skin that extended amidships from the forward end of the No. 6 Boiler Room aft throughout the full length of the boiler and engine rooms.

This new inner skin was riveted to inner frames placed inside the hull and extended above the waterline. Requiring no working openings for access, it was sealed off from the inside. In essence, *Olympic's* double bottom had been extended right up the sides of the ship. This was thought to increase her safety significantly by restricting any breach in the hull of the type that occurred in *Titanic* to the area within the new double hull. It requires little imagination to imagine the amount of work it took to accomplish this. Some of the most major modifications took place in Boiler Room No. 5. Here,

Olympic after *Titanic*'s sinking but prior to her refit.

located at the point in the hull where the sides began to taper toward the bow, the subsequent loss of internal space caused by the inner skin no longer gave enough space for five boilers to stand abreast. The centre one was removed and replaced with one of a smaller diameter, and the boilers on either side were moved inwards.

At the same time, Harland & Wolff took the opportunity to incorporate major changes to upgrade *Olympic*'s ventilation system, passenger accommodations and other areas. A large number of ventilating fans and their associated intake ducts were enlarged or reconfigured and extra cowls added to correct the insufficient ventilation in many areas. The Officers' Quarters deckhouse was extended forward by approximately 10ft to allow for the incorporation of more First-Class staterooms at the aft end of the structure. The straight-line forward bulkhead of the Wheelhouse was removed and a flat bulkhead was fitted in its place to match *Titanic*'s.[2] *Olympic*'s Bridge wing cabs were extended about another 2ft over the sides of the superstructure, again mirroring *Titanic*. The large First-Class *à la carte* Restaurant had proved so popular that it was enlarged, extending all the way out to the side of the ship. Passengers now had an unobstructed view of the ocean, just as they had on *Titanic*. A reception room was added on the starboard side at the expense of a wine cellar and two three-berth rooms. To further mirror *Titanic*, a Café Parisien was added by enclosing the starboard side promenade opposite the Restaurant. This feature eased the turnaround time in the Restaurant, because coffee could be served after dinner out on the wicker tables of the Café.

The outboard weather screens along the forward half of the Promenade Deck, which served to immediately distinguish *Titanic* from *Olympic*, were never added. Additional staterooms were added in some places and removed from others.

Externally, at the end of her refit *Olympic* appeared practically unchanged except for the additional windows along the starboard side of B Deck in way of the Café Parisien and the expanded Restaurant on the port side, and the removal of bulwarks on both sides of the Boat Deck where extra lifeboats were added. However, because of the high demand for lifeboats at the time, only sixteen of the thirty-two planned boats were available. To have *Olympic* ready for her next voyage, Harland & Wolff installed ten Berthon and six Henderson collapsible lifeboats as a temporary measure until the proper boats were ready for delivery. *Olympic* would eventually be fitted with a lifeboat capacity of 3,484 in 1913, and with the increased passenger accommodations the gross tonnage would jump from the original 45,324 to 46,359.

Throughout the refit, the White Star Line maintained its service between Southampton and New York with the *Oceanic* and *Majestic*. By mid-March 1913, the work on *Olympic* was completed and she left Belfast for Southampton on 22 March. She would resume her place on the Atlantic on 2 April. The White Star Line advertised the newly refitted liner in many publications of the time, giving much attention to her new inner skin and added safety features. However, *Olympic* soon lost her status as the world's largest ship because only one month after *Titanic*'s sinking the Germans launched the 52,000-ton *Imperator*. But even though *Olympic* had lost this largest-ship distinction, 1913 turned out to be a very good year, one in which she would have the second-highest passenger count of her career. Under the command of Captain Haddock, she was a very popular ship.

In 1914, the prospects for the White Star Line appeared to be improving despite rumours of financial problems within IMM (International Mercantile Marine). On 26 February, *Britannic* was launched in Belfast and if all went well she would be in service within the year. Plans for a new *Germanic* were also underway, although the *Germanic* was never intended as a replacement for *Titanic*. The White Star Line appeared to be moving on and prospering, and the *Titanic* tragedy was becoming a thing of the past. However, world events would put that prosperity on hold and ultimately decide the fate of both ships.

On 4 August 1914, Great Britain and France entered into a conflict against Germany and Austria-Hungary that would come to be known as the Great War. The British economy was soon forced to concentrate its efforts on supplying the war effort as the merchant fleets prepared for the long struggle ahead. *Olympic* was en route to New York when war was declared, and even though the ship was close to the coast, Captain Haddock ordered blackout conditions as a precaution against being spotted by German submarines. After they reached New York, the crew spent the four days in port blacking out the windows and painting the funnels and superstructure grey. On 9 August, Captain Haddock sailed *Olympic* back to what would be her new home port for the duration: Liverpool. Carrying no passengers and taking the safest route through the U-boat-infested waters off the northern coast of Ireland, she arrived safely on 15 August.

By that point the war effort was placing great demands on the merchant marine. Steamship companies were becoming hard pressed to keep up with their war duties while still supplying passenger service from England to America. As one consequence of the war, booking offices were thronged with Americans fleeing Europe and British nationals trying to get home. All available berths on every ship were occupied. First-Class passengers even took Third-Class berths when none better could be had. There was no complaining, as the conflict in Europe was escalating and anyone who managed to secure passage was grateful for their good fortune in doing so.

Olympic would make only a handful of runs out of Liverpool until 3 October, when she had to return to a new, temporary port at Greenock, Scotland. On 9 October *Olympic* departed for New York; it would be her last New York departure until the war ended. Following a zigzag course for safety, she arrived in New York seven days later. She departed New York on 21 October, setting a course for Belfast, where she would be laid up until her wartime role had been decided. Less than a day from safety *Olympic* found herself approaching the area where the 2nd Battle Squadron was patrolling. The battleship HMS *Audacious*, which had struck a mine off Tory Island, was lying crippled directly ahead. Because of the possibility of U-boat attacks, the Admiralty had ordered the rest of the fleet to leave the area while the light cruiser HMS *Liverpool* and a number of smaller vessels remained to assist the damaged warship. At 10.30a.m. *Olympic* was sighted by the *Liverpool* and ordered to help evacuate the crew of the *Audacious*. After 250 or so of the warship's crew were taken off, the destroyer HMS *Fury* assisted in getting a towing hawser from *Audacious* aboard *Olympic* in an attempt to tow the 23,400-ton warship back to port. *Olympic* and her new charge steamed slowly towards Lough Swilly with all going well until the steering gear on *Audacious* failed. By this point the sea was beginning to get rough and with *Audacious* unable to be controlled, the towing hawser snapped. A second attempt was made to tow the warship, but within 15 minutes the cable became entangled in the *Liverpool*'s propellers. A third attempt was made to secure a tow, this time to the collier *Thornhill*, but again the line parted. Captain Haddock was advised to stand by while a final attempt was made. By 5.00p.m. *Audacious* was foundering, her Quarter Deck under water, and it was decided to evacuate the remaining crew. By 6.30p.m. all were aboard either *Olympic* or the *Liverpool*. At 8.55p.m. there was a massive explosion in the battleship's magazine and she sank stern first.

Olympic anchored in Lough Swilly that evening to disembark those members of the *Audacious* crew who were aboard. Captain Haddock was ordered to stay out of sight of the Grand Fleet that was also anchored in the area, because there was a fear that some of *Olympic*'s German-American passengers were German sympathisers and would inform the Kaiser's government of the fleet's presence. As American citizens they could not be arrested, but they could be held for questioning if necessary. It was already too late to keep them from seeing what had happened to the *Audacious*, but they need not see anything further that might compromise the safety of the fleet. The passengers were confined to the ship and could send no communications. The only people permitted to leave were the crew of the *Audacious* and Chief Surgeon John Beaumont, who was being transferred to the White Star liner *Celtic*. On 2 November, *Olympic* was finally allowed to sail for Belfast, where the passengers were finally disembarked. Captain Haddock stayed on at Belfast, where the Admiralty appointed him to command a squadron of merchant ships disguised as warships in an attempt to mislead the enemy.

It was no doubt a melancholy reunion as *Olympic* joined her unfinished younger sister *Britannic* at Harland & Wolff. Both were laid up and could be seen berthed side by side, with only a maintenance crew from the shipyard aboard. She lay dormant for another ten months as the Admiralty decided what to do with the large merchant liners that were unsuitable for military service. Originally it had been intended to use them as armed cruisers, but in practice this proved unfeasible. The *Oceanic* had been declared a total loss after grounding on a reef off the island of Foula in the Shetland Islands in September 1914. In another incident, the *Aquitania* collided with the Leyland Line's *Canadian*, illustrating just how unsuitable these huge liners were for patrol duty. In fact, the *Aquitania* remained as an armed merchant cruiser for only two weeks. Because of the size of the great liners and the high cost of operating them, by the spring of 1915 *Olympic, Britannic, Aquitania, Mauretania* and *Lusitania* were either laid up or kept in standard company service.

On 7 May 1915, the Cunard liner *Lusitania* was torpedoed and sunk off Old Head of Kinsale, Ireland, with a huge loss of life. Initially Cunard announced that the *Mauretania* would be continuing with the next scheduled sailing to New York, but before this came to pass the Admiralty approached Cunard with the intention of using *Mauretania* as a troopship. The Admiralty offered a specified rate per gross ton, and given the sharp drop in bookings after the *Lusitania*'s loss, Cunard accepted. The *Mauretania* was officially requisitioned on 11 May for service in the Mediterranean. A key problem with large ocean liners carrying such large complements of men is that they were highly desirable prey for German submarines, and if one should be sunk, the loss – militarily and otherwise – would be high. But there appeared to be no other feasible alternative, as the use of many smaller ships would be needed to achieve what could be accomplished with a single liner of *Olympic*'s size. The liners also had the advantages of speed. All in all, they could transport more men, were faster, and could be fitted out more cheaply than the equivalent number of smaller vessels. Considering this, the Transport Department finally conceded that the use of the liners was a necessity, and on 18 June the *Aquitania* was also requisitioned as a troopship.

While the *Aquitania* was being prepared for war service, the Admiralty began opening negotiations with the White Star Line for the use of *Olympic*. General Manager Harold Sanderson conferred with Harland & Wolff and advised the Admiralty that *Olympic* could be refitted for military use without a problem. Her on-board cabin arrangements could be converted into table-and-hammock accommodations for up to 7,000 troops. The ship's bunker capacity would allow her to maintain a speed of 21 knots from Southampton to Mudros, a British port on a small island in the northern Aegean used as a disembarkation point for troops. However, although *Olympic*'s conversion was eminently feasible, she had spent many months idle at the yard and would need to be dry docked for the removal of the accumulated growth on her bottom. The tide would not permit the use of the Thompson Graving Dock until the end of the month, and the Gladstone Dock in Liverpool was occupied by the *Aquitania*. Perhaps fortunately, the Admiralty informed the White Star Line on 22 June that *Olympic* would not be needed just yet. Although the tide of the war was shifting dramatically, and troop movements to the Mediterranean were heavy, the number of casualties was beginning to overwhelm the Transport Division and hospital ships were now a priority. Earlier in the war, the Admiralty had used some twenty merchant vessels, called 'black hospital ships', to transport stores and troops to the battle areas and return with sick and wounded soldiers. The problem with this was that the ships carried no markings to identify them as carrying casualties, and the ships were not well-equipped to care for large numbers of men requiring medical attention. To solve this problem, the Admiralty requisitioned vessels to be used exclusively as hospital ships. This new classification of liners would be painted with Red Cross markings and therefore protected under the terms of the Geneva Convention. With their high speeds, the *Mauretania* and *Aquitania* were ideal for this use, and in September 1915 both were converted to hospital ships, leaving an opening for other ships to serve as troop transports.

On 1 September 1915, Harold Sanderson was instructed to get *Olympic* ready for war service. While Harland & Wolff began planning the necessary work, Sanderson negotiated the terms of the ship's charter. It was agreed that the Admiralty would pay only about £23,000 per month, out of which the White Star Line would have to pay the crew. The Admiralty did agree, however, to pay any costs the insurance company would not cover in the event of the ship being lost.

The work to convert *Olympic* to a troopship was no less involved than her original fitting out for passenger service. Many of the peacetime fittings were removed and stored, and the portable Third-Class accommodations were converted for the use of thousands of troops. Some of the public rooms were similarly fitted for berthing while others were converted to mess arrangements. However, the cleaning of the hull could not be carried out at Belfast. The Thompson Graving Dock was not available, and in any case *Olympic* would need to return to Liverpool for provisioning and coal. She left Belfast on 12 September, and upon arrival at Liverpool was placed in the Gladstone Dock that had recently been vacated by the battleship HMS *Barham*. Harold Sanderson originally intended Captain Haddock to resume command of *Olympic*, but the Admiralty turned him down because Haddock was needed to command the 'ghost fleet' of merchant ships masquerading as naval ships. Sanderson thus went to his second choice, Captain Bertram Hayes, formerly of the *Adriatic*.

Olympic as a troop transport in grey paint.

When Hayes boarded his new command at Liverpool, he found the situation to be one of 'utter confusion'. His initial meeting with the naval transport officer in charge did not go well; Hayes had a run-in with the officer over the fact that Hayes was not in uniform. It was common for captains of the merchant fleet to wear civilian clothes while not on the ship; therefore, it was in this state of dress that Hayes reported. Hayes also reported later that he felt obliged to speak up for his officers who were not in the naval reserve. Hayes insisted that if his assistant commander was not given a rank higher than sub-lieutenant, then Hayes would have him wear his company uniform while on duty to command a higher rank. The principal naval officer shook his finger at Hayes and said: 'Take care, sir. Remember you are talking about the King's Commission, and if you are not careful your commission may be taken away from you.' Hayes retorted that the reserve had done nothing for him in way of money, and in fact had been an expense to him, and that although the officer could take away his commission, he could not take away his employment, which provided his livelihood.

When *Olympic* departed the Gladstone Dock in Liverpool for the Mediterranean, she was fitted with a 12-pound gun on her Forecastle Deck and a 4.7in gun aft. Her official transport designation was T2810, and she was now known as HMTS

(His Majesty's Troop Ship) *Olympic*. On board were 6,000 troops, mostly from the Southern Counties Yeomanry, and a number of troops from the Welsh Horse Division with their glee-singers, who provided entertainment on the ship.

On 1 October, while steaming off Cape Matapan, Greece, *Olympic's* lookouts sighted lifeboats from the French steamer *Provincia*, which had been sunk by an Austrian submarine at 9.00a.m. that morning. Hayes ordered *Olympic* to be stopped while the thirty-four survivors were picked up, coming aboard by means of the pilot ladder. After the men were aboard the gun crews on board sank the lifeboats by gunfire, and *Olympic* continued her journey to Mudros. Although this was a gallant move by Hayes, in doing so he had placed his ship at risk for a U-boat attack. Later a U-boat was sighted, but Hayes altered course and outran it after firing on it. After arriving at Mudros, the French crewmen of the *Provincia* were disembarked to the SS *Aragon*. The French Admiral recommended that Hayes should be given the *Medaille de Sauvetage* (Life-Saving Medal) by a grateful French government. The Naval commander-in-chief (CIC) in the eastern Mediterranean was not pleased that Hayes had left his ship open for attack with more than 6,000 troops on board. The CIC was so incensed that he circulated a bulletin headed 'Indiscretion Shown by the Master of a Transport' in which others were warned not to do what Hayes did.

Hayes was given his next orders to sail to La Spezia, a port on the western coast of Italy, where he would take on coal and then depart as soon as possible for Liverpool. However, because of the disorganisation at Mudros, the troops aboard did not fully disembark until eight days later. It was not until the evening of 11 October that *Olympic* was cleared to depart. The ship arrived at La Spezia virtually empty except for her crew. On arrival Hayes found that inadequate provisions had been made for coal and water, leading to another delay of eight days in port. During the eventual voyage home to Liverpool it was discovered that the water was contaminated, and on the ship's arrival on 31 October 1915, many of the crew were sick with stomach

Sir Bertram Fox Hayes, KCMG, DSO, in the uniform of a commander, RNR.

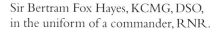

problems. *Olympic* made two more runs to the Mediterranean with the usual stop at La Spezia for coal and water. On her return to Liverpool on 21 December she had a reunion with *Britannic*, commissioned six weeks earlier, which also was tied up. The two ships would meet again only one more time, except for one time late in August 1916, when they passed at sea.

Olympic was not ready to depart Liverpool for Mudros again until 4 January 1916, as the crew was given time off to celebrate Christmas and New Year's Eve at home with their families. On 12 February, *Olympic* arrived at Southampton to embark troops, and it was here that she would meet the *Britannic* for the last time, *Britannic* having arrived three days earlier with her second load of wounded troops from the Mediterranean. On 13 March, *Olympic* completed her fourth and final troopship run to Mudros. *Olympic's* role was now uncertain, as a debate was in progress between Sanderson and the Admiralty over the cost of victualling the troops aboard ship. The company had been spending about £3,000 out of pocket because of the discrepancy between the Admiralty's payment and the actual cost of feeding the troops. As a result, by the spring of 1916 *Olympic's* continued use as a troopship was seriously in doubt.

With the massive evacuation of Allied troops from Gallipoli in December 1915, huge liners for troop and hospital transport between England and the Mediterranean were no longer needed. Plans were then drawn up to use *Olympic* as a troopship to India. The problem with voyages to India mostly concerned the ship's ability to carry sufficient coal for the journey. In order for the ship to be able to reach Cape Town, South Africa, where she would need to be coaled for the remainder of the trip, the reserve coal bunker would have to be enlarged by cutting a hole in the bulkhead between the Nos. 2 and 3 holds. In addition, in her double bottom she would need to carry much more fresh water than normal to supply drinking water for all the additional 'passengers' aboard. Because of this, a new problem arose: with the added weight the ship's draught increased, from about 34½ft to 38ft. This meant that in order for *Olympic* to coal, she would have to sit some 1,200 yards out from the dock, and at Bombay (now Mumbai) on the west coast, she would have to anchor 2 to 3 miles out to sea. Although Trincomalee on the island of Ceylon (now the Republic of Sri Lanka) would provide a good place to anchor, the coaling facilities there were inadequate and extra ships would be needed just to transport the troops from the liner. The idea was wholly impractical, and the officer investigating the possibility of *Olympic's* use for this particular theatre of operations agreed. On 8 February, the plan was dropped, once again leaving *Olympic's* future war service in question.

At midnight on 22 March 1916, *Olympic* left Liverpool to travel across the Atlantic for the first time in eighteen months. The Canadian government had requested extra ships to transport soldiers from the port of Halifax, and *Olympic* was perfect for the job. It would be while under this assignment that *Olympic* would again write herself another entry in the history books.

The ship made her maiden voyage to Canada on 28 March, but Captain Hayes was concerned about how his ship would be used. The original plans called for *Olympic* to be part of a protected convoy, but when he heard that convoy speed would be no more than 12 knots[3] he was worried that his ship would be an easy target for German U-boats. Hayes argued vehemently to the Canadian authorities to allow *Olympic* to run unescorted, using her speed as her best defense. *Olympic*, he said, had zigzagged up and down the Mediterranean, which was supposedly more infested with U-boats than the Atlantic, and had never had a problem. Hayes convinced them, and on 5 April *Olympic* sailed with a full complement of Canadian troops for Liverpool. The only mishap en route was a collision with the patrol boat that pulled alongside *Olympic* to disembark the pilot. There were no casualties, but the mast of the patrol boat carried away two lifeboats on the port side, damaging one of the davits in the process. Nevertheless, *Olympic* went on her way, arriving in Liverpool on 11 April.

Olympic made ten voyages between Halifax and Liverpool without serious incident. However, she did not escape bad luck throughout the year: on 29 October she grounded while at anchor outside Halifax for 4½ hours. There was concern about hull damage, but after the ship floated off she was sounded and no damage was found. On 5 November a fire broke out in the flue of the Third-Class galley that required more than 2 hours to extinguish. Some structural damage resulted, but it was only patched up because the ship was to go in for a refit for additional war service after the next scheduled voyage. On 30 December 1916, *Olympic* completed her tenth run to Halifax and back. After spending the first week of the new year at Liverpool she departed for Belfast, arriving on 12 January 1917. For the next three months she remained at Harland & Wolff for a refit while Captain Hayes was transferred to the *Celtic*. His first trip on his new command was cut short, however; just as his ship was approaching the Isle of Man it ran into a mine. The explosion blew a hole between the Nos. 1 and 2 holds, but thankfully the damage was shored and the *Celtic* was safely returned to Liverpool. Hayes then took passage on the *Adriatic* for New York, after which he was ordered to rejoin *Olympic* at Glasgow.

By the end of March, work on *Olympic* was coming to a close, and the White Ensign on the flagstaff was officially raised on 4 April 1917. *Olympic* was again commissioned as one of His Majesty's Transport Ships. This time she would look very different. Her grey war colours were gone, and at some point in 1917 a new type of camouflage, known as dazzle paint, was applied.[4] This new scheme would incorporate a series of geometric shapes painted on her hull, superstructure, funnels and lifeboats. The intended purpose was to confuse any U-boat captain who might be trying to ascertain the liner's heading and distance. The dazzle paint was intended to make it difficult to determine which way the ship was heading and to break up her outline. Later, the Admiralty would change the configuration of the dazzle paint to ward off the possibility of the enemy being able pick out bearing points on the hull by familiarity with the pattern. As a result, changes were made to the shapes and

Olympic in Halifax.

colours of the dazzle paint several times throughout the war and images of *Olympic* in dazzle paint are among the most dramatic of her career.

In addition to the contrasting colours of his ship, Captain Hayes found that *Olympic* had been fitted with six 6in guns while in Belfast and that his crew had been augmented by about forty naval ratings under the charge of a Gunner's Mate.

On 6 April 1917, the United States declared war on Germany. *Olympic* continued her Halifax-to-Liverpool transport route until Christmas Day of 1917, when she returned to her pre-war terminal in New York to embark American troops. However, the Hudson River was so choked with ice that coal barges could not be brought alongside until 11 January. The American authorities, eager to get as many troops over to the war as soon as possible, wanted *Olympic* to carry about 2,000 men more than she was designed to carry. Captain Hayes, knowing the overcrowding that would result and its consequences, convinced the Americans to reduce the number. The troops would not, he said, be in any condition to fight after arriving after a trip in such conditions.

Olympic made her second journey to New York carrying the new British ambassador to America, Lord Reading. Lord Reading made a point of mentioning how fine the food was aboard *Olympic* and that the men were being fed better than the

Olympic leaving port in her new dazzle paint.

Prime Minister himself. Captain Hayes informed him that the food was brought on at Halifax or New York, as surplus food in England was needed for the war cause. Lord Reading went on to ask Captain Hayes his opinion of the *Olympic-Hawke* collision, because Reading had appeared before the Admiralty in the hearings. Hayes replied that 'the Admiralty must have had the better lawyer as they certainly hadn't the better case.'

The spring of 1918 arrived with *Olympic* having more than two and a half years of distinguished service under the Crown, but her moment of glory was yet to come. Just before 4.00a.m. on the morning of 12 May, near the English Channel, her lookouts sighted a surfaced U-boat 500m (about a third of a mile) ahead. The submarine was not aware of *Olympic*'s presence because the larger ship was masked in darkness, but *Olympic* could see the submarine because of the sunrise behind it.[5] *Olympic*'s gunners opened fire and the submarine began to dive. Hayes ordered the helm put over to turn the ship into the submarine, striking her just abaft the conning tower. The hull of the massive liner rode over the fatally damaged submarine and the port propeller sliced through the pressure hull.

Another one of *Olympic*'s dazzle paint schemes.

The impact startled Hayes and the officers on the Bridge as they felt the shock through their feet. Hayes later said he had always thought that a submarine would be more fragile than that; he even questioned whether they had actually hit the submarine or if they had struck something else. He relaxed when he observed the conning tower and deck guns as they passed. While *Olympic* continued her voyage, the American destroyer USS *Davis* remained behind to pick up the thirty-one survivors of the sunken U-boat. However, *Olympic* did not come through the incident unscathed. After returning to Southampton, divers found that the hull had sustained damage: there were a number of dented plates, the starboard paravane[6] chains were torn away, and the stem was bent about 8ft out of alignment to port.

Hayes was praised for his seamanship and quick thinking by being awarded the Distinguished Service Order. The lookout that spotted the submarine was also awarded a medal and received a £20 bonus from the White Star Line: this was a standing reward given to any crewman who first sighted a submarine from which his ship escaped. The lookout in the Crow's Nest also laid a claim to the prize, stating that he had been in the process of calling the Bridge after sighting the submarine when the other lookout called it out. In the end, the two men split the reward money. There was also a reward from the Admiralty and Lloyds of London of some £1,000 to be distributed among the crew for successfully destroying an enemy submarine. The officers of one of the regiments on board also collected a sum of money and gave it to the purser for the purpose of commissioning a plaque somewhere on the ship. Later, when *Olympic* was being refitted after the war, this plaque was positioned in the landing of the forward First-Class Stairway. The inscription on it read:

> This tablet, presented by the 59th Regiment
> United States Infantry, commemorates the sinking
> of the German Submarine *U103* by *Olympic*
> on 12th May, 1918, in lat. 49, 16 N. long. 4, 51 W.
> on the voyage from New York to Southampton
> with American Troops.

By mid-1918 the war was coming to an end, with the British naval blockades resulting in starvation on the German mainland. The German push to drive France out of the war had failed, and the Kaiser's army was forced to give up nearly all of the territory they had occupied. Surrender finally came in November 1918. *Olympic*'s crew received the initial news of the armistice while bound for New York. Captain Hayes read the official announcement in the morning paper as he stayed at the New York apartment of some close friends after arriving in port late the night before. His ship had performed well through the conflict, and over her four years of war service had carried some 200,000 troops and thousands of civilian passengers.

After the victory celebrations in New York, *Olympic* returned to Southampton with only a handful of passengers. For the first time since before the war, she was

Olympic's twisted stem, damaged after running over *U-103*.

able to run without her lights blacked out at night. For the passengers this signified that the war was really over, but Hayes knew that it would be some time before the ship could be returned to regular service. All of the American and Canadian troops in Europe had to be brought back home again, and the big liners would be required to do the job. It was only natural that the first troops to come home aboard *Olympic* were Canadians. Upon the ship's arrival at Halifax, she was met by a crowd that was so noisy in their cheers that the docking instructions had to be transmitted with signals. The Haligonians so loved *Olympic* and her crew – which they treated like family – that they nicknamed the ship 'Old Reliable'.[7] For his service to the war and the people of Halifax, Hayes was awarded with plaques and a loving cup from the mayor of Halifax and the Halifax Board of Trade for all of his service to the war effort and to the people of Halifax.

For the rest of 1918, *Olympic* sailed between Europe and North America. Then in February 1919, *Olympic* was taken out of service and underwent inspection at Liverpool. During this inspection an 18in dent was found in the shell plating 14ft below the waterline between the Nos. 2 and 3 funnels. In the middle of this dent was

a 6in crack. The void between the inner and outer shell plating had been flooded, but because this area was inaccessible and the water had been contained it had not been noticed. This dent was not there during the last time *Olympic* was put in the dry dock, so Captain Hayes could only assume that it must have been caused by an unexploded torpedo striking the ship. One can only imagine Hayes' relief at finding out that his ship had escaped so narrowly.

At noon on 16 February 1919, *Olympic* departed Liverpool with a large number of American troops bound for America. When the ship approached the dock in New York, the men crowded onto the side of the ship closest to the pier. The accumulated

'Old Reliable'.

Olympic bringing troops back home. The remains of her dazzle paint is still evident at the bow.

weight of the troops on one side of the ship, in her lightened condition (low on stores and coal), caused a considerable list to the point that docking operations had to be suspended. The soldiers had to be ordered to move in order to trim the ship; otherwise they would have carried away the shed while pulling into the berth

Olympic made five more voyages to Halifax before returning to Belfast on 16 August for the second major refit of her career. Throughout the autumn and winter of 1919–20 the ship was virtually gutted as the interior fittings that had been stored away before the war were replaced. When *Olympic* returned to service, First-Class passengers found the *à la carte* Restaurant temporarily unavailable as a separate dining venue as it had been converted to an extension of the main Dining Saloon. The former Restaurant Reception Room was now also an extension of this area, with tables to accommodate 200 passengers.

In a fuel-saving measure, the boilers were converted to burn oil fuel instead of coal. *Olympic* would be the first of the large ocean liners to undergo this conversion. The transition would require the replacement of the old furnace fronts with burner units, and the coal bunkers would require considerable modification to be made suitable for the storage of liquid fuel. Although oil was more expensive than coal, it made refuelling easier and faster, cutting down the time required to replenish the bunkers from a number of days to a few hours. Oil also eliminated the never-ending problem of coal dust permeating the ship's decks and interiors. No longer would there be a haze of coal dust surrounding the ship and covering every surface while the ship was coaled. A further inducement was the reduction in engine room personnel from 350 to sixty men. With the original 'black gang' gone, there would be no visible difference between a Fireman and a Seaman.

It was also at this time that the lifeboat arrangement on *Olympic* would change. With the installation of the Murray's nested lifeboats there would be a line of twelve 30ft boats on each side of the ship. Nested inside each 30ft boat was a 28ft boat, with the two 26ft emergency cutters stowed inside the forward sets.

Post-war refit at Harland & Wolff, 9 September 1919.

With *Olympic* scheduled to return to service in the summer of 1920, White Star Line Manager Harold Sanderson was busy reconfiguring the other White Star ships for the next decade of passenger service. *Celtic, Cedric, Baltic* and *Adriatic* had survived the war but were compatible running mates with *Olympic* due to their lesser size and speed. With the loss of *Titanic, Britannic* and *Oceanic*, Sanderson faced some challenges ahead, as rebuilding the company's fleet would take time and money. Construction on *Homeric*, yard No. 470, had been brought to a halt because of the war, and it seemed that she would never pass far beyond the planning stage even after the signing of the armistice. In any event, she was never intended to be an express liner like the *Olympic*-class ships.

In the end, Germany surrendered unconditionally. Its merchant fleet was reduced to nothing, as any ship of worth was taken by the Allies as war reparations. Great Britain, France, and the United States haggled for months over how Germany's ships should be divided up. On 17 November the British shipping controller was finally able to release a list of ships allocated to Great Britain. Cunard had first choice, as it had sustained the heaviest loss: twenty-two ships. For the White Star Line, Sanderson

People line up to view the newly refitted *Olympic* on 12 June 1920.

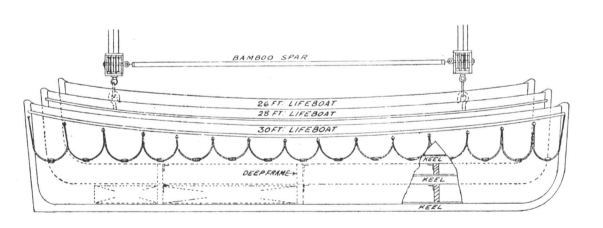

General arrangement of Captain Murray's Nested Lifeboats.

chose the 35,000-ton Norddeutscher-Lloyd (North German Lloyd) liner *Columbus* and the HAPAG (Hamburg American Line)[8] liner *Bismarck*. Although the *Bismarck* would require another nine months before it was completed for service, these two vessels were suitable to operate out of Southampton as running mates for *Olympic*.

In Belfast, *Olympic's* refit came to an end with a two-day public inspection of the now 46,439-ton, oil-fired flagship of the White Star Line. On 17 June *Olympic* departed Belfast for Southampton under the command of Captain Hayes, now Sir Bertram Hayes after being knighted for his war service. Harold Sanderson was on board and headed a banquet in celebration of the liner's return to the Atlantic service. Among the dignitaries and guests were Hayes, Viscount and Lady Pirrie, Lady Pirrie's sister Miss Carlisle, and Field Marshal Sir William Robertson. At the banquet, they inaugurated the new dance floor that had been added to the First-Class Reception Room.

On 26 June 1920, *Olympic* left Southampton Docks for her first commercial voyage after her reconditioning. *Olympic* was spick and span – like a new ship, according to Captain Hayes. The conversion to oil was well received by the passengers; for the first time they did not have to deal with cinders falling from the funnels and getting in their eyes while on the outer decks. (Perhaps most pleased with the change to oil was the ship's surgeon, who would no longer have to attend to passengers with complaints of 'something in my eye' day and night)

Several years after the war, the White Star Line and other steamship companies were just starting to pull out of the slump of the war and once again becoming competitive when a change in American immigration laws took place that would forever change the way the companies did business. In May 1921, the American government passed the Dillingham Immigration Restriction Act, which limited immigration after 1 July 1921 to just 3 per cent of the foreign-born population of the American 1903 census. This meant that only 360,000 immigrants per year would be allowed to enter the United States. This was a harsh blow; emigrants were the lifeblood of the big transatlantic steamship companies, and the large numbers of Third-Class passengers provided the revenue that kept the companies profitable and justified the building of such large liners. With this new law, the White Star Line found itself with the door being slammed in its face.

On 12 December 1921, while on an eastbound crossing for Cherbourg, *Olympic* ran into heavy weather that required her to reduce speed. At 3.44a.m. the ship was struck by several large waves that staved the glass in from five galley sidelights, necessitating a further reduction in speed. Five hours later a number of sidelights on the starboard side of the First-Class Reception Room were also staved in, and the forward tackle of the starboard emergency cutter was damaged. By 2.05p.m. that afternoon the seas had become so large that they caused the ship to undergo a series of quick rolls. This loosened the clamps holding one of the watertight doors open, causing it to close on the foot of a Third-Class passenger. Another died when a door slammed shut on him, dislodging his vertebrae and compressing his spinal cord.

Hayes sailed in command of *Olympic* for another two years, and on 7 January 1922, he arrived at Southampton for the last time before being transferred to the new *Majestic* (ex-*Bismarck*), which was still being completed in Hamburg. During his last trip on *Olympic* he had his successor aboard, Captain Alec E. Hambelton, ex-*Adriatic*. Hambelton was aboard to become acquainted with the ship he would soon command, one twice the size of those he had been used to. Much later, in his autobiography, Hayes would write that Hambelton was known throughout the company 'as being the biggest liar crossing the Atlantic when recounting some of his experiences'. Hambelton was noted for being plagued by foggy weather when making the Nantucket Lightship, whereas Hayes said that with regard to fog, he had 'only seen it twice in a number of years'. On the outbound crossing as *Olympic* was nearing New York, Hayes sent an officer down to wake Hambelton and invite him to come on the Bridge to see the lightship so he could recognise it if he were fortunate enough to see it again. On receiving Hayes' invitation, Hambelton rolled over in his bed and said 'I will take his word that it has not been altered in character since I saw it last' – and then went back to sleep.

While Hambelton's command continued to be the largest ship in the fleet, a newer and even larger running mate would soon be completed in Hamburg. On 15 February 1922, the *Homeric* (ex-*Columbus*) was released to join the Southampton–New York route as the second ship given to the White Star Line as part of the German war reparations. The first was the *Arabic* (ex-*Berlin*), which made one voyage from Southampton to New York before being put on the New York–Mediterranean route. Then on 12 April 1922 the *Majestic* completed her sea trials under Captain Hayes. At 56,551 gross registered tons and 23.5 knots, the *Majestic* was now the largest ship in the world and the fastest liner the White Star Line would ever own.

Captain Hambelton's year in command of *Olympic* would be uneventful. At the end of January 1923 he handed over command to Captain Hugh David, who, like Hambelton, had also commanded the *Adriatic*. On 21 November of the same year command of *Olympic* changed again as David handed over the reigns to Captain Frank B. Howarth, who remained in charge until the end of the year when *Olympic* would return to Harland & Wolff for her annual overhaul.

On 20 February 1924, *Olympic* left Southampton for her first scheduled voyage after her yearly maintenance was completed. The year 1924 would be the turning point that forever altered the character of the transatlantic steamship service. In this year, the American government lowered the immigration number to 2 per cent of the foreign-born population based on the American census of 1890. Before the war the number crossing the Atlantic was approximately 1 million each year; now only 160,000 would be allowed to make the trip. It would be another severe financial blow.

On 22 March 1924, *Olympic* was backing out of Pier 59 at New York as the Bermuda-bound Furness-Withy liner *Fort St George* was steaming downriver past her stern. *Olympic* collided with *Fort St George*, breaking her mainmast in two and causing damage to lifeboats, decking, and railings over a length of some 150ft. *Olympic* came away from the third major collision in her career (the first being with HMS *Hawke* and the second with *U-103*) with damaged plating and a cracked sternpost. The latter was particularly troublesome as it was an important structural component of the ship. The sternpost, cast in steel as one piece, carried the rudder and formed the aperture around the centre propeller as well as housing the centre propeller shaft bearing. Because of the complexity of the repair and the lead time needed to order a new casting, temporary patches had to be put in place until the sternpost could be replaced. This would be carried out during the following winter's refit and would be the first time a repair of this type had been carried out.

On 20 June, *Olympic* returned to Queenstown, Ireland, for the first time since the war. It marked the end of an era for Harland & Wolff, as the body of Lord Pirrie was aboard. He had died while aboard the SS *Ebro* on 7 June while returning from South America with Lady Pirrie on a business trip, having never really recovered from the shock of *Titanic*'s sinking. Lord Pirrie's body was transported to Belfast where he was buried on 23 June. Incorporated on his gravestone was an image of *Olympic* as a remembrance of his crowning achievement.

On 25 October *Olympic* left New York with His Royal Highness the Prince of Wales aboard. Prince Edward's presence was the social highlight of the year for those on board. Captain Howarth invited His Royal Highness up to the Bridge, permitting the press to photograph Prince Edward and himself on the starboard bridge wing. Later, His Royal Highness would be photographed in different areas of the Boat Deck.

Olympic was regarded as a difficult ship to handle in confined waters, as evidenced by the many near-misses and collisions she had with other vessels over the years, but she was a strong ship in heavy-weather sea. Although she had a tendency to roll when other liners were seen to be heaved to, *Olympic* would just plough right through the waves. In February of 1925 during a bad storm, a rogue wave reaching a height of 72ft engulfed the Bridge, breaking a window. In the same month a year later, the ship went through a storm so fierce that waves flooded the Crow's Nest, carried away 30ft of railing from the starboard bow and two deck ladders from Boat Deck, staved in four Bridge windows and tore up 10ft of Bridge planking.

At the end of February 1925, a new captain, William Marshall, took command of *Olympic*. With his new command came a change of policy in April 1925, handed down from the North Atlantic Conference.[9] A new class of travel known as 'Tourist Third Cabin' came into effect. On *Olympic*, passengers travelling in this new class were given either the less attractive Second-Class accommodations or the best of the Third-Class accommodations and paid just slightly more than the normal Third-Class fare.[10] This was a direct consequence of the harsh immigration restrictions enacted by the United States, which were starting to catch up with the British shipping industry in general and with *Olympic* in particular. The number of emigrant passengers had fallen sharply in response to the new law and the steamship companies had no choice but to adapt.

Captain Howarth and His Royal Highness, the Prince of Wales on *Olympic*'s starboard bridge wing.

In January 1926, *Olympic* damaged a number of shell plates on her starboard side after striking a fender while leaving her berth. A subsequent inspection of the hull revealed a number of cracks from the C-Deck portholes amidships to the drain holes directly below. The repairs made were considered to be adequate by surveyors from the Board of Trade, but when similar cracks were found on the port side the following year they concluded that *Olympic* should be put on their confidential watch list and monitored for any sign of further cracking. After a five-year period, it was found that these cracks had not lengthened or enlarged and the rivets nearby were all tight and sound.

On 28 December 1926, *Olympic* left New York to return to England, but this time there was a change in the air for the British companies within the International Mercantile Marine. The IMM conglomerate had become one of the rare failures among J.P. Morgan's many investments. If not for the war, the IMM might have collapsed years earlier, but by the mid-1920s it was still managing to remain solvent. In the summer of 1925, Sir Frederick Lewis of the Furness-Withy Line tried to purchase the Oceanic Steam Navigation Company (the parent company of the White Star Line), but the British General strike of 1926 caused the deal to fall through. The next round of negotiations would be opened by Sir Owen Phillips, better known as Lord

Lord Kylsant, *c.*1925.

A post-1927–8 refit photo of
Olympic at Southampton. The
B-Deck windows have been
changed to the Utleys pivoting
type because of the extension of
the staterooms.

Kylsant, chairman of the Royal Mail Steam Packet Company. Lord Kylsant purchased the Oceanic Steam Navigation Company for £7 million on 25 November 1926, and on 1 January of the following year the White Star Line became a part of the Royal Mail Group. Those aboard *Olympic* heard of the sale while at sea, travelling from New York. *Olympic* was now officially a British-owned ship after sixteen years of service.

In the winter of 1927, just before her next refit was due, *Olympic* was again caught in a storm so intense that it staved in a sidelight in the Firemen's berthing area on the lower decks. Water poured in every time the seas rose against the hull and a significant amount of flooding resulted. In order to secure the porthole against further flooding, *Olympic* had to heave to while a plug was fitted into the opening.

In 1928 Tourist Third Cabin became its own separate class, with public rooms and public spaces dedicated to the class. The times were changing, and in an attempt to adapt the ship to changing passenger expectations there was even a makeshift cinema added in the First-Class lounge. It consisted of nothing more than rearranging the chairs to face a projection screen positioned in front of one of the bay windows, but it was a novelty nonetheless.

In September of 1928 Captain Marshall, having served since 1925, was given command of the *Majestic* and his place aboard *Olympic* was taken by Captain Walter Parker, who had been transferred from the *Homeric*. Marshall's departure from *Olympic* was an emotional event for him. Parker even offered to take the *Majestic* for him in order that he could remain aboard *Olympic*, but Marshall replied: 'I suppose I ought to be honoured. She is, after all, the largest ship in the world, you know, Parker – but I am leaving the best to you, for all that.'

WHITE STAR LINE R.M.S. OLYMPIC 46,439 TONS
FIRST CLASS LOUNGE & CINEMA

The makeshift cinema screen.

When *Olympic* was brought in for her 1928–9 refit some major changes took place. On A Deck, most of the rooms forward of the main First-Class entrance were gutted and sixteen new staterooms extending out to the sides of the ship were created. Each of these had a private bath created from space formerly occupied by smaller inside staterooms. These new and larger staterooms were approximately the same size as the deluxe B-Deck staterooms which had been located between the two First-Class stairways on *Titanic*. One of the few problems that *Olympic* had, which became more pressing in later years, was that she was built at a time before private bath rooms became the expected standard by many passengers. In contrast, passengers of the Edwardian era were not concerned about the lack of private baths, even in First Class. This form of cabin upgrade would continue into the 1930s, with subsequent refits adding private baths at the expense of reducing the total number of passenger accommodations. By the time *Olympic* re-entered service in 1929 two-thirds of First-Class passengers had their own bath rooms, and even some Tourist-Third cabins had private baths.

With the reduction in passenger numbers also came a change to the First-Class Dining Saloon. The central area amidships, where once there had been a great oval table, was covered over in parquet and converted into a dance floor, and a podium for an orchestra was added at the forward end of the room. This was one of the few instances where an orchestra played for dancing between courses and after one's meal. Prior to this, dancing had been restricted to the Reception Room outside.

Another minor but no doubt confusing change to *Olympic* during this refit was that her decks were renamed. Previously, the Promenade and A Deck had been one and the same. Now, the Promenade Deck would be known only by that name. The former B Deck was renamed A Deck, C Deck was renamed B Deck, and so on down in a corresponding manner.

Captain Parker was in command of *Olympic* when, on 18 November 1929, a most peculiar event happened. While the ship was at latitude 42°, 12' North, longitude 56°, 56' West, a sudden tremor was experienced that lasted for about 2 minutes. Parker was in the Chart Room when it happened. Stepping onto the Bridge, the watch officer advised him that there had been no collision. The possibility of a thrown propeller was out of the question as the engines were running smoothly and there was no sign of a wreck in their wake. Except for a short loss of power in the Mail Room, the ship was just fine. Captain Parker suspected an underwater earthquake; this was confirmed when messages started coming in. The 1929 Grand Banks earthquake had resulted in a massive underwater landslide that severed many transatlantic telegraphic cables. The earthquake happened 2½ miles below *Olympic*'s position on the sea, not affecting her otherwise, and she arrived safely at New York. At the end of the next voyage, Parker and Chief Engineer J.H. Thearle both retired. Thearle had been with *Olympic* since she entered service in 1911. Following Parker's retirement *Olympic* would see yet another commander in Captain E.R. White, again from the *Adriatic*.

Olympic's new dance floor in the centre of the First-Class Dining Saloon.

Just as the Great Depression was taking its toll on the worldwide economy and the shipping industry, age was taking its toll on *Olympic* in small ways. In 1929 the new stern frame was showing signs of pitting caused by an undetermined electrochemical reaction, and the special cement applied to reinforce the pitted areas proved ineffective. In 1930 the stern frame was showing increasing signs of pitting, so Harland & Wolff applied a white metal sheath over the affected area and this appeared to stop the problem.

In 1931, an unspecified inspection revealed that the cracks discovered in 1927 in the B Deck portholes were getting worse.[11] This was brought on by a winter of horrific weather earlier in the year. Completely replacing shell plating on a ship *Olympic's* age was not economically feasible however. The White Star Line compromised by using extensive welding combined with the placement of doublers[12] to reinforce the fractured areas. By this point the British Board of Trade was concerned that the repairs would not last permanently, and consequently would only issue a certificate of seaworthiness for six months. The repairs were checked again at the end of this period and were found to be in perfect condition by the surveyors, so a certificate was given for an additional six months. When the hull was inspected again the next year, the repairs were found to still be holding, and *Olympic* was given the full twelve-month certificate of clearance.

In October, 1931, Second Class and Tourist-Third Cabin merged to form Tourist Class alongside First and Third Class. *Olympic* was back to being a three-class ship, although Third Class had slightly fewer cabins than when the ship was new owing to the best of those now being included in Tourist Class and some Third-Class cabins being converted to crew accommodations.

In 1932 *Olympic* steamed over 70,000 miles at an average speed of 21.8 knots. On 14 October 1932, she returned to Southampton for a routine engine adjustment and to perform some unforeseen repairs. Cracks had been found in the engine bedplates and part of the crankshaft. When the engines were raised to service the bedplates, it was noticed that the double bottom was in generally good condition apart from a few loose rivets. The most significant deficiency noted was with the riveting of the thrust blocks, which was rectified at this time.

On 1 March 1933, *Olympic* returned to service after 12 hours of sea trials, looking like new. The Chief Engineer was very impressed at how the engines and thrust blocks showed little sign of movement for the first time in months. On the passenger decks, in an attempt to modernise her, much of her beautiful wood panelling had been painted forest green, with its carved detailing picked out in gilt. *Olympic's* owners had enough sense, however, to leave the oak and mahogany untouched in the First-Class Lounge and Smoking Room.

On the management side, Lord Kylsant was buying up other lines that were stricken by the Depression, borrowing money to the point that he compromised his own investments. He became far too confident in acquiring these lines to expand his shipping empire. Kylsant also had control of Harland & Wolff when he placed an order for the new *Oceanic*, a 60,000-ton liner intended to be added to the White Star Line. The *Oceanic* would never be completed, because by the autumn of 1929 Kylsant's empire was already starting to collapse financially. Work on *Oceanic* was said to have been suspended because of problems with the new type of propelling machinery employed (turbo-electric technology) but in reality the problem was that Kylsant simply could not come up with the funds. Kylsant was still having difficulty paying back the British government loans that had been granted to expand the Royal Mail fleet in the early 1920s, and his financial troubles were finally catching up with him. The future of the White Star Line was tied to Kylsant's financial solvency, and its days were numbered.

In September 1931, Lord Kylsant was charged and imprisoned for publishing misleading statements in the 1928 Royal Mail prospectus. The death knell for the White Star Line was when the Australian government refused to extend the company's payments on the Commonwealth Line. This resulted in a loss of nearly £1,500,000 to the White Star Line. In a last attempt to save what was left of White Star, one of the managers, Colonel Frank Bustard, approached none other than J. Bruce Ismay in an attempt to put together some form of a bailout. He did not succeed, and in 1933 the White Star Line listed another yearly loss. It was too late. The Treasury stepped in.

Meanwhile, the drop in business in the North Atlantic steamship trade was also being felt by Cunard, the White Star Line's historic rival. The British government

Olympic in 1933, looking like new.

agreed to provide a loan to ensure the company's financial solvency, but only if Cunard agreed to merge with its rival. After both agreed, the government would release an amount of up to £9 million to support the new company. On 30 December 1933, the board members of both companies met to outline the terms of the merger and on 10 May 1934, the Cunard–White Star Line was officially registered. The White Star Line would contribute about ten ships to the new company, but before the end of the year the consolidation of assets would result in the *Adriatic, Albertic* and *Calgaric* being sold for scrap, leaving *Olympic's* future in question.

Before the new company was even a week old, *Olympic* experienced yet another collision that would recall some of the bad luck she had experienced with the *Hawke* in 1911. On 15 May, *Olympic* was bound for New York under the command of an exhausted Captain John Binks, who was suffering from lack of sleep. At 10.50a.m. the ship was nearing the Nantucket lightship in heavy fog. *Olympic's* radio operator was having a hard time keeping in touch with the directional beacon of the lightship, when at 10.56a.m. the signal abruptly ceased. The crew on *Olympic's* Bridge heard the lightship's foghorn but could not determine her bearing. The only thing they knew, on the basis of the strength of the last radio signal, was that *Olympic* was within 30 miles of the lightship. Tragically, she was much closer than that. At 11.06a.m. the red hull of the lightship appeared out of the fog directly in *Olympic's* path. Binks ordered 'Full Astern', but it was too late. The hull of the huge liner cleaved the lightship in two.

Damage caused to *Olympic*'s bow from the collision with the Nantucket lightship.

Binks later stated that *Olympic* was not making more than 3 or 4 knots, but the mass of the huge liner was no match for the much smaller vessel regardless of her speed.

Having come to a stop, *Olympic* lowered a number of her lifeboats to look for survivors. The boats returned with three bodies and four survivors of the lightship's original eleven-man crew. By 12.29p.m., looking for the remaining crew proved to be fruitless and *Olympic* continued on to New York.

On 17 May an inquiry into the accident opened in the New York Customs House. Captain Binks found himself in the hot seat, much like what Captain Smith would have faced had he survived the sinking of his own ship. The inquiry determined that it was not uncommon for liners to pass within a close proximity of the lightship at high speeds; in fact, two close calls had happened the night before. In response to this, the captain of the lightship had ordered his crew to wear their life jackets and swing the emergency boats out. Another point made during the inquiry was the inability of the liner's radio operators to identify the Cape Cod and Pollock Rip lightships from their radio signals because of a code change. The *Olympic*'s radio operator had lost contact with the Nantucket lightship, but not because of a failure in *Olympic*'s radio system; he had been able to receive the transmissions of other beacons. As with the *Hawke* incident, Cunard–White Star once again had to take responsibility for an acci-

Rescued crewmen of the lightship (right to left): Roberts, Perry, Marshall.

Captain Binks with the wounded captain of the lightship.

dent involving *Olympic*; however, it won an appeal against the judgment of $500,000 in claimed damages, reducing the amount to $325,000 by 1936.

Olympic's arrival at New York on 5 June marked the last time that she would berth at the old White Star Pier 59. From that point on she docked five blocks south, at Cunard's Pier 54. Sadly, the end of her career was less than a year away, because liners of her age were no longer needed on the Atlantic run. When *Olympic* struck the Nantucket lightship, she was only carrying about 200 passengers. By this time many of the big liners had been reduced to making weekend cruises because the Depression had resulted in a sharp drop in transatlantic bookings.

In January 1935 *Olympic* sailed for one more spring season. Her days were finally numbered. On 27 March, she left Southampton for New York for the last time. The honour of commanding her on her final voyage went to Captain Reginald Peel. On 12 April she arrived at Southampton to end her career. Interestingly, aboard as one of the crew was Frederick Fleet, who had been a lookout on *Titanic* twenty-three years earlier.

For the next six months *Olympic* was tied up and abandoned at Berth 108, located at Southampton's new Western Docks. For a time there were rumours that she would be used by the British Admiralty or sold to the Italian government as a troopship. These rumours were dispelled when, in September 1935, she was sold for £97,500 to Sir John Jarvis, who in turn sold her to Thomas Ward & Sons, a ship-breaking firm in Jarrow in the north-east of England. The move was nothing more than a gesture by Sir John, a member of parliament, to provide employment for his constituents.

Perhaps the saddest moment in Old Reliable's history occurred at 4.12p.m. on 11 October 1935, when, under the command of Captain P.R. Vaughan, she sailed past

Mauretania and *Olympic* at Southampton's Western Docks.

Olympic's Promenade Deck.

the Ocean Dock where the *Homeric* and *Majestic* were moored. *Olympic's* house flag was dipped, and the whistles blew one last salute as she was given an honorary escort down Southampton Water by speedboats owned by Mr Hubert Scott Paine.

After a two-day journey, *Olympic* arrived at Jarrow, where she awaited the tide to make her way up the Tyne River to the breakers. There was a large reception for *Olympic* on her arrival, with tugs and boats all responding to her whistles, which consisted of three long blasts – the liner's traditional signal of thanks and farewell. By 3.00p.m. *Olympic* had arrived at Palmers Yard where she would be broken up. At 5.00p.m. Captain Vaughan rang down to the Engine Room for the final time the order 'Finished with Engines'.

In the weeks before the final dismantling began, there was an auction of many of the ship's salvageable fittings, comprising a list of some 4,456 lots. The auction company called in to do the work on Tuesday 5 November was the London firm of Knight, Frank & Rutley. Among the fittings that were auctioned and sold to many private parties and hotels were chairs, light fixtures, sconces, doors, windows, wooden panelling and many other articles, some of which still exist today.

The final dismantling took nearly two years to complete. On 19 September 1937, the remaining hulk of the hull was towed to Inverkeithing, Scotland, for final scrapping.

Another view of *Olympic* at Southampton's Western Dock.

Perhaps *Olympic*'s end also brought about the end of one of the men who conceived her: J. Bruce Ismay. On 17 October 1937, Ismay – who had lived life as a recluse after surviving *Titanic*'s sinking – died after suffering a stroke. The Last Grand Lady would be gone forever, but not forgotten. She touched many people, not least of whom were the mariners who had served aboard her. Perhaps the most heartfelt tribute was voiced by Captain Sir Bertram Fox Hayes, the man who commanded her from 1915 to 1921. In his memoirs, Hayes wrote that *Olympic* was 'the finest ship in my estimation that has ever been built or ever will be.'

Olympic's final journey from Southampton:

Her whistles blow farewell.

Her funnel billowing smoke.

Reliable to the end.

Olympic arrives at Jarrow.

Olympic's whistles sound for the last time.

Olympic's woodwork displayed for auction in 1991. (*From the catalogue sold by the auctioneers, Anderson & Garland / Authors' Collection*)

A stern view of *Olympic's* hull at the breakers.

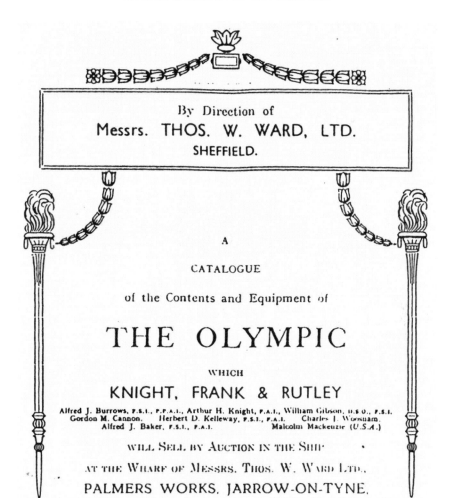

By Direction of
Messrs. THOS. W. WARD, LTD.
SHEFFIELD.

A

CATALOGUE

of the Contents and Equipment of

THE OLYMPIC

WHICH

KNIGHT, FRANK & RUTLEY

Alfred J. Burrows, F.S.I., F.F.A.I., Arthur H. Knight, F.A.I., William Gibson, D.S.O., F.S.I.
Gordon M. Cannon.   Herbert D. Kelleway, F.S.I., F.A.I.   Charles J. Worsnam.
Alfred J. Baker, F.S.I., F.A.I.   Malcolm Mackeuzie (U.S.A.)

WILL SELL BY AUCTION IN THE SHIP

AT THE WHARF OF MESSRS. THOS. W. WARD LTD.,

PALMERS WORKS, JARROW-ON-TYNE.

On TUESDAY, NOVEMBER 5th to FRIDAY, NOVEMBER 8th,
MONDAY, NOVEMBER 11th to FRIDAY, NOVEMBER, 15th,
and MONDAY, NOVEMBER 18th, 1935.

AT ELEVEN O'CLOCK PRECISELY EACH DAY.

Private View (admission by Catalogue only, price 5 - each) on
Thursday, October 31st, from 10 to 5 o'clock.

Public View (admission by Catalogue only, price 2/6 each) on
Friday, Saturday and Monday, November 1st, 2nd and 4th, from
10 to 5 p.m.

Catalogues from the Auctioneers, at their Offices.

20, HANOVER SQUARE, LONDON, W.1

Telephone: Mayfair 3771 (ten lines)   ALSO AT
Telegrams: Galleries, Weedo, London   41, Bank Street, Ashford, Kent

Printed by H. Davy, Manfield House, Strand, W.C.2, England.

Olympic – The Ship Magnificent.

HIS MAJESTY'S HOSPITAL SHIP *BRITANNIC*

When Lord Pirrie and J. Bruce Ismay initially discussed the design for their new class of liners, they originally planned for two (*Olympic* and *Titanic*) to be built immediately, with the third to follow at a later date. On 20 June 1911, before *Olympic* arrived in New York City on her maiden voyage, the order for the third ship was placed. The keel was laid for yard number 433 on 30 November 1911, in slip No. 2, the original construction berth of her eldest sister *Olympic*.

Progress on the hull slowed dramatically after the sinking of *Titanic* on 15 April 1912, as White Star awaited the outcome of two government inquiries into the disaster. The White Star Line had originally intended the new ship to be in service by the end of 1913, but due to the retrofitting of a second 'inner skin' after the inquiries, it would take longer than that.

Following the tragic loss of *Titanic*, White Star named their newest liner *Britannic*. Though hotly denied by J. Bruce Ismay that there ever was any intention to name this ship *Gigantic*, an ex-employee of Harland & Wolff made that claim years later. Regardless, after the *Titanic* disaster, the White Star Line immediately returned to their former policy of using names associated with geographical locations and historical periods. Names that even hinted at a ship's strength or invulnerability to the forces of nature were immediately discarded. Instead, the name *Britannic* was chosen to evoke nationalism and pride in Great Britain and also in memory of to a beloved White Star ship that had served earlier in the company's history.

Like her infamous sister *Titanic*, *Britannic* would never complete a commercial voyage. In fact, *Britannic* would never even make it into company service. She was requisitioned by the British Admiralty as a hospital ship and served in this capacity during the First World War, striking a mine in the Kea Channel off the coast of

Builder's model of the *Britannic* at Harland & Wolff.

Greece and sinking before she was even a year old. It is an ironic twist of fate that *Britannic* would rest forever in Greek waters.

On 26 February 1914, at 11.15a.m., twenty-seven months after her keel was laid, *Britannic* left her construction berth and slid down the ways. In a light drizzle, the massive hull took 81 seconds to launch, achieving a speed of 9½ knots, accompanied by sirens and cheering from the large crowd in attendance. Dignitaries attending the event included Lord and Lady Pirrie; Harold Sanderson, who had replaced J. Bruce Ismay as chairman of the White Star Line; and Captain Charles Bartlett, the White Star Line's Marine Superintendent at Belfast. Financier J.P. Morgan, whose empire had played a major part in the creation of the *Olympic*-class ships, was not present as he had passed away in Rome nearly a year before.

At the time of *Britannic*'s launch she was the largest British-built liner in terms of gross registered tonnage, and would remain so until the launch of the *Queen Mary* some twenty years later. *Britannic* had an overall length of 882ft 9in and a moulded breadth of 93ft 6in or 94ft extreme when measured to the outside of the shell plates. This represented an 18in increase in beam over that of her sisters.

By early on 14 February, *Britannic* was almost ready for launch. She was constructed in the same slip that gave birth to *Titanic*. In the No.3 slip off to the side sits Harland & Wolff yard No. 436, Holland–America Line's *Statendam*.

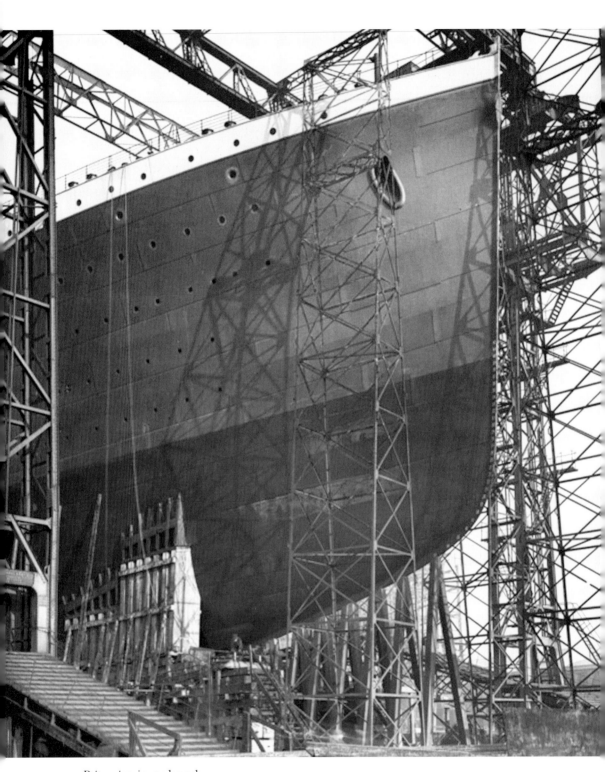

Britannic prior to launch.

Britannic's main competitors would be the HAPAG and Cunard Line ships. This is most likely the reason for the many exaggerations of *Britannic*'s length and beam. It appears that someone at the White Star Line did not want the actual measurement of 882ft 9in revealed to the general public too early. Even the much-admired *Shipbuilder* magazine had *Britannic*'s length overall listed as 'about 900 feet'. With the new *Aquitania* planned at 'about 900 feet', it is no mystery as to why the actual numbers had been 'adjusted' over time. However, builder's plans of *Britannic* that still exist show the same number of construction frames as her older sisters and the scale drawings indicate an identical length of 882ft 9in.

Britannic would have a displacement of over 53,000 tons at a maximum load draught of 34ft 7in. Her gross tonnage of 48,158 would be 1,830 tons larger than *Titanic*'s and her wider beam would add greater stability. She had accommodations for 2,579 passengers and a crew of 950. As with her sisters, there was no attempt to make *Britannic* an ocean-going greyhound. She would have a service speed of 21.5 knots in all weather, half a knot faster than the other two *Olympic*-class liners.

It is frequently and incorrectly stated that *Britannic*'s beam was widened amidships as the result of the inner skin added after *Titanic*'s loss. Records available from Harland & Wolff contradict this, showing that the decision to widen *Britannic* was made by October of 1911, well before *Titanic* met her fate. The void between the inner and outer shell plating was 3–4ft deep on both sides, so an increase of 18in to her beam would do nothing to accommodate the lost space caused by the inner skin. The added weight on the upper decks of *Britannic* and the experiences with *Olympic* made this increase in beam a necessity.

Each successive liner launched at Harland & Wolff represented a distinct advance over the preceding ship. In *Britannic*'s case her size was not materially increased, but her passenger provisions would be improved over those of *Olympic* and *Titanic*. The public was pleased with *Olympic* and her popularity continued even after *Titanic*'s loss, as the White Star Line had a keen grasp of what its passengers wanted in way of comfort and luxury.

Externally, her wartime hospital ship markings aside, *Britannic* can be readily identified by her huge unsightly lifeboat davits on her upper decks. It is almost certain that prior to 15 April 1912, *Britannic* was originally designed to be a nearly identical running mate to *Olympic* and *Titanic*. With no requirements of 'lifeboats for all' prior to *Titanic*'s sinking, *Britannic* would have emerged as a slightly refined version of *Titanic* had that ship survived. Certainly the internal arrangements of the hull would have been much the same. However, after the sinking of *Titanic* there were some improvements made for safety purposes. Along the hull, the 'inner skin' that had been retrofitted to *Olympic* was built into *Britannic* from the start. It encompassed the machinery spaces and the boiler rooms, and extended about 3½ft above F Deck. The inner skin as fitted to *Britannic* was claimed to be superior to the arrangement used in the Cunard ships, which relied for their watertight integrity on longitudinal

Britannic at the Fitting Out Wharf.

coal bunkers located along both sides of the hull. The theory behind this design was that any flooding caused by a breach in the hull would be confined to the space within the bunkers. However, Harland & Wolff felt that the concept of coal bunkers acting as inner skins was flawed, as the possibility of an open door in the bunkers would permit water to enter unchecked in the event of a failure of the shell plating. Additionally, it was felt that one or more bunkers filled with water as well as coal would cause an excessive list that would make the lowering of lifeboats on the high side of the ship very difficult.[1] However, Harland & Wolff's inner skin design was not without its drawbacks either, the main one being that it could not be accessed, and, if unknowingly flooded as was the case with *Olympic* during the First World War, corrosion could occur within the cellular spaces. Harland & Wolff did not consider this any great risk, however, as it considered that these spaces might be used for the storage of fuel oil in the future.

In areas where extra stress on the hull was normally expected, not only were areas of doubled plating used (such as on the upper strake of plating along B Deck) but

Harland & Wolff also quadruple riveted those areas that were triple riveted on the earlier two sisters. In addition, *Britannic* would benefit from the addition of an extra transverse watertight bulkhead. She would have sixteen transverse watertight bulkheads against her sisters' fifteen, creating seventeen watertight compartments instead of the original sixteen that were planned. Five of these bulkheads extended 40ft above the deepest load waterline to B Deck, while the other eleven extended over 21ft above the waterline to E Deck. These improvements would give *Britannic* the ability to stay afloat with a six-compartment standard instead of the four-compartment standard enjoyed by the other two ships of the class. In addition, there would be an indicator on the Navigating Bridge to show whether the watertight doors were open or closed; this feature would also be fitted to *Olympic* in 1913.

The propelling machinery and engines would be much the same as fitted on *Olympic* and *Titanic*. The two reciprocating engines generated 32,000 horsepower at their normal service speed. However, a notable difference in *Britannic* was that her centre turbine was larger than the ones used on the earlier ships. Built entirely by Harland & Wolff in the Belfast shops, *Britannic*'s turbine engine could generate 18,000 shaft horsepower against *Olympic* and *Titanic*'s 16,000. Weighing about 500 tons, *Britannic*'s exhaust steam turbine was the largest on any liner in the world. As on her sister ships, this turbine operated in the ahead direction only and at speeds of half ahead and above, characteristics common to all exhaust turbines.

Her designers intended that *Britannic* would have upgrades to all classes of accommodation. At this time in history private bath room facilities were becoming popular in ocean liners. Accordingly, a large number of *Britannic*'s First-Class staterooms were single-berth rooms with a water closet and either a bath or shower. Many of the double-berth rooms were also similarly equipped, and *Britannic* would have over four times the number of private bath facilities that *Olympic* did in 1911.

On the Boat Deck, there would be a children's playroom and the customary First-Class Gymnasium, both with 9½ft ceilings. Also to be added – a first for any ocean liner – would be a ladies' hairdressing salon. The dog kennel would be located abaft the fourth funnel on the Boat Deck as opposed to the past practice of placing the kennels below deck. The Promenade Deck would be like *Titanic*'s in that there would be windows fitted to protect strolling passengers from ocean spray while allowing for an unobstructed view of the open sea. Also included would be the same Smoking Room, Lounge and Verandah Cafés in First Class, as well as an *à la carte* Restaurant and Restaurant Reception Room, both of which would span the entire width of the ship at the cost of eliminating the Café Parisien.

On *Titanic*, most of the former B Deck enclosed promenade space had been converted into deluxe First-Class staterooms except for the aftermost sections that were used to expand the *à la carte* Restaurant and add the Café Parisien. On *Britannic*, B Deck would be configured closer to *Olympic*'s original arrangement. The B Deck promenade would be partially retained, to run from the forward end of the deck to the forward First-Class entrance. The Private Promenade suites would be retained, but the one on the starboard side would have the length of its promenade reduced from 50ft to 25ft; the promenade would be renamed a 'verandah'. This new floor plan created more spacious sitting rooms which were furnished with a dining table with chairs and four armchairs. Instead of the usual wicker furniture, the verandah was furnished with three settees and tables, two armchairs and two round-back chairs. The port side private promenade would remain at 50ft in length, being essentially unchanged from its counterpart on *Titanic*. Two additional parlour suites would be added on C Deck.

For added elegance, the forward Grand Staircase was to be fitted with a huge Aeolian organ complete with storage chests for music rolls. For convenience, the three First-Class electric elevators located here would travel up to the Boat Deck and a fourth elevator would be added near the after First-Class Grand Staircase. As with *Olympic* and *Titanic*, the Turkish Baths, Squash Court, Swimming Bath and the First-Class Dining Saloon would also grace *Britannic*.

In Second Class, accommodations would be the same as on *Britannic's* sister ships, with the addition of a Second-Class Gymnasium. The Third-Class accommodations would also be much the same, save for an increase in stairways and drinking fountains, and an external feature that would make *Britannic* visually different from her two sisters: enclosed well decks that would double as Third-Class promenades. When examining photos of *Britannic*, one cannot miss the covered well decks with the cargo-loading apparatus mounted on top of the roofs over these areas. At the stern of the ship, the Third-Class Smoking Room was relocated to the area above the Third-Class General Room, and this changed the appearance of the Poop Deck.

A new sanitation feature, quite likely introduced for the first time in a seagoing vessel, ended the age-old practice of discharging waste from lavatories and sinks via numerous waste pipes located along the hull just above the load waterline on each side of the ship. Instead, waste water was collected in tanks in much the same manner as in a municipal sewage system. When the level in these tanks neared capacity, a float switch activated pumps that discharged the contents into the ocean beneath the waterline.

In the Marconi Operating Room, a notable addition was the installation of a pneumatic tube to transport messages directly to the Navigating Bridge. The room was also soundproofed against external noise; the noise from the steam venting from the exhaust pipes on the funnels during *Titanic's* sinking had made it difficult for the wireless operators to hear incoming messages through their headphones.

In her electrical system, *Britannic* had a separate Accumulator Room above the waterline. In this room were not only a mass of emergency batteries, but also two electric generators used to charge the batteries while under load. They could also power the emergency circuit and would power the electric service of the ship while in port.

With the increase in lifeboats mandated by the new British Board of Trade requirements, *Britannic* would not simply have them added to the Boat Deck as on *Olympic*.

Instead, *Britannic* was to be fitted with huge Harland & Wolff-built gantry-style davits that flanked the Nos. 1, 3 and 4 funnels, and were also located aft on top of a newly designed Shade Deck built over the existing Poop Deck. These electric davits were fitted with electric lights to illuminate the surrounding deck space and were designed to lower their lifeboats to the water even if the ship were to take on a heavy list. The wire ropes for the falls at each end of each davit were wound on drums attached to the same shaft so that the lifeboats would descend evenly, but the drums could also be worked independently if needed. The ship was designed to carry forty-four 34ft lifeboats, two 26ft cutters and two motorised (gasoline-powered) cutters, each with its own Marconi apparatus.

Britannic's expected completion date of September 1914 was pushed back for numerous reasons, not least of which was a series of almost continuous labour disputes and strikes. Eventually it was announced that the ship would not be completed until the spring of 1915. This latest delay was not due to any strike activity, but because Harland & Wolff was at full capacity completing other contracts, unlike when *Olympic* was under construction. Then the final fitting out was interrupted by the outbreak of war. Without government contracts, Harland & Wolff found it difficult to acquire the materials needed to complete its ships and work slowed. Soon Harland & Wolff found itself laying off some 6,000 workers, most of whom promptly enlisted into the service. *Britannic* would enter the graving dock in September for the fitting of her propellers, but would then sit until November of 1915. At about this time Harland & Wolff did receive work from the government; when the need to augment the Grand Fleet became apparent, it received several large contracts centred on converting small merchant ships into dummy warships. This ruse, attempted at the beginning of the war, was intended to confuse the enemy as to the number of ships that were actually in the fleet. Harland & Wolff would mount phony gun turrets and towers made from wood and canvas on these decoy ships. However, Harland & Wolff now had to complete their pre-war contracts and their government contracts with a shortage of employees at hand.

Olympic was laid up after her last voyage from New York, arriving in Belfast on 3 November 1914. It was at this time that Harland & Wolff's photographer captured an image of the two sister ships moored together side by side. In the picture on page 272, the funnels of *Olympic* can be seen in the background behind the silent and incomplete *Britannic*. The two ships would remain together for ten months.

In May of 1915 Harland & Wolff informed Harold Sanderson, chairman of the White Star Line, that *Britannic* had passed her basin trials, when they turned over the engines while moored securely in the water-filled graving dock, and that *Britannic* could be ready for war service, if needed, in ten to twelve weeks. Her fate would ultimately rest on the British evacuation of Gallipoli and the huge numbers of casualties from the Dardanelles campaign. She would become a hospital ship. Liners had previously been used as such, but had proved entirely inadequate without the specialised arrangements that were needed to carry and care for wounded men. The White Star

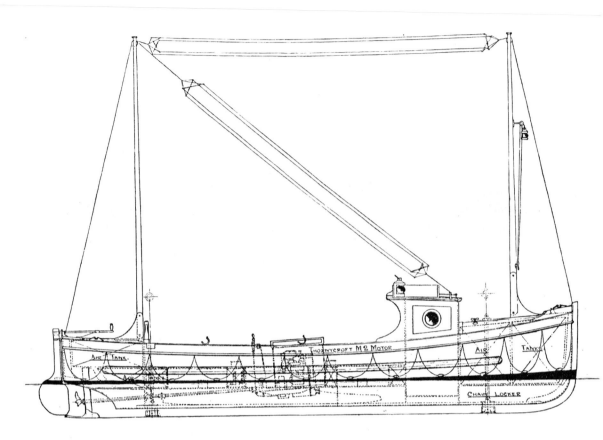

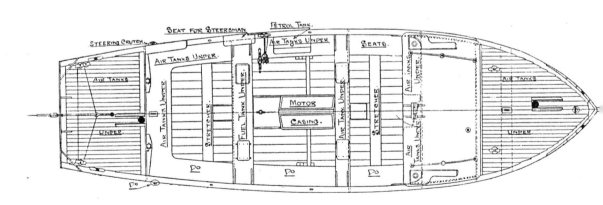

Plan of a motor lifeboat similar to that fitted on *Britannic*. At 34ft x 10ft x 4ft, these were 4ft longer than the original wooden lifeboats fitted to *Olympic* and *Titanic*.

A model of *Britannic*'s davits.

Line would charter *Britannic* to the Admiralty for approximately £24,000 a month with the Admiralty fully insuring the vessel. Unlike negotiations regarding *Olympic*, there was no need to determine depreciation of *Britannic* as she was, for all intents and purposes, new.

Britannic in the foreground with *Olympic's* funnels in the background.

Work on *Britannic* resumed at a feverish pace. Many of the luxury fittings already installed were removed and stored. The still-incomplete interiors were now converted to accommodate wounded soldiers and hospital staff. The First-Class Lounge, Smoking Room, Reading and Writing Room, Gymnasium, Children's Playroom and Restaurant were converted to medical wards. The First-Class Dining Saloon and adjoining Reception Room on D Deck, both with unobstructed access to the main staircase and elevators leading to the Boat Deck, were eminently suitable for the operating theatres and main ward. The enclosed promenades were fitted with cots and hammocks. Staterooms and cabins were converted into berths for hospital personnel. When all the work was completed, *Britannic* had the capacity to carry 3,309 wounded.

Because *Britannic* had been incomplete when she was rushed into conversion to a hospital ship, some of the intended accommodations and features were never installed. Among these were the gantry davits intended for the Shade Deck structure on the Poop Deck and the davits intended for the forward end of the Boat Deck on the port side of the No. 1 funnel. Instead, twelve standard Welin davits would be placed along the open spaces on the Boat Deck amidships with their corresponding fourteen lifeboats and collapsibles below. Further aft, two davit sets were installed on the Poop Deck in the locations where the gantry davits were originally intended to be fitted. The total complement of lifeboats came to fifty-five. There were supplemental stacks of wooden Carley floats[2] stacked on the Boat Deck along with numerous boxes containing life preservers.

The ship was painted in the standard Red Cross colours mandated by the Geneva Convention. The hull was painted white with a green horizontal band 1.5m (almost 5ft) wide on both sides parallel to the waterline. At three intervals on each side the green band was interrupted by huge red crosses. Her funnels were painted a golden yellow and green lights were fitted along the Promenade Deck to identify the vessel as a hospital ship at night. An illuminated red cross was hung between the Nos. 1 and 2 funnels and two large red crosses were mounted on the bulwarks on both sides of the Boat Deck, each illuminated by 125 electric light bulbs. However, the cross mounted on the starboard side bulwark interfered with navigation on some hospital ships at night as its glow overpowered the starboard (green) running lamp on that side. The solution was a switch installed on the bridge enabling the Bridge Officer to turn the cross off at the approach of another vessel.

Britannic left Belfast on 11 December 1915 with the assistance of five tugs. The voyage would include sea trials and war service preparations under the command of Captain J.B. Ranson. She would return from sea trials only long enough to disembark some Engine Room officers. Due to the many delays interrupting her construction, *Britannic* had taken a year and a half longer than *Olympic* to complete, accumulating nearly four years from keel laying to entry into service.

Britannic arrived in Liverpool under armed escort on 12 December 1915 as the HMHS *Britannic*. Her classification as one of His Majesty's Hospital Ships would afford her immunity from enemy attack. She was ready to accommodate a medical staff of 52 officers, 101 nurses, 336 orderlies plus a crew of 675. There were 2,034 berths and 1,035 cots to transport injured soldiers. The medical staff on board was rotated after each voyage so that the ship's staff could accompany their assigned patients back on shore. The onshore personnel would then rotate to the ship. An exception was the matron (head nurse), Miss Elizabeth Ann Dowse. Dowse, a veteran of the Boer War, would not rotate off the ship and would oversee the Voluntary Aid Detachment (VAD) nurses who cared for the wounded.

On 14 December 1915, Captain Charles A. Bartlett took command. He had been chosen by the White Star Line because Captain Haddock could not be released from his assigned duties with the Admiralty. Bartlett, with White Star since 1894 and at one time commander of the *Cedric*, had been the company's Marine Superintendent at Belfast and had been present during *Britannic*'s construction and launch.

Britannic left on her first voyage on 23 December 1915, bound for the Mediterranean in the Dardanelles service but stopping first at Naples to take on coal and water. It would be at Mudros, off the island of Lemnos, that she would serve with the *Mauretania*, *Aquitania* and her sister ship *Olympic*. Too large to dock, the ships anchored off the coast and embarked the sick and wounded from the military hospital on Mudros via smaller ships based at the port. Two days out of England the Christmas holiday was celebrated on board. On 29 December, her coaling completed, *Britannic* departed for Mudros where she would usher in the New Year and take some 3,300 wounded on board.

Aboard ship, staff and patients alike were required to follow the schedule and regulations set forth by the Admiralty. Ambulatory patients were issued hospital suits

His Majesty's Hospital Ship *Britannic*.

consisting of blue trousers and jackets with brown facings. No patients were allowed on deck unless wearing these clothes to prevent the enemy from seeing a large number of men on deck in service uniforms and mistaking the ship for an armed troop transport. At 6.00a.m. patients were awakened so that the wards and passageways could be thoroughly cleaned. The patients were served breakfast between 7.30 and 8.00a.m. after which the tables, benches and water closets were cleaned prior to Captain Bartlett and Chief Medical Officer Colonel Henry Anderson making their rounds at 11.00a.m. Lunch was served at 12.30p.m., after which the medical areas were cleaned and disinfected. Tea was served at 4.30p.m. and patients who were officers could receive a ration of wine or spirits if their medical condition allowed.

The patients were put to bed at 8.30p.m., half an hour before an officer would make the final rounds. Patients' diets were regulated in accordance with the injury or sickness. The Chief Medical Officer would provide Chief Purser Claude Lancaster with a list of the meal requirements needed for the following day and the chef was then responsible for fulfilling them.

Britannic returned to Southampton with her first load of wounded on 9 January 1916. As with all hospital ships, upon approach to Southampton she advised authorities of the numbers of dysentery and enteric cases on board so that appropriate preparations and routing destinations could be made for the trains awaiting their arrival for transportation of the wounded to London.

The second voyage would begin from Southampton shortly after noon on 20 January and would be much shorter than anticipated. After arrival in Naples on 25

January to take on wounded, Captain Bartlett signalled ahead to Mudros that *Britannic* would arrive around dawn on 28 January. Instead of just receiving an acknowledgement, Bartlett was ordered to remain at Naples to receive injured from five other ships en route from Mudros to Naples. *Britannic* took on 438 patients from the *Grantully Castle* and 393 from the *Formosa* on 28 January; 594 from the *Essequibo* on 1 February and 493 from the *Nevasa* on 2 February. The last ship to transfer patients would be the *Panama* with 319. After the final transfer of sick and injured on 4 February, *Britannic* returned to Southampton, arriving on 9 February.

The third voyage was uneventful. *Britannic* arrived at Naples to take on water and coal and departed for the port of Augusta on the nearby island of Sicily two days later to take on wounded. She returned to Southampton on 4 April 1916 to discharge her wounded. Upon leaving port, she anchored off the Isle of Wight for four weeks. With Gallipoli evacuated, the Admiralty no longer needed as many hospital ships. *Britannic* returned to Belfast on 18 May 1916, and was officially released from service on 6 June 1916. But less than a month later, on 1 July, British troops participated in an offensive on the Somme in France and on the first day alone suffered 20,000 fatalities and 40,000 casualties. Suddenly the need for hospital ships was again acute. On top of this, even after the evacuation of Gallipoli, the Allies had maintained a presence at Salonika in neutral Greece. When the troops in this area attempted to block German supplies from being brought into Turkey, it would result in a new offensive to begin in September of 1916. This, along with a two other battles with the Turkish Army, revived the need for hospital ships to once again service the medical evacuation port of Mudros.

Following *Britannic*'s arrival at Belfast, Harland & Wolff had began to refit her for commercial service. Pictures taken at that time show that some onboard apparatus was changed or updated after the first three voyages. With the large numbers of casualties now coming out of the Mediterranean however, her services were again required as a hospital ship. She was reinstated in service on 28 August with Captain Bartlett once again in command, and left Belfast for Southampton to be provisioned as a hospital ship. After provisions had been loaded, she anchored off Cowes while a new crew was assembled. *Britannic*'s fourth voyage began out of Southampton on 24 September 1916, with the usual stop at Naples before continuing on to Mudros. Having taken on wounded there, she returned to Southampton on 11 October.

Britannic's fifth voyage involved transporting a contingent of Royal Army Medical Corps personnel and stores to Egypt, Malta and Salonika. Departing on 20 October, *Britannic* arrived at Naples five days later. After arriving at Mudros on 28 October, she embarked wounded both from shore facilities and six other hospital ships. Unfortunately, the outbound transportation of personnel to other parts of the war theatre was an abuse of the hospital ships in the eyes of the Germans and was one reason later used to justify unrestricted submarine warfare against them.

This particular voyage of *Britannic* also resulted in an embarrassment for the Admiralty. While at Mudros, an Austrian invalid named Adalbert Messany was trans-

Another hospital ship, the SS *Panama*.

ferred aboard from the hospital ship *Wandilla*. Messany was a twenty-four-year-old opera singer and Austrian national captured in Egypt at the outset of the war. Messany was to be returned to England and then repatriated to Austria. While on board *Britannic* Messany witnessed the transfer of supplies and personnel to the *Wandilla* and observed onboard activities of the ship. Upon returning to Austria, Messany issued a statement that *Britannic* was carrying some 2,500 armed troops below deck and claimed twenty-two abuses by the Allies in the operation of the hospital ships. This information supposedly came from discussions with two officers on board named Harold Hickman and Reg Taplay who were returning to England with some of their injured troops. The British government vehemently denied Messany's claim, stating that there were no armed troops, nor had there ever been, on board *Britannic*, explaining that many of the men who were convalescing and ambulatory wore their uniforms instead of hospital dress.

On this particular voyage, the ship was carrying 3,022 wounded soldiers. After an investigation by the Admiralty, it was determined that Taplay was a private in the RAMC being transported to Southampton with a case of dysentery. Hickman was identified as a private in the Welsh Hussars being treated for malaria. Both Taplay and Hickman denied having any discussion with Messany on the matter. In addition, even if it were physically possible for *Britannic* to accommodate 2,500 armed troops, plus over 3,000 wounded, such an increase in passengers would hardly go unnoticed. It would have been impossible to maintain secrecy and would have left the hospital ship open for attack.[3]

At the end of October 1916, an event occurred that would eventually result in *Britannic*'s demise: the German submarine *U-73* commanded by Kapitänleutnant

Gustav Siess left Cuxhaven, Germany, with instructions to lay mines in the Mediterranean shipping lanes.

As *Britannic* arrived at Mudros on 28 October on her fifth voyage, she was unaware that enemy submarines were keeping close watch. The log of *U-73* reported that hospital ships had been sighted at 8.15p.m. on the evening of 27 October and again at 3.25a.m. on 28 October. Supposedly it was because he observed the hospital ships travelling along the same route that he decided to lay the mines in the Kea Channel off the coast of Greece, a passage regularly used by ships travelling between the Aegean Sea and the Mediterranean.

On the return leg of the fifth voyage, *Britannic* encountered heavy seas from a storm that severely damaged the hospital ship *Aquitania*. As a consequence, the *Aquitania* had to be laid up at Southampton for repairs and *Britannic* – which had just returned some 15,000 injured and sick soldiers to England – had to depart again for Mudros on 12 November 1916, after only four days in port. This would be her sixth and final voyage.

This sixth voyage differed from previous voyages as there was no medical staff or personnel to be transferred to other duty ships. With no passengers on board, Matron Elizabeth Dowse removed the ropes that cordoned off the decks so that the nurses could walk about the ship, play deck games and use the Swimming Bath. *Britannic* arrived at Naples on Friday 17 November, took on coal and water, and prepared to leave port. Weather conditions delayed her departure, and she sailed four days later under clearing skies, bound for Mudros. On the morning of 21 November *Britannic* entered the Kea Channel leading to the Aegean, less than a day out of Mudros. One of the passengers, Revd John Fleming, would write later that he was so overtaken by the beauty of the morning and the islands they were passing, that they didn't even notice the 8.00a.m. breakfast gong being sounded. It was shortly after the breakfast gong that an explosion was heard. Revd Fleming wrote: 'I was just leaving my cabin late for breakfast, when there was a great crash, as if a score of plate-glass windows had been smashed together; and the great ship shuddered for a moment from end to end.' Further aft, crewman Percy Tyler would state that he 'felt a violent bump which sent him forward a few paces then back again'. Some of the other men assumed that *Britannic* had hit another ship. To avoid a panic, Major Harold Priestly of the Medical Corps assumed control of the situation and advised everyone to return to their meal as the Captain had not sounded the alarm. After about 5 minutes a man ran in and instructed everyone to get their belts and head to the Boat Deck.

Britannic had struck one of the mines laid three and a half weeks earlier by *U-73* and was mortally wounded. The mine had exploded against her hull at nearly the same point that *Titanic* had struck the iceberg. The damage was near the bulkhead joining holds No. 2 and No. 3, approximately 150ft aft of the bow on the starboard side. It is believed that the doors at the after end of the Firemen's tunnel and the door between Boiler Room Nos. 5 and 6 were damaged and did not close, allowing water to run further aft. The bulkhead between the Nos. 1 and 2 holds was apparently also damaged. What ultimately sealed her fate however was the water that began pouring through all of the open portholes aft of Boiler Room No. 6 after the ship started listing. It was hot in the Mediterranean, and many of the sidelights were open for ventilation.

Unlike in peacetime, when all watertight doors were normally kept open, under wartime conditions all watertight doors were kept closed to protect against the very event that had just occurred. But during the change of watch every morning at 8.00a.m., it was standard procedure to open the watertight doors. It is ironic that *Britannic* would sustain damage at the precise moment she would be most vulnerable. She was designed to allow six watertight compartments to flood without foundering. If the explosion had happened just moments later, the doors would have been closed as per regulations and the flooding would have been contained.

In a desperate attempt to save his ship, Captain Bartlett turned towards land with the intent of beaching her. The emergency alarm sounded and distress signals were sent while the lifeboats were prepared. The nurses were advised to retrieve their belongings and report to their lifeboat stations. From her position on the Boat Deck, Matron Dowse recorded the name of each nurse as she passed by to her assigned lifeboat. Dowse refused to leave until all of her nurses were accounted for.

Because Captain Bartlett was attempting to beach the ship, he delayed issuing the final orders to lower the lifeboats all the way to the water. He would not give this order until it became apparent that the ship could not be saved and the propellers had stopped. During that delay, Fifth Officer G. Fielding allowed two of the port lifeboats to be lowered within 6ft of the water, but halted them at that height while he waited for the propellers to stop turning and the order to proceed.

As the ship sank by the head and the stern rose, the propeller on the port side was still turning as it broke the surface of the water. Two of the lifeboats, launched without direction, were drawn into the blades and capsized. These boats were heavily loaded and would be the only casualties resulting from the sinking.

One of the few to survive the violent destruction of these two lifeboats would be a VAD nurse named Violet Jessop. Jessop had not only survived *Titanic*'s sinking but had been aboard *Olympic* during the *Hawke* collision. This time she stopped to collect her toothbrush before she left her cabin: in recounting the sinking in her memoirs, she wrote that she had yearned for a toothbrush when she was aboard the *Carpathia* following *Titanic*'s sinking and was determined not to leave *Britannic* without it. In the capsizing of the lifeboats she sustained an injury to her head that she allowed to go untreated for many years. Years later, through X-rays, it was discovered that she had actually suffered a skull fracture. She would later blame this injury for losing her hair in old age.

One of the last to leave the ship was Captain Bartlett. Assured that no one else remained on board, he simply stepped into the water off the sinking ship. He had witnessed *Britannic* being born and now witnessed *Britannic* dying.

HMHS *Britannic*.

Britannic sank beneath the waves at 9.07a.m., leaving thirty-five lifeboats and hundreds of survivors scattered in the water. From sea trials to sinking, *Britannic* would live only 351 days – not quite one year. The 1,106 survivors included all the women on board (approximately seventy-six nurses and four stewardesses); thirty died in the sinking.

The final resting place of His Majesty's Hospital Ship *Britannic* is 5 miles from the area originally indicated on the Admiralty charts, off the island of Kea. *Britannic's* wreck was found on 3 December 1975 at a depth of 390ft by world-renowned oceanographer Jacques Cousteau after significant encouragement from the late William H. Tantum IV and Ed Kamuda of the *Titanic* Historical Society. Her bow is bent and twisted on the ocean floor as a result of her striking the bottom while the stern was still afloat. She lies on her starboard side, hiding the damage caused by the explosion, with her stem buried in the sediment. The government of Greece exercises control and protection over the wreck under laws protecting archaeological sites and no dives or artefact recoveries can be made without authorisation. *Britannic* has become a living reef, teeming with maritime life, and today her value for biological studies ranks equal to her importance as a historical shipwreck.

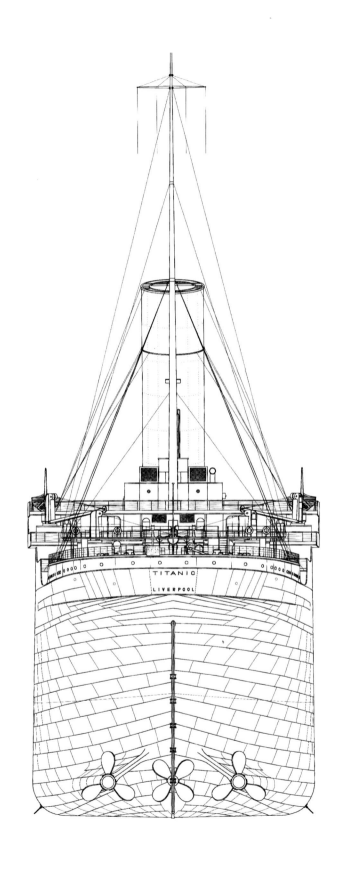

ENDNOTES

Chapter 1

1   Garzke, W., *et al.*, 'Titanic, the Anatomy of a Disaster: A Report From the Marine Forensic Panel' (SD-7), 1997.
2   British Board of Trade regulations specified lifeboat capacity in cubic feet, not number of persons.
3   Holmes, A. Campbell, *Practical Shipbuilding*, 1918, p. 374.

Chapter 2

1   *Olympic*'s hull was actually painted in a light grey while the upper strakes of plating were painted white. The colour is often described as white, and though it appears as such in the black and white photographs, a closer examination shows that the hull shade is a bit darker than the white of the sheer strakes.
2   A recent discovery in the British archives by researcher and historian Mark Chirnside has revealed that *Titanic*'s centre propeller may have had three blades.

Chapter 3

1   All courses are given in the form used in 1912, followed by the course in the form that would be used today.
2   The *Hawke* was an Edgar-class 'protected cruiser'. Unlike armoured cruisers, which were constructed with a belt of armoured plating around their sides, protected cruisers were designed with lighter armour (127/76mm in thickness) on their upper decks only. This was primarily to protect them from plunging shell fire of a calibre smaller than or equal to that of their own guns. These warships were designed more with an eye toward bombarding land-based fortifications than engaging in ship-to-ship combat. However, she did have a cement-reinforced ram bow built for the express purpose of sinking other ships. It also improved hydrodynamic efficiency by reducing turbulence about the hull, as the Royal Navy had known for several decades. For this reason the ram bow continued in warship design even though by the late 1800s its usefulness in sinking other ships was dubious.
3   It must be clearly understood that helm orders in 1911 were given in relation to the rudder head and not the rudder – in other words, opposite to the direction the ship's head would turn. Thus a

reference to putting the helm to port referred to turning the ship to starboard. In the port helm order referred to by Bowyer, he intended to swing the ship's head to starboard so that the stern of the ship would move away from the *Hawke*.

4   As in the previous reference, the helm orders given would have the effect of swinging the ship's head in the opposite direction referred to. Blunt, in this case, was ordering a hard turn to starboard.

5   Had the *Hawke's* speed been greater, she would have been found at fault, as an overtaking vessel has the duty to keep clear of the vessel being overtaken under the international 'Rules of the Road'.

6   'Hogging' describes the stress upon the hull of a vessel if a large wave were to pass under the centre of the vessel and leave the bow and stern less supported. 'Sagging' describes the stress resulting from the hull passing over a large wave trough such that the area of the hull amidships was less supported.

7   In 2005, an expedition to the wreck found a short section of the double bottom that was completely separate from either the bow or stern sections of the wreck.

8   N 44° 20', W 38° 36'.

Chapter 4

1   The uniform of Ordinary Seamen and Able Seamen aboard White Star Line ships was a blue pullover called a guernsey, with 'White Star Line' embroidered across the front.

Chapter 5

1   The term 'falls' refers to the free end of a rope that is paid out from the deck to lower the boats to the water.

Chapter 6

1   H-1636.

2   Information given to the authors by correspondence, 1987.

3   Presented as a web document, 1998.

4   *Titanic and Other Ships*.

5   Senior Officers, also known as Bridge Officers, were the Chief Officer, First Officer and Second Officer. The Third, Fourth, Fifth and Sixth Officers were known as Junior Officers.

6   *Herald, Hornby, Huskisson* and *Herculaneum*.

7   The Third-Class Dining Saloon did not see nearly as many emigrant passengers on westbound trips, and since it was divided into four sections, it would have been easy to close one section off.

Chapter 7

1   One book that discusses this practice is *Titanic – Belfast's Own* by Stephen Cameron, and a widely reprinted image in which this can be seen is H-1557. This image shows six men working on or around *Titanic's* starboard propeller shaft, but a seventh man has been erased from the picture. His outline can be seen just to the left of the rightmost man.

2   The rivet heads along much of the hull were also flush with the surface of the plating, and are rarely visible. For this reason the plates often appear welded together, but they were not.

3   Photographs usually caption this colour erroneously as white. It was not, although it was nearly so.

4   Technically, a porthole is an opening cut in the hull or bulkhead of a ship, whereas 'sidelight' is the proper term for the steel or brass frame set within the opening to hold the circular glass that provides illumination. The term 'porthole' has been used here since we are speaking of openings in the hull.

5   The reciprocating engine casing is the deckhouse structure between the Nos. 3 and 4 funnels that has a large skylight on top. In photographs the four skylight hatches are usually propped in the open positions. Inside the skylights a vertical shaft led directly down to the Reciprocating Engine Room, and provided a key means for heat to escape.

6   On any wooden boat or ship the gunwale (pronounced 'gunnel') is the uppermost strake of plank-
    ing, or the upper edge of the boat.

Chapter 8

1   In point of fact, *Titanic*'s lookouts were never issued binoculars, having only been given the loan of
    the Second Officer's set on the trip from Belfast to Southampton.
2   At the British Wreck Commissioner's Inquiry, Naval Architect Edward Wilding calculated that
    16,000 tons of sea water entered the ship in the first 40 minutes following the collision.
3   A number of discoloured patches are also visible just above the waterline. These light-coloured
    patches are areas where the paint had been peeled off by the pounding action of the waves.
4   The Lizard is an extension of a peninsula in southern Cornwall, England, with a ridge of sub-
    surface rocks that have claimed countless ships over the centuries. The wreck of the *Suevic* is famous
    for being the largest rescue in the history of the Royal Naval Lifeboat Institution. In a dense fog and
    heavy seas over a period of 16 hours, RNLI lifeboat volunteers rescued 456 passengers, including
    seventy infants.
5   'The Fire Below: Spontaneous Combustion in Coal', DOE/EH-0320, Issue No. 93–4.
6   Since this book was written, the stern lettering indicating the name '*Titanic*' and the port of registry
    have been verified during James Cameron's 2001 IMAX dive. However photographic images have
    yet to be released.
7   The Firemen's tunnel was a horizontal shaft-like structure that ran from the from the forward-most
    boiler room beneath the Nos. 2 and 3 holds to a set of spiral stairs leading up to the crew quarters in
    the fo'c'sle. This permitted greasers, firemen and trimmers to get to and from their quarters without
    having to pass through the loaded holds at sea.

Appendix I

1   The name 'Sirocco' may have come from the name of a hurricane-like wind that comes from the
    Sahara Desert. In this section the term 'Sirocco' is used generically to refer to the fan unit plus its
    associated ducting, base and attached intake.
2   The stokeholds were the areas in front of the boilers where the Firemen stoked the furnaces.
3   Close study of the railings along the edge of the Officers' deckhouse roof in this area will reveal a
    series of eye loops. These were used for securing the awning at its outboard edges.
4   The function of these pipes within the water supply system is beyond the scope of this text; inter-
    ested readers should consult *Titanic: The Ship Magnificent*, volume 1, pp 361–70.
5   These comprised the lowest row of portholes in the white-painted area of the hull.

Appendix II

1   In actual fact, the job of Fireman required far more skill than most laymen would have given them
    credit for. The coal had to be spread evenly within the furnace, laid neither too thickly or thinly,
    levelled and watched with a practised eye to ensure neither too much nor too little air was getting
    to the fire. In addition, 'clinkers' – hard chunks of incombustible matter – had to be 'sliced' from
    the fire and broken up, and the underside of the furnace grates had to be regularly raked to remove
    ashes and clinker fragments. It was a vital job, and the ship's performance and fuel economy could
    suffer drastically from an inexperienced stokehold crew.
2   In this and many areas, *Olympic* saw improvements that had been incorporated into *Titanic*'s con-
    struction based on what was found unsatisfactory with *Olympic* in her early service.
3   Ships in a convoy, by necessity, must reduce their speed to that of the slowest ships in the convoy.
4   It is uncertain whether this paint scheme had been applied by 4 April or if it was done later the
    same year.
5   According to intelligence reports, the submarine – *U-103*, under the command of
    Korvettenkapitän Claus Rücker – had spotted *Olympic* at 3.37a.m. and were getting ready to fire

torpedoes at her, but the ship came up so quickly that they weren't aware of her until they came under fire.

6   Initially developed to destroy naval mines, the paravane can be likened to an underwater glider. It would be towed from the bows of the ship on a long cable attached to the towing ship by chains. The wings of the paravane ensured that it streamed out and away from the ship. If the paravane cable snagged a cable anchoring a mine to the bottom it would either cut the mine's cable, allowing the mine to float to the surface where it could be destroyed by gunfire, or it would pull the paravane against the mine and cause it to explode away from the ship.

7   This nickname was so unique to the people of Halifax that at one point during the war a Canadian sailor at a military checkpoint became confused when Captain Hayes referred to his ship as the 'Olympic'. The sailor had known the ship only as 'Old Reliable'.

8   HAPAG is an acronym for Hamburg-Amerikanische Packetfährt-Actiengesellschaft, which translates to Hamburg-America Steamship Company. In 1968 this company would merge with Norddeutscher-Lloyd to become HAPAG-Lloyd.

9   The North American Conference was a member organisation consisting of all the major steamship lines. Its purpose was to agree on matters such as fares and other matters in order to stabilise competition.

10 Until 1928, Tourist Third Class was not a true class of its own, as it had no public rooms or spaces dedicated to the class.

11 Recall that the decks were renamed in the 1928–9 refit.

12 A doubler is an extra plate fitted over the regular plating either for extra strength or to compensate for strength lost due to an opening in the plating.

Appendix III

1   Flooding the compartment on the opposite side of the ship would moderate the list in such a case, but could introduce other problems such as putting a machinery space out of commission due to the high water.

2   Carley floats had the appearance of oval rings and were made from a length of copper or steel tubing 30–50cm (12–20in) in diameter, surrounded by kapok or cork for buoyancy and then covered with a layer of waterproof canvas. The floor of the raft was made from a wood or webbed grating. Paddles, water, rations and survival equipment were lashed to the floor grating. The largest could accommodate up to fifty men, half inside the raft, and the others in the water holding onto the grab ropes.

3   Captain Arthur Rostron of the *Mauretania*, formerly of the *Carpathia*, stated in his autobiography that 'no troops were ever transported aboard the large hospital liners'.

SELECT BIBLIOGRAPHY

Behe, George, *Titanic: Safety, Speed & Sacrifice* (Transportation Trails, 1997)

Beveridge, Bruce, *et al.*, *Titanic: The Ship Magnificent*, 4th edition (The History Press, 2012)

Klistorner, Daniel, *et al.*, *Titanic in Photographs* (The History Press, 2011)

Chirnside, Mark, *RMS Olympic – Titanic's Sister* (Tempus Publishing Ltd, 2004)

Chirnside, Mark, *The 'Olympic' Class Ships – Olympic, Titanic, Britannic,* 2nd edition (The History Press, 2011)

Eaton, John P. and Haas, Charles A., *Titanic: Triumph and Tragedy*, 3rd edition (Haynes Publishing, 2011)

Garzke, William H., & Woodward, John, *Titanic Ships - Titanic Disasters: An Analysis of Early White Star and Cunard Superliners* (The Society of Naval Architects and Marine Engineers, 2002)

Gittins, Dave, *Titanic: Monument & Warning* (Self-published electronically, 2005)

Griffiths, Denis, *Power of the Great Liners* (Patrick Stephens Ltd, 1990)

Holmes, A. Campbell, *Practical Shipbuilding*, vol.I and II, 3rd edition (Longmans, Green, 1918)

Jessop, Violet, *Titanic Survivor: Memoirs of Violet Jessop Stewardess* (Sheridan House Inc., 1997)

McCaughan, Michael, *The Birth of the* Titanic (The Blackstaff Press, 1998)

McGreal, Stephen, *The War on Hospital Ships: 1914–1918* (Pen & Sword, 2008)

Mengot, Roy, and Woytowich, Richard, 'The Breakup of *Titanic:* A Progress Report from the Marine Forensics Panel (SD-7)' (published as an online document by the Society of Naval Architects and Marine Engineers, 2008)

Moss, Michael, and Hume, John R., *Shipbuilders to the World: 125 Years of Harland & Wolff, Belfast 1861– 1986* (Blackstaff Press, 1986)

Plumridge, John H., *Hospital Ships and Ambulance Trains* (Seeley, Service & Co., 1975)

Warren, Mark D., *Distinguished Liners from 'The Shipbuilder', 1907–1914*, vol.2 (Blue Riband Publications, Inc., 1997)

THE AUTHORS

Steve Hall lives in the small coastal town of Angels Beach in New South Wales, Australia. He is a renowned *Titanic* visual historian, having collected, studied and researched the ship's photographic record for over three decades. He has consulted to the media, auction houses and museums around the world and holds one of the largest privately held collections of *Titanic* photographs in the world. He has co-authored several landmark books on the subject, including *Titanic: The Ship Magnificent* volumes 1 and 2 (2008), *Titanic in Photographs* (2011) and *Report into the Loss of the SS Titanic: A Centennial Reappraisal* (2012). He retired from the information technology industry several years ago and now devotes his spare time to writing a series of children's novels.

Bruce Beveridge has been a history buff for many years, centring on early civilisations, the Crusades, and famous ships. He is also the senior historical archivist for his local community library and spends his time away from *Titanic* working on local history projects. Bruce has established a reputation in the *Titanic* community as being one of the foremost visual and technical historians of the *Olympic*-class ships. He has advised on *Titanic*'s visual and technical specifications for exhibitions, professional modelling firms, the Danbury Mint, the auction firm of Henry Aldridge and Son and other organisations requiring specialised consultation on the ship. Bruce's highly sought-after General Arrangement plans of the ship, released in 2003, were the most highly detailed and accurate plans released to date and were subsequently used by dive teams investigating the wreck. Bruce's research on the ship ultimately led to the book *Titanic: The Ship Magnificent*, a two-volume tome coordinated and co-authored with Steve Hall, Scott Andrews, Daniel Klistorner and Art Braunschweiger and which has become the defining reference for information on the ship.

Art Braunschweiger has had a long-standing interest in maritime and naval history, focusing on the British Navy of the period 1750–1820, Second World War submarine warfare in the Pacific, and the Atlantic convoys of the Second World War. He is an accomplished ship model builder and, along with Bruce Beveridge, is a trustee of the Titanic Research and Modeling Association. Art also assisted in writing and researching *Titanic: The Ship Magnificent* and *Titanic in Photographs*. He devotes his spare time to ship model building and beekeeping.

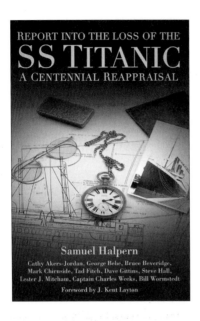
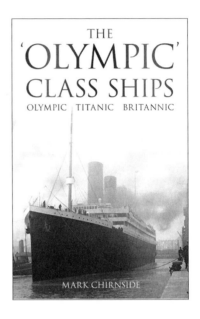
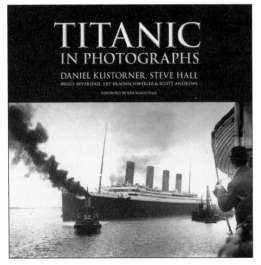
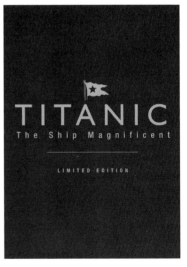